My
Mind
Consciousness

Mysticism
Mind
Consciousness

Robert K. C. Forman

STATE UNIVERSITY OF NEW YORK PRESS

For
Rosha Nicole Kraus Forman
and
Avram Michael Kraus Forman

Contents

Preface

This book is the product of a lifetime.

I have been thinking about the issues discussed herein since my early twenties, when I took up the practice of meditation and began having some of the experiences we students of mysticism like to investigate. I have been puzzling over the philosophical problems that such experiences bring up since my very first semester of graduate school at Columbia University's Department of Religion, where I first was confronted with them in a class conducted by my esteemed professor and challenge-mentor, Wayne Proudfoot. I have been exploring them through my years of thinking about Hinduism, mystical Christianity, Buddhism, and the riot of spiritual programs alive in the modern West.

Thus what you have in your hands is the product of an adult life of thinking, writing, pondering, and wondering about the nature of conscious experience and especially mystical experience; and that life's halting attempts at making sense of them.

Those of you that know my work will find here some that is familiar and some that is entirely new. Some of these paragraphs have been published before, many have not. This book is more than a collection of my essays, for it makes its own points more coherently than that might imply. Think of it as a collection of the last two decades of my thoughts on a particular subject. I like to think that the arguments herein are fleshed out to their fullest and strengthened by force of proximity. But to the reader who is already familiar with my work, portions of chapters 1, 3, and 6 are amplifications of work published in *The Problem of Pure Consciousness,* and portions of chapter 7 were previously published in *The Journal of the American Academy of Religion.* The present work is more than a mere recapitulation of those essays however. It both fleshes out the thoughts of those essays and adds to them in significant ways.

It is my hope that this book will serve to finally close the door on the possibility that one can assume without further justification that mysticism is constructed, and will open the door to much broader and more far-reaching debates on both the deeper character of mysticism, and on what mysticism has to show us about the nature of human consciousness and life.

There are countless people to whom I would like to express my thanks. In the two decade development of this work, I have learned from my graduate school professors, especially Wayne Proudfoot, Ewert Cousins, Joel Brereton, Peter Awn, Norvin Hein, and Robert Somerville. Because they set the issues and clearly articulated the conundrums I've pondered, I owe an enormous amount to my professional colleagues and sparring partners, Steven Katz, Jerry Gill, and Robert Gimello. Much of my insight has been gleaned from my co-authors in earlier volumes and colleagues in various venues, notably Anthony Perovich, R. L. Franklin, Paul Griffiths, Donald Rothberg, Scott Lowe, Jeff Kripal, Sally Katz, and G. William Barnard. Finally, or perhaps firstly, I learned more at the feet of three teachers than from anyone else: Maharishi Mahesh Yogi, Ram Dass, and Meister Eckhart. To all these people I cannot express my gratitude deeply enough, for together they have given my life meaning, direction, and value.

I also owe a debt of gratitude to my students at Vassar and Hunter Colleges. They have taught me where my thoughts are muddy, clear, or occasionally inspiring. They have helped show me the real value of this query. My mysticism students especially have been sources of a great deal, and a great deal of joy.

Finally my thanks are unending to my beloved and ever-patient wife, Yvonne, whose tireless support, sane council, and thoughtful feedback have made both me and this book unquestionably stronger. She also kept me from selling Earth Shoes.

Finally, I thank my wonderful children Rosha and Avi, for the love we share, and for putting up with their often preoccupied dad.

Chapter One

Mystics and Constructivists

Introduction

What, or who (or perhaps Who), causes mysticism? What does it signify? From whence does it come? Is it an authentic experience of something real, or a revered self-delusion? Some of each perhaps? Are mystics the fools of God, or merely fools?

Over the last quarter of a century, scholars—who are rarely mystics—have come to generally agree that it's not a Who but a what that plays the key formative role in mystical experiences. The "what" is the mystic's background: his or her beliefs, expectations, hopes, wishes, needs, questions, etc. In academic shorthand these are commonly referred to as the mystic's conceptual "framework" or background "set." This approach to religious experience, along with a range of relatively minor variations and shadings with which it is taught, is called "constructivism." Constructivism is the view that in significant ways the mystic's conceptual and linguistic scheme determines, shapes, and/or constructs his or her mystical experiences.

Constructivism has come to dominate an astonishing array of recent books and articles about not only mysticism, but about religious experience, spirituality, and indeed much of religion as well. It is the engine that drives most historical, theological, and contextual studies of religious individuals: scholars of particular religious people commonly trace how that person's experiences were influenced by his or her tradition or background. But this is to maintain—however unconsciously—that that individual's religious tradition shaped and/or constructed his or her religious experiences.

In the literature concerning Meister Eckhart's mysticism, for example, with which I am somewhat familiar, scholars have shown how Eckhart's thought and experiences were influenced by Neo-Platonism,[1] Augustine,[2] Thomism,[3] etc., etc. Hidden in all these accounts is the claim that the mystical experiences to which Eckhart avers must themselves have been influenced by his background. Typically, such articles do not argue for the purported connection between background set and mystical experience. They don't have to argue for it: given the general scholarly agreement on this approach, they can assume it. Those that are alert enough to recognize that they need to justify this connection, do so by merely referring the reader to the recent theoretical literature (purportedly) establishing this link. Among Eckhart scholars, for example, both Bernard McGinn and Kenneth Clark refer to Steven Katz's well-known article for an articulation of this connection.[4]

Hence, to understand the linkage between background and mystical experience the reader must turn to the philosophical literature that defends this claim, the so-called "constructivist" claim. William Wainwright,[5] Ninian Smart,[6] John Hick,[7] Terence Penehelum,[8] Jerry Gill,[9] Wayne Proudfoot,[10] Peter Moore,[11] and others have all offered excellent defenses of constructivism. Steven Katz, with his two articles, "Language, Epistemology and Mysticism" and "The 'Conservative' Character of Mystical Experience," is perhaps the most outspoken and renowned defender of the constructivist claim.[12] So frequently glossed are these articles, especially those of Katz, that this view became virtually the received view in the 1970s and '80s on mysticism.[13] Because it has been so central to the recent discussions, I will focus much of my thought and attention on this viewpoint.

I will explore constructivism by both addressing the key articulating articles of this position, especially those of Katz, as well as the theories of the construction of experience in general. For mystical constructivist philosophers are writing squarely from within the great constructivist traditions of British and American analytical philosophy. Proudfoot, Katz, and Gill are the grandsons of philosophers like G. E. Moore, Gilbert Ryle, and Ludwig Wittgenstein; and the great-grandsons of Immanuel Kant. In his *Critique of Pure Reason*, Kant maintained that we cannot experience reality in itself (which he called the "noumenon") directly. Rather, we can only encounter the world through a limited number of categories—space and time, the concept of unity, etc. We humans supply these categories, he said. We can see only in their terms. These concepts and categories "mediate" any possible experience. If some experience came to us in other terms, we simply could not entertain it—we would have no category for it.

Wittgenstein, in his suggestive and evocative way, dispensed with the notion that our concepts mediate, for any human being, some unidentifiable *noumenon* "out there." Rather, his dominant model is that we "construct" our world in and through our language, concepts, beliefs, and actions. The world does not come "at" us, he said, with our concepts passively filtering certain things out. Rather, we more actively "construct" our experience. The world is as we build it. And having built it, we live in what we have ourselves built. In living and understanding it in certain ways—which we learn from language, culture, behavior patterns, etc.—we *construct* our sense of the real.

This insight, that we construct our own reality, has had enormous impact on modern Western humanities and social sciences. I cannot begin to demonstrate the full ramifications of this constructivist model, but here are a few of its more obvious ones: the sociology of knowledge and anthropology have both detailed how a culture's world view structures and controls perception and beliefs.[14] Psychologists since Freud (and perhaps before) have argued that childhood concepts and experiences control, shape, and determine adult emotions and perceptions.[15] Historians of culture and of ideas, and, of course, of religion all write explicitly out of this model. Even fields like Modern Art[16] and Art Criticism[17] may be viewed as grappling with the notion that we see only what we are conditioned to see. Writers work with it: Iris Murdoch, for example, said, "man is a creature who makes pictures of himself and then comes to resemble the picture."[18] Thus, when we explore the thesis that all experiences (including mystical ones) are constructed, we are in effect exploring a room whose corners are inhabited by the full panoply of humanists and social scientists.

Because this model is shared by so many, a challenge to such a widely accepted way of looking at things is likely to be either ignored, scoffed at, or seen as a threat.[19] Be that as it may, challenge it I will. For I am, in effect, asking in this book, is there a *limit* to the constructivist model of human experience? Are there any experiences, types of experiences, or phenomena that a human being may consciously undergo, which may plausibly be said to be *not* determined or constructed by the subject's set? Can anyone, i.e., a mystic or anyone else, escape the self-constructed world, even for a moment?

If the answers to my questions are affirmative, as I believe they are, then we will be faced with another question: if the mystic does not construct her own experience, then what does cause and/or shape the experience(s)? This means we must offer our own theory of mysticism, one that is more adequate to the task. And, given the deep acceptance of the constructivist thesis in general, our answer may turn out to have ramifications that reach far beyond the narrow confines of mysticism studies.

A Definition of Mysticism

Before analyzing the constructivist model in detail, I want to define mysticism as I will use the term. The word *mysticism,* like *religion, truth,* and *modernity,* is pivotal but murky. It can denote the unintelligible statements of an illogical speaker, a schizophrenic's vision, someone's hallucinations, a drug-induced vision, the spiritual "showings" of a Julian of Norwich or a Mechthilde of Magdeburg, the unspoken, silent experience of God that Meister Eckhart called the "Divine Desert," or the Buddhist Nagarjuna's empty *shunyata.* Clearly, before we can progress we must be more precise about our field of inquiry.

Roland Fischer has put forward a "cartography" of states of conscious arousal which includes all of these so called "mystical" states.[20]

Hallucinations, acute schizophrenic states, and the visions and auditions of a Julian of Norwich fall on the ergotropic side of the chart. These are states of hyperarousal: cognitive and physiological activity are at relatively high levels. On the trophotrophic side are hypoaroused states, marked by low levels of cognitive and physiological activity: here we find Hindu *samādhi, mushinjo* in *zazen,* the restful states associated with *The Cloud of Unknowing's* "cloud of forgetting," or Eckhart's *gezucket.*

Levels of metabolic excitation, emotional arousal, mental activity, etc. indicated on the trophotropic and ergotrophic scale move in opposite directions. Physiological parameters such as heart rate, skin temperature, spontaneous galvanic skin responses, etc. increase on one side of the chart, and decrease on the other. Electroencephalogram (EEG) patterns differ sharply. Given such different signatures, these two scales are unlikely to have identical psychological characteristics, mental features, and, most interesting, causes. One should not explain feelings of love as if they were just like the feelings we have in a foot race, at least not without further rationale.[21] We must be careful, for models developed to explain phenomena on the ergotrophic scale may very well not explain trophotropic phenomena.

I propose reserving the term *mysticism* for trophotropic states. I will call ergotrophic phenomena such as hallucinations, visions, auditions, etc. "visionary experiences." Thus, the following vision record of the thirteenth-century Christian, Mechthild of Hackeborn, however fascinating, is ergotrophic:

> The King of glory once appeared in indescribable splendor in the fullness of his joy, wearing a golden robe embroidered with doves and covered by a red mantle. This garment was open on two sides to indicate that the soul has free access to God.[22]

The Beguines, St. Teresa when she speaks of her visions and auditions, Mohammed, Isaiah, Nichiren, etc. are all known for being visionaries.

I will reserve the term *mysticism* only for those people who write about experiences on the trophotropic side of our chart. Such authors as Eckhart, Dogen, al-Hallaj, Bernadette Roberts, and Shankara are all, in my usage, "mystics" rightly so called. A passage like the following, from the Hindu Bhagavad Gita, then is "mystical" as I will use the term:

> But with desire-and-loathing-severed
> Senses acting on the objects of sense,
> with (senses) self-controlled, he, governing his self,
> Goes unto tranquillity.
>
> In tranquillity, of all griefs
> Riddance is engendered for him;
> For of the tranquil minded quickly
> The mentality becomes stable.[23]

I can thus concur with Ninian Smart's definition of mysticism: "Mysticism describes a set of experiences or more precisely, conscious events, which are not described in terms of sensory experience or mental images."[24] In so restricting the term *mysticism* to experiences not described with sensory language, I believe I am in accord with the original meaning of "mystical," i.e., "to close," and to the overtones of the term as it was brought into the Christian lexicon by Pseudo-Dionysius, that is, separate from the sensory ("rapt out of himself").[25]

Let us focus the searchlight of our inquiries even narrower. W.T. Stace distinguishes between "introvertive mysticism" and "extrovertive mysticism."[26] In extrovertive mysticism one perceives a new relationship—one of unity, blessedness, and reality—between the external world and oneself. This Stace distinguishes from introvertive mysticism, the nonspatial experience of a void awareness or "pure consciousness." Although he does provide seven characteristics of each type, he overlooks what seems to me to be the central fact that distinguishes them. It can be seen most readily in a distinction made by twentieth-century Hindu mystic Ramana Maharshi between *samādhi* and *sahaja samādhi*.[27] *Samādhi* is a contemplative state, and is thus "introvertive" in Stace's sense of the term. *Sahaja samādhi* is a state in which a silent level within the subject is maintained along with (simultaneously with) the full use of the human faculties. It is, in other words, a state that is *continuous*—either permanent or lasting a long time—through activity. The distinction between a state maintained only during meditation and one maintained along with activity seems to be key here.

Because it involves several aspects of life—that is, external activity and some sort of internal and quiet aspect—and the relationship(s) between them, *sahaja samādhi* seems inherently more complex than *samādhi*. And it seems to be a more advanced state in the sense of coming later in the developmental process.[28] It seems to me that much misunderstanding has arisen because people have looked at the more advanced, sophisticated, and perhaps more interesting form of experience—*sahaja samādhi,* extrovertive—prematurely, that is, without first understanding the simpler more rudimentary form(s) of mystical experience. In this book I will first look at this more rudimentary stage, and then, with our understanding of it firmly in hand, turn to a more advanced form. That is, I propose to begin at the beginning.

In so doing I want to emphasize one point: while I will start by looking at the pure consciousness event (PCE)—one quite interesting and relatively common form of introvertive mysticism[29]—I do *not* claim that this form of mysticism is the only important mystical phenomena. There are many other interesting mystical phenomena, *sahaja samādhi* being one, and we will turn to that one toward the end of this inquiry. I will first focus on the pure consciousness event because:

1. it is relatively common;

2. it is rudimentary and hence may indicate key features of more advanced mystical phenomena;

3. most important, it seems an excellent philosophical case study of one of the peculiarities of mysticism, one that stands as a *prima facie* counterexample to the constructivist model.

I want to emphasize that I do not claim, and I do not believe, that it is everywhere believed to be ultimate or salvific. Indeed, I do not regard it as salvific in and of itself, although it may play an important role in the more advanced forms of the mystical life.[30]

Structure of the Book

In sum, my question is, how shall we best account for mysticism? By mysticism I mean "trophotrophic" mystical experiences. I will look at two common types of them, a transient experience called the pure consciousness event (PCE), and a permanent or semipermanent experience called the dualistic mystical state, (DMS). What is the best way to understand these experiences?

The book is divided into three parts. In Part I I will look primarily at the pure consciousness event, and ask whether constructivism adequately accounts for it. Here I will, of course, detail several reports of this sort of experience (chapter 2) and then explore constructivism and its philosophical underpinnings (chapters 3 and 4). The question here is, does constructivism adequately account for these events? I will argue that is does not.

In chapter 5, I will show how a well-respected ninth-century Eastern thinker, Paramārtha, tends to support my thesis that constructivism does not adequately account for these pure consciousness events. Paramārtha offers an account of ordinary experience that is in profound accord with the current constructivist model, but goes on to say that it is not applicable to mysticism.

The hypothesis of Part I then is that constructivism is ill suited to explain these "introvertive" mystical experiences. But that leaves us with the problem of offering a more adequate account. This I will offer in Part II. Because constructivism so focuses on language, in chapter 6 I will explore in some detail the role of language in bringing on the pure consciousness events. In chapter 7 I will turn to the place of consciousness in them.

But this touches only on the pure consciousness event. In Part III I will turn to the dualistic mystical state. First, in chapter 8 I will present some data about its existence and precise phenomenological character. In chapter 9 I will explore this interesting experience by drawing a parallel between Sartre, Hui Neng, and the observations of several mystical thinkers. With that in hand I will offer what seems to me a more sensible account of human consciousness, which both makes sense of the insights of the mystics and also has a lot to say about the nature of ordinary human consciousness. And this may serve to call into question some of the academic orthodoxy about the constructed nature of all human awareness and experience.

Part 1

The Pure Consciousness Event

Chapter Two

Reports of Pure Consciousness Events

B efore beginning our philosophical investigations, I want to put several reports of mystical phenomena on the table, so we know just what it is we are discussing. In Part III of this book we will look at a permanent experience, the DMS, the Dualistic Mystical State, which is something that lasts continuously. In this first part, we will look at something more short lived and hence, as William James' put it, transient: the Pure Consciousness Event (PCE).

An Upanishadic Description

Let us begin by looking at several classical descriptions of pure consciousness events. The first is taken from a fairly late Upanishad, the Maitri 6:18–19.

To the unity of the One goes he who knows this. (18) The precept for effecting this [unity] is this: restraint of the breath (prāṇāyāma), withdrawal of the senses (pratyāhāra), meditation (dhyāna), concentration (dhāraṇā), contemplation (tarka), and absorption (samādhi). Such is said to be the sixfold Yoga. . . .

(19) Now it has elsewhere been said, "Verily when a knower has restrained his mind from the external, and the breathing spirit (prāṇa) has put to rest objects of sense, thereupon let him continue void of conceptions. Since the living individual (jiva) who is named "breathing spirit" has arisen here from what is not breathing spirit, therefore, verily, let the breathing spirit restrain his breathing spirit in what is called the fourth condition (turya). For thus it has been said:

11

> That which is non-thought, [yet] which stands in the
>   midst of thought,
> The unthinkable, supreme mystery!—
> Thereon let one concentrate his attention
> And the subtle body (linga), too, without support.[1]

This is a passage that touches upon many of the themes commonly seen in mysticism. It is obviously concerned with some experience. It mentions meditation, something ineffable ("the unthinkable, supreme mystery"), an experience of unity ("the unity of the One"), etc.

Our passage first tells us what it takes to bring on the experience its author has in mind. Clearly, it takes place while sitting quietly in something like meditation, *dhyāna*. One undergoes *pratyāhāra*, withdrawal of the attention from the senses. One focuses one's attention, *dhāranā*, until one gains full absorption. Another way of saying the same thing is that one has "put to rest objects of sense" (6:19). One is thus not seeing anything, noticing some tactile sensations, hearing sounds, etc. One is also not thinking during this event: one "continues void of conceptions." Not thinking, restraining the mind from the external and sensory, one is left fully focused but devoid of any sensory or imagined object for the mind. Thus one becomes fully "absorbed," gaining the state known as *turya*.

Turya means "fourth," and in the Upanishads denotes the state gained in meditation that later came to be more commonly known as *samādhi*. By "fourth" is meant the fourth "condition." The first three mentioned in the Upanishads are the waking, dreaming, and deep sleep "conditions," (what we might call "states of consciousness"). It is sometimes also called *caturtha*, which is the ordinal numeral adjectival form of four, but it is more commonly named *turya*. Later philosophical treatises more typically use the form *turīya*, which came to be the accepted technical term. *Turīya*, then, is the fourth state of consciousness, after waking, sleeping, and dreaming. Unlike any of them, it involves neither sensing nor thinking. Indeed, it signifies being entirely "void of conceptions," by which I understand that there one one does not encounter images, imagined sounds, verbalized thoughts, emotions, etc. In short, in *turīya* one encounters no content for consciousness.

Now, one might think that one has some sort of mental object herein, for it says, "To the unity of the One goes he who knows this." Is one aware of some One, as one might be aware of a vision of God or of the number one? This, I believe, would be a mistake. "To the unity of the One" needn't necessarily mean one becomes *consciously aware* of some thing. Rather, I believe that our passage is saying something *analytically* (that one moves into a state of unity with the One), not *descriptively* (that one thinks or feels some One). If one was thinking or feeling some one thing, then we would not read that one has "put to rest objects of sense" or remains "void of conceptions." Rather, it would say one experiences the one, or thinks the one, or some such. But here one is said to move to that which is "non-thought, yet which is in the midst of thought." Thus, one is not perceiving or thinking *about* some thing, even a one, but rather is coming to be that one thing which one inherently is, if you will, without any additional mental content.

In other words, as I understand this passage, it is suggesting that one moves to a condition of being entirely without any sensory or mental content, or without any intentional content for the awareness. One simply persists "without support."

Eckhart on Gezucken

Meister Eckhart (c. 1260–c. 1328) was a Dominican friar, prior, abbot, lecturer, and preacher.[2] Although in his earlier university days he wrote several Latin works in scholastic style—the Parisian Disputations and Prologue to his Opus Tripartitum[3]—he is most renowned for his later German Sermons and Tractates. While it is not his focus, in them he not infrequently alludes to an experience he calls "gezucken," or rapture.

One of the clearest characterizations of *gezucken* is found in the sermon *Dum Medium Silentium*, a sermon on which we will focus.[4] Eckhart there introduces the medieval notion of the powers of the soul.

Whatever the soul effects, she effects with her powers. What she understands, she understands with the intellect. What she remembers, she does with the memory; if she would love, she does that with the will, and thus she works with her powers and not with her essence. Every external act is linked with some means. The power of sight works only through the eyes; otherwise it can neither employ nor bestow vision, and so it is with all the other senses. The soul's every external act is effected by some means.[5]

In addition to the five senses there are six powers: three lower (lower intellect, desire, and anger) and three higher (memory, higher intellect, and will). It is by their activity that the soul enters into and interacts with the external world.[6] We look at objects with our eyes, hear sounds with our ears, etc.[7] The activity of the six higher powers generates thought and desire, that is, willing and cognitive or mental activity. Eckhart is here using fairly standard scholastic psychology.

Having introduced the powers and alluding thereby to the normal phenomenon of the mind's attending to some thought or sensory object, Eckhart goes on to describe the *gezucken* of St. Paul, his archetype of someone having the mystical experience he wishes to describe.

> [T]he more completely you are able to draw in your powers to a unity and forget all those things and their images which you have absorbed, and the further you can get from creatures and their images, the nearer you are to this and the readier to receive it. If only you could suddenly be unaware of all things, then you could pass into an oblivion of your own body as St Paul did, . . . In this case . . . memory no longer functioned, nor understanding, nor the senses, nor the powers that should function so as to govern and grace the body. . . . In this way a man should flee his senses, turn his powers inward and sink into an oblivion of all things and himself.[8]

As we saw in the Upanishadic passage, Eckhart specifically asserts the absence of sensory content ("nor the senses") in this experience, as well as mental objects ("devoid of" memory, understanding, senses, etc.). One has become oblivious of one's "own body" and "all things." One even loses the awareness of oneself. In short, in this phenomenon of *gezucken* one is "unaware of all things," i.e., devoid of all mental and sensory content.

In another passage Eckhart specifically notes that the contemplative "withdrawal" from cognitive activity includes both "internal" and "external" powers. "If a person wanted to withdraw into himself with all his powers internal and external . . ." The "external" powers are the senses, the lower intellect (common sense), anger, and desire—the powers by which we notice and respond in rudimentary ways to the external world. The "internal" powers are intellect, will, and desire, the "higher" powers with which we generate thought and desire. Hence, withdrawal of both implies that neither the powers of thought nor of sensation "flow out" into their usual activities. In other words, both the sensing and the thinking aspects of the mind are inactive. Responding to his conditional, Eckhart continues, " . . . then he will find himself in a state in which there are no images and no desires in him and he will therefore stand without any activity, internal or external."[9] With both internal and external powers withdrawn, one experiences neither thought, affective feeling, sensation, nor vision.

In *gezucken,* then, one is aware of, according to Eckhart, neither thought, word, speech, or even vague daydreams. Even oblivious of "himself," such a man becomes completely silent and at rest, without cognitive content: he is contentless yet open and alert. Restated, according to this passage in *gezucken* the subject is merely awake, simply present, but devoid of a manifold for awareness, either sensory or mental. Once again, we have a description of a state in which there are no thoughts, no sensations, no cognitive content: a nonintentional, yet wakeful moment.

Being without Thoughts in Zen Buddhism

Zen, as is well known, teaches a disciplined technique of sitting in a prescribed, erect fashion and concentrating the mind on an object assigned by the Roshi. While *koans* are in the West the most famous of these meditative tools, these are used principally by the Rinzai tradition. Soto Zen, the other main school, frequently teaches its novices to focus the attention on the breath. The aim of such a technique has nothing to do with some knowledge of respiratory physiology. Rather, it is designed, in part, to help one temporarily cease having any objects for consciousness.

This process and its meditative experiences are described in one of the earliest and most renowned Soto texts, the *Fukan Zazen-gi,* by Dōgen, the abbot who is traditionally credited with bringing Soto Zen from China to Japan. It was written in 1277, soon after its twenty-eight-year-old author had returned from China. Needing a brief work in which his teachings about *zazen* were codified and stated simply, he set down this relatively short work. He must have considered it important since toward the end of his life he undertook to reedit it.[10] It introduced Zen so clearly and successfully that it has become quasi-canonical: "the Soto sect's single most cherished writing, being recited at the regular night sitting in Soto Zen temples and at other appropriate occasions."[11]

When the *Fukan Zazen-gi* was written, Rinzai, which emphasized koan use, was the dominant Zen school. By laying such a stress on the differences between those who had "answered" the koan and those who had not, Dōgen believed that this school's teachings could lead to "word attachment"—i.e., differentiating between enlightenment and the ordinary samsaric world.[12] Dogen taught a more straightforward "just sitting" (*shikan taza*) or "wall gazing" technique which was intended to help eliminate the disjunction between *samsara* (the world) and Nirvana (enlightenment). Dōgen did not consider *dhyāna* (meditation) to be a means *to* Nirvana, but rather considered it to be fundamentally one *with* Nirvana.

According to Dōgen, the problem that prevents one from realizing this is the tendency to discriminate, especially between what one thinks is "good" and "bad." One must simply stop discriminating. "Do not judge things as good or evil, and cease such distinctions as 'is' and 'is not.' Halt the flow of the mind, and cease conceptualizing, thinking, and observing."[13] Dōgen advocated being rid of all "dualistic (relational) thinking."[14] "Zazen is a practice beyond the subjective and objective worlds, beyond discriminating thinking."[15] Rather than discriminating and thinking, according to the *Fukan Zazen-gi*, in Zazen one should simply allow all thoughts to subside. After having given instructions about posture, breathing, etc., Dōgen states, "When your body posture is correct, breathe in and out [once deeply]. Sway left and right [several times] and then sit firmly and resolutely. Think about the unthinkable. How do you think about the unthinkable? Do not think. These are the essentials of Zazen."[16] In a gloss to this important but aphoristic passage, Waddell and Masao state,

> These words derive from the following dialogue, which is the central subject of [Dōgen's] Shobogenzo Zazenshin:
>
> > A monk asked Yueh-shan, "What does one think of when sitting immobilely in zazen?" Yueh-shan replied, "One thinks of not thinking."

"How do you think of not-thinking" asked the monk.

"Non-thinking," answered Yueh-shan.[17]

The key element in both these passages is that the Zen practitioner is to gain a state in which no thinking occurs. At that time the mind is simply present; one "just sits," if you will, without any mental cogitations or perceptions. Being simply present is a sign that one is no longer making any discriminations, not attentive to any of the "ten thousand things."

As things one does not think in Zazen, Dōgen expressly includes all thoughts of Nirvana, becoming a Buddha, and any of the other Buddhist notions. "Give up even the idea of becoming a Buddha. This holds true not only for zazen but for all your daily actions."[18] This emphasis will become important in the next section.

In this claim, Dōgen is neither idiosyncratic nor even atypical. Such experiences are described and thought to be significant in both earlier scriptures and later Zen writings.[19] Indeed, according to Conze, reports of non-thinking can be found in the full range of Indian Buddhist Scriptures.[20]

An Autobiographical Account

Modern academic studies of mysticism have focused virtually exclusively on textual reports and analysis of traditions of them. Some have even gone so far as to argue that texts are our *only* source of data about mysticism.

> [T]he only evidence we have . . . is the account given by mystics of their experience. These are the data for study and analysis. No scholar can get behind the autobiographical fragment to the putative "pure experience"—whatever one holds that to be. Whatever the truth of the nature of the commingling of theory, experience and interpretation that goes into the mystics' "report," the *only* evidence one has to call upon to support one's analysis of this material, and hence one's description of this relationship [between set and experience], is the given recording of the mystic—the already "experienced" and "interpreted" first person recording.[21] (Emphasis mine)

Professor Katz is here arguing that the only evidence we have about mystical experiences are *post hoc* reports and descriptions. Inevitably, interpretation is involved in such reports. Katz amplified this thought at a recent conference, where he added that there are only a limited number of subjects, the "great mystics," whom he regards as the legitimate subjects of inquiry.[22]

While I would not like to lay too much stress on what may have been an ill-advised comment, I do believe it fairly represented both his personal attitude (as shown in his articles) and those of his colleagues. For texts by "classical mystics" are certainly the primary if not the exclusive focus of both of Katz's edited volumes as well as most scholarly literature on mysticism. But whether this is intentional or not, this approach does mean that the constructivists' study of mysticism is a study of highly interpreted, generally famous texts, whose authors (the great mystics) have typically long since died.

Whether intended or not, this selection process may be skewing our understanding of mysticism. First, while the so-called great mystics—the St. Teresas, Meister Eckharts, Nagarjunas, and Dōgens—may be among the most articulate and therefore most historically significant mystics, they are certainly not the *only* mystics. For every highly revered St. Teresa, there have been many many colleagues and disciples, some of whom have no doubt had some mystical experiences. Even the constructivists will agree that there have likely been non-renowned people who have had extraordinary mystical experiences. A mystical experience does not guarantee fame. Nor does a mystic's fame guarantee that his or her experiences have been either unusual even particularly interesting. A mystic's fame derives from the quality of their writings, and perhaps the influence of their followers. Writings and followers make a "great" mystics great, not the depth or idiosyncrasy of their experience.

An unnoticed side effect of this particular focus is that our information about and understanding of mysticism may be skewed toward the writing, educated elite. Great writers may not be the greatest mystics.

Secondly, texts are, by their nature, complex. A religious text is written within a particular intellectual, historical, and faith context. A mystical author writes to a particular audience, and is, in part, generally trying to persuade that audience of the truth of a particular position or to explain something. If mystical authors describe their experiences, they may do so in the service of their rhetorical goal(s). Thus, their primary agenda may or may not be—indeed, rarely is—to describe their experiences accurately or clearly. In the service of an author's agenda, descriptions may be nuanced, shaped, or even misleading. Furthermore, even as descriptions texts are often unclear. Their authors may not have a talent for description, they may have been edited or transcribed by another (as were St. Teresa and Meister Eckhart), etc. Thus, as sources for philosophical analyses, classical texts may be themselves flawed.[23] Since their authors have long since passed away, it is impossible to verify the accuracy of the descriptions we have. Mystical texts may make interesting reading, but unreliable phenomenology.

Third, modern scholars who claim that texts are influenced by their faith context may be unconsciously or perhaps consciously *limiting* their sources to textual ones as a way to protect their thesis. Complex texts certainly *are,* at least in part, shaped by their context. If we recognize no other descriptive sources than these, then it is easy to argue that these descriptions are clearly shaped by their context, and thus that the experiences also must have been so shaped.[24]

But analyzing such complex, apologetic texts is not the only available methodology to identify the phenomena of mysticism. For today, in both America and Europe, we are not limited to such texts. There are thousands upon thousands of people practicing meditation of one variety or another, and again thousands have had mystical experiences.[25] Since many of these people are alive, it is possible to ask them questions about their experiences per se, and to pursue something when it is unclear, as many textual descriptions are. In a personal interview, one can ask certain obvious questions that would confirm or deny the constructivists' thesis: "Did you take this 'as' Brahman while it was going on, or was that a later naming?" Another is, "Did you know about thus and such *before* you underwent this?" Negative answers to either question would *prima facie* call the constructivist hypothesis into question.

Interviews with people who changed traditions might also be instructive: "Have you changed how you think about this experience?" "Do two different words adequately describe that phenomenon?" If someone said that they did not know of, e.g., Brahman before undergoing *samādhi,* or if someone only regarded it "as"

Brahman after some experience, this too would call the constructivist hypothesis into question.

Finally, I also believe that it is appropriate to include autobiographical descriptions. While the normal academic posture is to remain aloof from one's own personal experience, I feel that in a discussion about mysticism, this may be counterproductive. In my case, I know that the way I read first person accounts, theoretical accounts, and philosophical analyses of mysticism is colored in ways great and small by my own experience. Thus, to help clarify the source of some of my thinking, I believe it is incumbent upon me to include an autobiographical account, and I will begin with that.

I have been practicing a Neo-Advaitan form of meditation twice daily since November 1969. The technique involves the use of a bija mantra, a short verbal sound, which is not said aloud but repeated mentally with minimal effort. Often when I meditate, the mantra seems to drift away from my attention, and I find myself lost in thoughts and dream-like imagery. Sometimes when the mantra fades away, my thoughts and perceptions also quiet down. Things seem to get very settled and vague, as if even my own thoughts and perceptions are vague and dim.

Occasionally my thoughts drift away entirely, and I gain a state I would describe as simply being awake. At those times I'm not thinking about anything. I'm not particularly aware of any sensations. I'm not aware of being absorbed in anything in particular. Yet I know (after the fact) that I haven't been asleep. I am simply awake, simply present.

It is odd to describe such an event as being awake or being present, for those terms generally connote an awareness of something or other. Yet in this experience there is no particular or identifiable object of which I am aware. I am driven to say I am awake for two reasons. First, I emerge with a quiet, intuited certainty that I was continually present, that there was an unbroken continuity of experience or of consciousness throughout the meditation period, even if there were periods from which I had no particular memories. I just know that I was awake without a break, that there was a continuity of myself (however we define that) throughout.

The second reason I am driven to say I am awake therein is that there is a difference in how I feel after a meditation in which this occurs and after a meditation in which I fall asleep. After a sleep in meditation I wake up groggy, and it takes a good while for my mind to clear to full alertness. On the other hand, after one of these experiences I am clearheaded, and indeed my perceptions have more clarity and vibrancy than usual. I also feel especially calm.

I tend to undergo this phenomenon more often when I have been getting enough sleep. Other than that, I have not been able to correlate this phenomenon with any other process: for example, it does not happen more often when I have eaten certain foods, wear certain clothes, or sit in a particular chair (though, since I have a bad back, being very uncomfortable tends to preoccupy me with pain, and thus discourage letting go of sensations).

I may undergo this PCE as often as several times a meditation or only once every few months. As the years have progressed it is my impression that it has happened with increasing frequency, though I have never kept careful count.

A Zen Abbot's Account

I interviewed John Daido Sensei Loori, the abbot at Zen Mountain Monastery in Mt. Tremper, N.Y.[26] A charming, lanky, fiftyish man, he was a scientist, an engineer, and a nature photographer before he became a Zen Roshi. Daido Sensei Loori trucks no pretense: he met me in jeans and a blue denim shirt with huge embroidered eagles. For one with so lofty a title, he was refreshingly frank, thoughtful, and open about both his own and his students' mystical experiences.

Daido Sensei Loori distinguished two types of (what I would call) pure consciousness events he and his students have undergone: *absolute samādhi*, a contentless state in which there is absolutely no possibility of a response to the world, and *working samādhi*, in which one can respond if necessary. His first experience of absolute *samādhi* came during a photography workshop with Minor White, before he had looked into Zen. He had been out on assignment, photographing this and that when he came on a tree,

> which was basically just a tree, just a plain old tree like a hundred thousand other ones. But this one was very special for some reason. And Minor used to say, sit in the presence of your subject until you have been acknowledged. . . . So I set up my camera and I sat with this tree, and it was in the middle

of the afternoon, and that's all I remember until it was dusk, the sun had gone down and it was cold. And I was feeling just totally elated, just wonderful.

From the fact that he had started in the early afternoon and came out after dusk, when it was cold, he deduced that he had been in front of that tree for roughly four hours. Yet he had no recollection of anything from that entire period.[27] He states that when he first came out, he hadn't thought anything odd had happened. I understood by this remark that he did not come out with the sense that he had blacked out or lost awareness. He was certain, he told me, that he had not slept.

His second experience of absolute *samādhi* came several years later, after he had been practicing Zen for some while. He was on a week-long meditation course, a *sessin*, and had been feeling excruciating physical pain. His teacher had told him, in typical Zen fashion, to "be the pain."

> D. I was desperately trying to figure out what he meant by "be the pain." It didn't make sense to me. And at one point he walked through the zendo, and his sleeve brushed against me as he went by. I realized that the pain was gone. And the second I realized it, it was back. And then shortly after that was the last thing I remember until the noon meal.
>
> Q. So it was probably how [long]?
>
> D. About six hours.
>
> Q. Can you describe the experience during that six hours?
>
> D. All I know is that I was in terrible pain one minute and the next minute I was carrying my bowl into the dining hall and the sun was up and everything was very, very vivid. The food which I normally hated tasted wonderful. . . . At first I didn't think that anything unusual had happened. But . . . after the meal I began to put two and two together, that there was a big part of that morning that I had no recollection of. I didn't get verification on these things until after the sessin. I found out that I had actually sat through [the entire work time] without moving.
>
> Q. Its not like you had [blacked out or] gone anywhere. . . . It was a simply being present. . . . Is that fair?
>
> D. I think so. It was [only] because somebody . . . told me that I had sat for that time [that I knew anything unusual had happened].

Had he been asleep, he told me, he probably would have emerged with a sense that he had been asleep. But here he was certain that he had not. Hence, he enjoyed a "continuity" of being awake.

He also associated a very good feeling—"just totally elated" — with this absolute *samādhi*. So I asked him,

> Q. I want to be real exact here. [Did] you become aware of how good you felt [during the event? or after it?] During [it] would you say there was any particular awareness?
>
> D. No. No awareness at all. No reflection on it at all.

He was not aware of any feelings of elation until he came out. Again, rather than any particular content, the distinguishing feature was the absence of content and the loss of time. All seemed normal enough, except that he "lost" some six hours.

Daido Sensei Loori also described a second type of *samādhi*, "*active samādhi*," in which the mind *can* respond to the world if needed. It has come to be quite regular for him as well as many of his students. I had earlier described my own experiences of pure consciousness to him (much as I described them above), and he described this active *samādhi* by saying,

> D. I do this thing that you do, I do it almost every period. . . . Now when I sit, and I sit for a long enough period of time, my mind is not moving. I know, when I finally become aware of the room and I'm getting up to move, I know that I was present during that whole period of time, and I'm confident that I didn't miss anything. Yet I have no awareness of what went on. . . . Sometimes that happens right before I give a talk. Usually right before a talk happens we sit for just two or three minutes. After [the microphones and lectern] have been taken care of and the cup of coffee is there . . . I usually close my eyes and drop everything. During that two minutes or three minutes there is nothing. I know that if something had happened I would be aware of it. But nothing is moving, there is no feedback that is happening to me.

In sum, Daido's absolute *samādhi* experiences were of a passage of time—four or six hours—in which he utterly lost all conscious awareness of the sensory and thinking world. He came out thinking all had been perfectly normal; that is, there had been no gap in awareness. He had not passed out, he knew, nor asleep. But more than that he couldn't say. This he distinguishes from a more regular "working *samādhi*," which is something that he gained from regular Zen practice and which happens "almost every period." In this phenomenon, he "drops everything," i.e., is without awareness of anything in particular. Yet he can emerge, he knows, if the need arises.

I have never undergone something like his absolute *samādhi*, but this latter experience sounded quite familiar to me. We discussed this similarity. I stated,

> Q. From what I can tell, and one can never get in the body of another, we are describing an identical experience here.
>
> D. It *could be.*

By this "could," I understood him to mean that he sensed that we *were* describing an identical experience, but we could never be absolutely certain of identity in such private matters. Later he said:

> D. I think when we talk about *samādhi,* that we are talking about . . . that we're probably very close to saying the same thing.

A Siddha Yoga Novice's Account

The second interview on which I would like to report was with Danielle, a twenty-one-year-old female practitioner of Siddha Yoga.[28] A somewhat nervous, energetic, and earnest student of mine at Hunter College, Danielle mentioned in a Hinduism class that she had had an experience much like those described in the Upanishads. I asked her to come to my office, and asked her if I could record her description of her experience, to which she agreed.

Unlike Daido Sensei Loori, Danielle's first experience of this sort happened while she was meditating. She had been feeling particularly anxious about something one afternoon, she said, so

> D. I went into [the room we] called "the cave." It's black, you can't see anything. . . . I was sitting there and I was only going to stay for like ten minutes. But I was out for four hours and I didn't even realize it. I didn't have any incredible experi-

ences, like seeing cosmic lights or anything. . . . I didn't even realize I was there for that long. . . . Time just passed. Time just didn't exist. I thought only ten minutes, maybe fifteen minutes [had passed]. . . .

Q. Would you say [during this experience that] you were thinking?

D. No. I mean, I was completely out. I didn't, well, no.

Q. Can you describe anything about that experience . . . during the four hours?

D. No. The only thing I know is just that I was sitting there. I was very very comfortable but I didn't know I was sitting there. It was like I wasn't even there. . . .

Q. Were you asleep?

D. No.

Q. How do you know?

D. 'Cause I know when I'm asleep. My head falls and I start dreaming or whatever. But, it was still up and I [just know I] wasn't.

She was quite adamant that she was not asleep. She reiterated it several times. So I wondered:

Q. [Did] you have the sense that you had been awake?

D. I don't know if I was awake. I wasn't sleeping. It wasn't like a lot of times during meditation[. When] I do fall asleep, my head falls and I know when I've been asleep. I know I wasn't sleeping but I don't know what I would call it.

Q. So, you weren't awake in the usual way.

D. No, not really.

Q. How would you distinguish it from being awake in the usual way?

D. Well, when I'm awake I'm thinking and I know what's going on. I wasn't thinking and not because I chose to. It just happened. It wasn't like I told my mind "okay, don't think. . . ."

Q. So you know you weren't awake and you know you weren't asleep. Well, *that's* funny . . .

D. No. I was in some other world; I don't know.

Q. Did you have an experience like being in another world?

D. I didn't have any experiences. I didn't feel anything. . . .

Q. When you came out, did you have any particular thoughts like, "oh, boy that was nice," or something?

D. Yeah. I loved it. I mean, I couldn't believe I was there for four hours in that spot. I didn't move once and I didn't want to get up.

Q. So, for once in your life you were doing nothing else, just sitting.

D. Yeah, I guess so.

Q. Would you describe it as like that? Just sitting?

D. Just sitting but not as if I just sat down on the floor right now and closed my eyes. I didn't hear anything. I didn't see anything. I didn't feel anything. I didn't think anything.

I was struck with how Danielle stated that she had no thoughts during the period: "I wasn't thinking," she said, "and not because I chose to. It just happened. It wasn't like I told my mind 'okay, don't think . . . ' " With this she communicates a sense of effortlessness, almost as if someone or something other than herself had turned a switch off. Rather than her actively trying to *not* think, she just found herself without thoughts. It seems clear that had she actively been trying not to think, that effort alone would have been enough to pull herself out of this state. The state seems to assume a total absence of effort. She also communicates that, rather than her being able to bring on this state at will, it just happened to her. Her mind seemed to just stop on its own, autonomously.

Daido Sensei Loori described the onset of *samādhi* as often coming with an "off sensation," as if some switch within the mind or body clicks off:

One of the things that happens is—and this is particularly true during sessin—is an "off sensation" usually sets in first. . . . If you sit for long periods of time, especially during sessin, you [sometimes] lose sensation of your body. . . . [W]hen you are not moving any more you lose [the tactile awareness of your body]. Yet you know your body is there. Your mind is still working. You can see it: you can look down [and see it]. The tendency is, when that first begins to happen, an involuntary thing like [a twitch] will happen. A person will just kind of jump. . . . That's the first thing that precedes *samādhi*. And then, usually, the mind stops reflecting.

I too have sometimes experienced something like a twitch, a sort of quiet "off sensation" that occasionally comes upon me before mental operations settle down. It seems to have, we might say, a will of its own. As Danielle described, it also feels to me somewhat autonomous.

Similarities and Conclusions

Several commonalties within these reports strike one.

1. For everyone involved, these events seem to be beneficial. After both of my interviewees' *samādhis*, the problems that had been plaguing them had lifted, and remained absent for many months after their experiences. Daido felt remarkably good for many months after both his experiences, he told me. After the experience in front of the tree, he said, "I was feeling just totally elated, just wonderful. All my questions and my problems had dissolved. All my problems I tried to bring them up and they just weren't there any more." After that experience, he continued,

> [T]he only thing that remained with me was my surprise at how good I felt, for months thereafter. All my questions had gone away. All these things that seemed like these impossible problems were no longer there. I mean like nothing had changed. All the things that were bugging me before were still present, but they somehow weren't bugging me. That was the astonishing thing.

The feeling of well-being stayed with him after his second experience for some six months. After his second *samādhi,* he told me,

> I felt terrific and I was experiencing things very intensely like the food—[this was] right after—and the smells and I remember it was a beautiful sunny day. The sunlight was coming right into the dining room. Everything, all the colors, seemed very vivid and warm and comfortable. I had incredible loving

feelings for all the people there. . . . I just felt an incredible presence of all these people. Everything felt good.

Although this feeling of well-being gradually became less intense, it stayed with him for six months.

Danielle reported a similar sense of well-being:

I just felt lighter. Like I went in heavy and depressed and nervous. I had all these bad feelings, anxiety, and that just all left. I walked out and I felt completely fine and better and peaceful.

Her problems had lifted. Although she did not mention how long her sense of well-being persisted, the day after her experience in the "cave" she left the ashram on a trip and resolved some long-standing family troubles.

In my own case, while I often feel particularly calm and clear-headed after pure consciousness events, I have never resolved any specific deep-seated problems immediately after one of these experiences. I am convinced that meditation as a whole has done me a world of good, but I cannot say that any *single* meditation experience has ever radically changed the way I felt. Perhaps this can be related to the fact that I have never had a multi-hour event like theirs.

I should emphasize, however, that none of us holds that it is these unusual quiet events which transform one permanently. Truly significant changes, I believe, result from a life of regular meditative practice. The emphasis I am placing on these events may suggest that they are the key transformative moments on a path, but I do not believe that they are. Far from it! The paths on which we have each embarked are long and complex meditative, conceptual, therapeutic, devotional, and existential paths which, hopefully, have and will continue to profoundly change each of us. The goal of such a path is not a flash that lasts for a few moments or even hours, such as those I am discussing, but rather a permanent life change. I see the *samādhi* events, as it were, as mile markers on a road, not goal posts. They have some effect, but only within the context of a path as whole.

2. A second feature of these reports is that while we all were certain that these experiences were not experiences of being asleep,

each of us had trouble categorizing these experiences. We all had trouble saying that we were awake in anything like the normal way. Yet we all emphatically denied that we were asleep. Asked how she would distinguish it from being awake in the usual way, Danielle said,

> D. Well, when I'm awake I'm thinking and I know what's going on. I wasn't thinking, and not because I chose to. It just happened. It wasn't like I told my mind "okay, don't think . . ."
>
> Q. Okay, so you know you weren't awake and you know you weren't asleep, well *that's* funny . . .
>
> D. No. I was in some other world; I don't know.
>
> Q. Did you have an experience like being in another world?
>
> D. No. I didn't have any experiences. I didn't feel anything. . . .

Like many of us, by "awake" she understands some activity of perceiving or thinking this or that. She "knows what is going on." Yet in this event, since she was not thinking or perceiving, she did not "know what was going on." She was entirely without perception. Nor did she know whether or not any auditory stimuli had been present. Thus she expressed perplexity in that she could say neither that in her pure consciousness event she was asleep nor that she was awake.

Daido Sensei Loori also had trouble categorizing his *samādhi* experiences. They were not sleeping:

> Q. [W]ould you distinguish it from being dead asleep?
>
> D. Yeah!
>
> Q. How?
>
> D. First of all, (*little chuckle*) you know that you weren't asleep. I mean, you know after the fact that you weren't asleep. If I've fallen asleep on the cushion; I know when I've fallen asleep. When you wake up from sleep, your mind is kind of groggy. When you wake up out of *samādhi* you mind is so sharp and focused, everything is so vivid and alive. Your body even feels that way. So it's different in that way.

But nor is it waking, if by waking we understand the process of perceiving, thinking, speaking, acting, etc. As the *Heart Sūtra* describes this event, said Daido Sensei, "there can be no "world" existing for its duration:

> D. The *Heart Sūtra* describes it. The *Heart Sūtra* says, no eye, ear, nose, tongue, body, mind; no color, smell, taste, touch phenomena. No world of sight, no world of consciousness. Because the mind has stopped functioning, and the senses have stopped processing, there can no longer be any "world of waking consciousness."

I too have trouble describing this sort of event as either waking or sleeping. When I come out it, I am certain that I was awake for the full length of meditation. But on the other hand, it certainly is not "waking" in the usual sense of the term: no objects, thoughts, etc. But I do want to apply the term "consciousness" or "wakefulness" to this event, because I know I was present, persisting, awake throughout. My sense is that it was only my consciousness itself that persists.

Perhaps this is why our Upanishadic passage resorts to such odd language as, "To the unity of the One goes he," or, "That which is non-thought, [yet] which stands in the midst of thought, the unthinkable, supreme mystery!" It must be spoken of in peculiar terms because, compared with ordinary intentional experiences, it *is* peculiar!

Now, the parallels between these accounts of *samādhi* are remarkable, are they not? We have a wakeful persistence going on for many hours, yet the subject recalls no content. All our subjects were certain that they were not asleep; there was no sense on emerging of having blacked out, of being groggy, as one is when waking up, or of a hiatus in the continuity of wakefulness. There was, rather, a gap in time: the two interviewees had "lost" some four to six hours.

Chapter Three

Of Horses and Horse Carts

The Borderless Anonymity of Perennialism

Now that we have seen several reports of pure consciousness events, let us see how several recent philosophers will account for reports like these. The dominant model for mysticism through the 1970s and and 1980s was, as I noted, constructivism. This model for mysticism emerged largely as a response to the so called "perennial philosophy." Perennialists—Aldous Huxley,[1] Rudolf Otto,[2] Evelyn Underhill,[3] Frithjof Schuon,[4] Alan Watts,[5] Huston Smith,[6] and perhaps W. T. Stace,[7]—claimed that all religious experiences are similar and, further, that those experiences represent a direct contact with a (variously defined) absolute principle. Religious traditions, they argued, all teach a cross-culturally similar philosophy that does not change over the centuries, i.e., a perennial philosophy. Perennialists claimed not only that all mystical experiences were parallel; in part because they are, there is a parallel in metaphysical philosophy or theology between the major, or perhaps the primordial, traditions.

Perennialists were criticized for two very good reasons. First, the general conceptual paradigm in the humanities shifted toward the notion that language and culture shape experience. As Philip Almond put this in an excellent recent article, perennialism

> was vitiated by what amounts to a contemporary paradigm shift in epistemology toward the view that there are no human

31

experiences except through the sociolinguistic relations which mediate them.[8]

Perennialists seemed to maintain that mystical experiences were *not* subject to this shaping process. Yet they never offered a credible philosophical account for why mysticism is not so shaped. Indeed, they studiously ignored the whole whirlwind of epistemological questions that were swirling through the academy, and they thus appeared epistemologically naive.

Second, in order to establish their philosophical and religious parallels, perennialists often seemed academically irresponsible. To establish their universal claims, they often misquoted, mistranslated, misrepresented, and misinterpreted their sources in order to make them appear identical. For example, Rudolf Otto's *Mysticism East and West* was an attempt to draw parallels between the mystical writings of Shankara and Meister Eckhart. Otto was rightly criticized for misrepresenting both, however. Shankara's key notions of *māyā*, superimposition, the two forms of Brahman, and other technical terms were never given clear exposition by Otto, and thus the distinctiveness of his philosophy was muddled. Similarly, little of the nuance of Eckhart's doctrines of the Birth of the Word, of the boiling up (*ebullitio*) of the Godhead, or of the breakthrough (*durchbruch*) were ever clarified; again, what made Eckhart distinctive was lost. Aldous Huxley, in his renowned *Perennial Philosophy,* quoted little bits and pieces out of context from one mystic after another; in his zeal to make them seem identical, he offered little if any exegesis of any of them. Perennialists like these thus benuded the individual mystics and mystical traditions of their specific teachings. The various traditions seemed to disappear into some bland, characterless anonymity.

Constructivism Defined

It was the constructivists who pointed out these failures, in effect plucking the traditions and the mystics out of this desert-like anonymity. While their thought had its forerunners in such early twentieth-century thinkers as Dean Inge[9] and Rufus Jones,[10] the constructivist case was argued by Bruce Garside,[11] R. C. Zaehner,[12]

H. P. Owen,[13] John Hick,[14] and others. But the most forceful and influential statement of this view undoubtedly came in 1978, with the publication of *Mysticism and Philosophical Analysis*, edited by Steven Katz, and especially Katz's own article, "Language, Epistemology and Mysticism."[15] This article was buttressed by other contributions to that volume, notably those by Robert Gimello, Peter Moore, Frederick Streng, and Ninian Smart, as well as by supporters like Jerry Gill. More recently, Wayne Proudfoot and William Wainwright have argued a similar case.[16] But Katz's essay so forcefully stated this position that it became virtually the received view on mysticism in the eighties.[17] Because it is so seminal and forceful, it has become a lightning rod, attracting much of the criticism of this view.[18] I will consider it, as well as similar articles, in some detail in this chapter.

In his response to perennialism, Katz maintains two interconnected theses which are linked by an unstated presupposition. He offers a negative version of the first thesis when he opens his essay with a renowned summation of his "single epistemological assumption."

> There are NO pure (i.e. unmediated) experiences. Neither mystical experience nor more ordinary forms of experience give any indication, or any grounds for believing that they are unmediated. . . . The notion of unmediated experience seems, if not self-contradictory, at best empty. This epistemological fact seems to me to be true, because of the sorts of beings we are, even with regard to the experiences of those ultimate objects of concern with which mystics have had intercourse, i.e. God, Being, nirvana, etc. (26).

This is similar to Hick's statement that when we experience the divine, we do so always through a set of conceptual filters:

> [T]he infinite Spirit presses in all the time upon the multiplicity of finite human spirits, and yet always so that our finite awareness of this encompassing reality is filtered through a set of human religious concepts.[19]

Hans Penner also assumes mediation: "The basic assumption of this essay is that there are not direct experiences of the world, or between individuals except through the social relations which 'mediate' them."[20]

None of these writers clearly define what they mean by "mediated" or "unmediated." We are forced to rely, as they themselves clearly do, on the enormous theoretical and empirical constructivist literature, glossed in chapter 1 above, which has articulated this model in detail. This is important: Katz and the other constructivists have applied a model to the trophotropic states of mysticism that was developed to explain our ordinary, everyday experiences of speaking, perceiving, thinking, etc. Not mysticism.

This term, *unmediated,* and *mediate,* derives from the Latin *mediatus,* to be in the middle. It means to transmit or carry as an intermediate mechanism or agent. This suggests a neo-Kantian picture, whereby one's concepts and set serve as a filter or conduit between the conscious self and an object of experience. Katz sometimes suggests such a filtering model, as when he states that "all experience is processed through, organized by, and makes itself available to us in extremely complex epistemological ways" (26). He seems to be assuming here that no experiences can avoid being processed through and thereby shaped by these conceptual filters. Thus he has been called a neo-Kantian.[21] His assumption that there are *"no un*mediated experiences" is thus a double-negative version of the first thesis, *the constructivist thesis* or model, which is his essay's controlling metaphor. According to this view, "[t]he [mystical] experience itself as well as the form in which it is reported is shaped by concepts which the mystic brings to, and which shape his experience" (26).

Before going on, I want to stress here that the truth and applicability of this model is thus *assumed* from the outset. It is not proven or even argued for. The argument is thus on very soft philosophical grounds. The position's rhetorical and logical force rests entirely on the fact that the model is taken over, *en bloc,* as an assumption from articles which have demonstrated its application to other, that is, *ordinary,* experiences. Neither Katz, Hick, Penner, nor anyone else for that matter has shown why it is appropriate to apply the constructivist model to another experiential mode. Again, they may be explaining the feelings of love on the basis of feelings like those we have in a foot race.

Although the second thesis is an unstated presupposition, it plays a key role in Katz's and others' article. With it, I believe, no right-thinking person would disagree. It is that different religious traditions provide their participants with different concepts and beliefs—different "sets." Subjects will come to their various religious or mystical experiences with different values, conceptual backgrounds, patterns of behavior, etc. Even within a single tradition, different schools, different periods, or even different teachers within the same school will provide their adherents with different sets. As the adept matures he or she will acquire new concepts and beliefs. Hence, even one person will come at different times with different concepts and beliefs (27, 59), and hence their experiences will necessarily differ as they age.

The third axiom of the article is the logical product of the first thesis (constructivism) and the above presupposition. This we may call the *pluralism thesis*. Since all mystical experiences are in part shaped and formed by the concepts and beliefs of their religious traditions, and different traditions and schools supply individuals with different concepts and beliefs, mystics from different religious traditions will necessarily have experiences that are conditioned and shaped differently. Religious experiences from different eras and traditions will necessarily differ.

> Thus for example, the nature of the Christian mystic's pre-mystical consciousness informs the mystical consciousness such that he experiences the mystic reality[22] in terms of Jesus, the Trinity, or a personal God, etc., rather than in terms of the non-personal, non-everything, to be precise, Buddhist doctrine of nirvana. Care must also be taken to note that even the plurality of experience found in Hindu, Christian, Muslim, Jewish, Buddhist mystical traditions, etc., have to be broken down into smaller units (27).

In other words, Katz, Gill, Hick, Penner, and many other constructivists argue for a pluralism thesis.[23] The pluralism thesis is important to them, in as much as it is their answer to the perennial philosophers' claims that all mysticism is *the same* across time and tradition and can thus serve to establish a "perennial" philosophy. In opposition to the perennialists, constructivists believe they can do justice to the full range of mystical experiences and traditions. The constructivists pride themselves, with some justification, on the success of their "plea for the recognition of differences" (25).

These two theses, constructivism and pluralism, are the twin theses of the constructivist position. Since the logical foundation of pluralism is constructivism, I will turn to it in a moment. Before doing so however, I want to clarify what we mean by a model.

Of Models, Explanations, and Causes

Constructivism is presented sometimes as an explanatory and some-times as a causal model. These are not the same. An explanation is intended to make a thing or a phenomenon (the explanandum) intelligible, or to say why it is as it is. A common procedure is to provide an account (the explanans) or model that reduces the un-familiar to the familiar, typically in a simplified way. This reduc-tion does not necessarily provide a cause, but rather a generalized or familiar *pattern* to which the explanandum conforms: all water heated to 100° C. at sea level pressure boils, this water has been so heated, etc. An explanatory model (sometimes called a descriptive model) is a detailed picture, often graphic, of the way a phenomenon works, i.e., heat is like billiard balls bouncing around rapidly. It pre-sents a picture in familiar terms that is analogous to the unfamiliar phenomenon. The explanatory model, to be convincing, must seem sufficiently near to the circumstances to warrant being applied.

A very common way of explaining something is to provide a causal model. Causal models are typically a subset of explanatory models.[24] They provide details of particular relationships within the explanatory model. Here is a causal model of heat: if I *intro-duce* a heat source into a closed system, the "billiard balls" will bounce around faster. The model shows the clear connection be-tween a cause and an effect within the familiar picture. A causal model demonstrates a relationship between two or more elements within an explanatory model.

Many successful causal models are nomological (or deductive): All A's are B, this is an A, therefore this is a B. "Anytime" you put a heat source into a closed system containing free atoms, the heat will increase; here is a heat source in this volume of air; therefore the air's temperature will increase. Technically, a causal model will elucidate the explanandum if the universal hypothesis (All A's are B's) is considered valid and if it is believed to be appropriately applied to the situation, that is, if the conditions of the universal hypothesis are fulfilled.

A causal model may be disproved in any or all of the following ways:

1. In the case of a nomological causal model, the universal hypothesis may be shown to be invalid. All A's are not B's or all actions A do not bring about B's. A necessary and sufficient cause may be shown to be merely sufficient, but not necessary.

2. The conditions are not fulfilled. This is not an A or a B, A does not precede B, etc.

3. The causal or explanatory model is awkward and inelegant; it "does not cut at the joints." Ptolemaic astronomy predicted the phenomena, but inelegantly. The introduction of a more elegant and satisfying model is often the best way to disprove a nomological model.

4. Subsidiary predictions implied by the causal model are not fulfilled. A does bring about B, but not the B_1 we would expect. This can be re-written as # 1 above. I include it because it often is the unexpected minor discrepancies that lead to the invalidation or adjustment of a causal theory. Relatively minor discrepancies in the behavior of light led to the assertion of its particle and wave characteristics, and ultimately to quantum mechanics.

With this clarification in hand, I want to present in greater detail the constructivist explanatory and causal model of mysticism as we have it from constructivists. Since mysticism is unfamiliar, it is only fitting that theorists should present an explanatory model, that is, present it in terms that are more familiar. The terms they have provided are, again, those of ordinary perception and perceptual psychology.[25]

Perceptual and Mystical Constructivism

Constructivists generally base their strategy on perceptual psychology, especially on visual and sense experiences. Katz, for example, provides us with a single "non-controversial example" of how an experience might be in part shaped or determined by someone's set. This is a very important passage, since it is the only one that offers the familiar account that purportedly shows how an experience might be shaped by concepts and beliefs.

> [B]eliefs shape experience, just as experience shapes belief. To take, for the moment, a non-controversial example of this, consider Manet's paintings of Notre Dame. Manet "knew" Notre Dame was a Gothic cathedral, and so "saw" it as a Gothic cathedral as testified to by his paintings which present Notre Dame with Gothic archways. Yet close examination will reveal that certain of the archways of Notre Dame which Manet painted as Gothic are in fact Romanesque. As Coleridge reminded us: "the mind half-sees and half-creates." (30)

(With all due respect, I believe it was Monet, not Manet, and the famous painting was of the Rouen Cathedral.)[26] This is a good example, for it is clear how Monet's experience might have been shaped by what he expected to see. The visual information on the church before him was of Romanesque (i.e., rounded) archways. Due to his expectation that he would see a Gothic (i.e., pointed) archway, he *altered* the visual information before him and instead "saw" pointed archways, as is shown by his painting. He overlooked what was there and substituted for it something that was not there.

When the perceptual psychologist E. H. Gombrich provides parallel examples of this phenomenon, he generalizes about the kind of process involved in such a perceptual error.

> The individual visual information . . . [is] entered, as it were, upon a pre-existing blank or formulary. And as often happens with blanks, if they have no provisions for certain kinds of information we consider essential, it is just too bad for the information.[27]

In this often-studied and fascinating process, we *replace* one segment of visual data with another based on what are called perceptual "automatizations," habits.[28] Katz is thus suggesting that by "shaped" or "colored" he means that we impose our blanks or formularies onto the manifold of experience, and thus encounter things in the terms our formularies supply. It is easy to see why Katz uses the term "mediate," for here the formulary or concept stands between (*mediatus*) the visual information and our perception of it.

Mystical experiences are, constructivists maintain, created by a process similar to this one. They differ from ordinary experiences only because they result from the superimposition of a *new* set of blanks and formularies which are applied to the objects of experience. The yogi, for example, imposes a new set of automatizations onto his experience, i.e., yogic.

> Properly understood, yoga, for example, is not an unconditioning or deconditioning of consciousness, but rather it is a reconditioning of consciousness, i.e. a substituting of one form of conditioned and/or contextual consciousness for another, albeit a new, unusual, and perhaps altogether more interesting form of conditioned-contextual consciousness. (57)

The mystic's acculturation, or rather re-culturation, might be analogous to, say, a Chinese painter who moves to Paris and learns to see with a new set of formularies, i.e., Gothic. If he imposes these onto Notre Dame he is doing something quite close to what the mystic is: superimposing a *new* set of formularies onto the manifold of experience.

Like his fellow constructivists, Katz is making an epistemologically heavy claim here. He is not asserting that previously held beliefs and concepts will come into play only in the *post*-experiential shaping of a mystic's *descriptions* of an experience. Beliefs and concepts will play their role in the shaping of the actual mystical *experience*(s) themselves:

> The *experience itself* as well as the form in which it is reported is shaped by concepts which the mystic brings to, and which shape, his experience. (26, emphasis mine)

> This process of differentiation of mystical experience into the patterns and symbols of established religious communities is experiential . . . it is at work before, *during* and after the experience. (27, emphasis mine)

> [A]s a result of his process of intellectual acculturation in its broadest sense, the mystic brings to his experience a world of concepts, images, symbols, and values which *shape as well as colour the experience* he eventually and actually has. (46, emphasis mine)

Just as Monet's expectations led him to "see" Gothic arches (not just paint them) so too the mystic purportedly sees in the terms his tradition provides. Katz repeatedly emphasizes that not only will the circumstances surrounding the mystical experience be formed by the tradition, but the actual character of the experience itself will be shaped and determined by the subject's expectations.

> This much is certain: the mystical experience must be mediated by the kinds of beings that we are. And the kind of beings that we are requires that experience be not only instantaneous and discontinuous, but that it also involve memory, apprehension, expectation, language, accumulation of prior experience, concepts, and expectations, with each experience being built on the back of all these elements and being shaped anew by each fresh experience. (58)

> The creative role of the self in his experience is not analogous to the passive role of the tape-recorder or camera. Even in mystical experience there seems to be epistemological activity of the sort we know as discrimination and integration and, in certain cases at least, of further mental activities such as relating the present experience to past and future experience, as well as traditional theological claims and metaphysics. (60)

In short, subjects undergo their experiences using terms provided by their backgrounds. Speaking technically, a complete phenomenological description of the experience itself will reveal traces of the subject's conceptual background.

Peter Moore makes a similar point when he emphasizes that a correct method of studying mysticism must include an analysis of doctrine:

> [T]o ignore the doctrinal elements in an account is to risk ignoring important features of the experience itself. For there is a complex interplay between experience and doctrine, both at the external level where doctrine affects the description of an experience, at at the internal level where doctrine may *affect the substance of the experience itself.*[29]

William Wainwright[30] and Wayne Proudfoot[31] make similar points.

So far we have an explanatory (or descriptive) model: the mystic is undergoing something like the imposition or superimposition of formularies (or blanks) onto his experience; hence he or she "experiences the mystic reality in terms of Jesus Christ, the Trinity, or a personal God, etc." (27). That is, he or she will have an experience "under a description" he or she will "experience as." When the Hindu has an experience, he or she will experience it "as" Brahman, imposing the term *Brahman* more or less consciously onto the manifold of experience. The associations of that term are thereby drawn into the experience, and with it, its full significance.

There are two or three possible interpretations of constructivism here. When Gimello writes that mysticism is "simply the psychosomatic enhancement" of the set, he suggests that there is a complete construction involved.

> [M]ystical experience is simply the psychosomatic enhancement of religious beliefs and values or of beliefs and values of other kinds which are held "religiously."[32]

Gimello's take is that the experience is one hundred percent shaped, determined, and provided by the set. A hallucination may be one such example, for no sensory input is involved. Only the set, given life by whatever idiosyncratic psychological processes, is playing a constitutive role.

Second, there may be an incomplete constructionism at work: *some* of the shape of the experience is provided by the set and some of its shape is provided by something else—sensory input or whatever. Monet's misperception was in part set-provided and in part a result of his response to the gray mass before him. Most sensory experiences seem shaped this way.

Incomplete constructivism is, on its face, the more plausible. But it cannot do the work required by the pluralism thesis. This is clearest in the case in which the role of the set is negligible, for then experiences from various traditions would be distinguishable only in negligible or insignificant ways. If construction is incomplete then the perennialist might say, as Ninian Smart does, that mysticism is to some extent the same but only "different flavors" accrue to those experiences as a result of the constructive activities of the subject.[33] If there are only different flavors to a common underlying type of experience, then the perennialist could base his claims of identity on that underlying parallelism, and Katz's plea for the recognition of differences would go unheeded. This is key: the best way, indeed probably the only way, to defend the pluralist hypothesis would be through a complete constructivism.

There is a third possible interpretation of mystical construction. We might call it catalytic constructivism. It is that the adept's generating problems lead him or her to hold to beliefs and perform practices that themselves act as catalysts for mystical experiences. The following passages may be read in this light:

> The respective "generating" problems at the heart of each tradition suggest their respective alternative answers.... The mind can be seen to contribute both the problem and the means of its overcoming: it defines the origin, the way, and the goal, shaping experience accordingly. . . . These constructive conditions of consciousness produce the grounds on which mystical experience is possible at all. (62–3)

The Buddhist experience of *nirvana*, the Jewish of *devekuth*, and the Christian of *unio-mystica*, the Sufi of *'fana*, the Toaist of *Tao* are the results, at least in part, of specific conceptual influences, i.e., the "starting problems" of each doctrinal, theological system (62).

> [O]ntological structures inherent in language and judgement pre-create the contours of experience . . . this structural matrix works to locate both experience and the experiencer (the mystic) in a given socio-historic conceptual field whose problems and problematic he or she adopts and aims to solve.[34]

The idea here seems to be that it is only because they hold to certain beliefs and have certain generating problems that someone will meditate and thereby come to experience *samādhi*. This however is not the epistemologically heavy version of the thesis which the pluralism claim demands. Someone may very well come to a mystical experience by performing certain mystical practices, yet that experience may not be epistemologically shaped by those problems or practices. That is, a complete phenomenological description of that experience might not reveal traces of the set.[35] The generative problems and meditative techniques may serve as a catalyst for the experience—leading someone to meditate, fast, or pray—but not play an epistemologically heavy role in shaping its character. Unless we can see on other grounds an epistemologically heavy connection between set and experience, the connection here is insufficient to make the constructivist's case.

> Occasionally Katz, Gimello, and others seem to argue for a causal model.

What I wish to show is only that there is a *clear causal connection* between the religious and social structure one brings to experience and the nature of one's actual religious experience. (40) (Emphasis mine)

Emphasizing the role of specifically spiritual models (Gurus, saints, etc.) Katz writes,

[O]ur deconstruction and re-conceptualization suggests that models play an important role in providing our map of reality and of what is real and, thus, contribute heavily to the creation of experience—I repeat to the creation of experience.[36]

Unfortunately, it is hard to say just what this "clear causal connection" might mean. Just how does a set "cause" an experience? How complete is this cause? Everybody has models, and thus everyone has similar "causes." Why do so few have mystical experiences? What are the mechanics of causation? Which are primary and which secondary "causes"? How can we distinguish a necessary cause from a merely contingent one? Thus the causal thesis is, at best, vague.

Constructivism Evaluated: The Cart and the Horse

This model has several not inconsiderable virtues. First, considering the plausibility and, for most phenomena, widespread acceptance of this picture of experience as, in part, shaped and constructed, it is certainly credible. It "seems to make sense." Second, with reference to mysticism the account certainly illuminates the distinctions between mystics from different traditions. Katz and his colleagues are to be congratulated for drawing attention to the differences—both great and small—between mystics in different traditions and within the same tradition. His "plea for the recognition of differences" has indeed been heard. They have successfully removed the mystics from the perennialists' borderless desert.

Despite its virtues however, this position has several major failings, some of which I have already mentioned. Its greatest and most damaging failing is that it is inadequate to the data it purportedly explains: it cannot plausibly account for many common forms of mysticism, among which is pure consciousness events such as those we saw in the previous chapter. Nor can it elegantly explain mysticism's unpredicted, surprising, or novel nature. I will argue these points in detail in later chapters. Furthermore, many constructivists rely on the philosophical notion of intentionality for part of their philosophical backing. This reliance is never argued, is counterintuitive, and is philosophically suspect, a point I will argue in the next chapter. For now, let me point out some of the problems with Stephen Katz's article. This may be seen as an instance of the first and third ways of disproving a causal model, showing that the universal hypothesis is invalid and showing that the theory is inelegant.

Structure of the Article

As I noted earlier, Katz opens with an assumption concerning the character of all experience, and assumes—tacitly—that it applies to mystical experience. This commits the fallacy of *petitio principii*, assuming what is to be proved. It is ironic that Katz claims that his is an improvement on the other approaches because, unlike theirs he maintains, his makes no "a priori assumptions" and proves its case by "convincing logical argument" (65). Just the contrary is true: once he has assumed that language enters and in part shapes and constructs all experiences, the remaining thirty-nine pages of the article provide virtually no further argumentation but only instances of the assumed relationship.

Here are two examples. After describing the pre-experiential set of the Jewish mystic, he writes, "that this complex pre-experiential pattern affects the actual experience of the Jewish mystic is an unavoidable conclusion" (34). After noting the differences in pre-experiential set between Jewish and Buddhist mystics, he says, "just setting this Buddhist understanding of the nature of things over against the Jewish should, in itself, already be strong evidence for the thesis that what the Buddhist experiences as *nirvāna* is different from what the Jew experiences as *devekuth*" (38). Merely setting the set of the Jew over against the Buddhist's serves as "evidence and documentation" of *only* the claim that these doctrines are different. It shows absolutely nothing about the differences between experiences unless we *assume* a connection between set and mystical experience. But that's exactly the point he claims to be proving.

In neither case has Katz shown just how a constructive process takes place, or how one experience actually had different phenomenological characteristics than another. All he offers are summaries of religious doctrines and restatements of his original assumption. These are *instances* of an assumed claim, not arguments for it.

Systematically Incomplete

I noted that one of the twin theses of Katz's articles and those of other constructivists is the pluralism thesis, their answer to the perennial philosophical claim that mysticism is everywhere the same. The implied argument here is that any change in religious concepts *ipso facto* means a change in mystical experience. If so, then differences in any single concept held by two mystics implies differences in their experiences.

It may be that a certain concept held by a subject will play a role in forming some experience(s), but, as Anthony Perovich has shown, it is an overstatement to claim that *each and every* concept held by a subject will necessarily play a role in shaping each and every experience.[37] Did the concept of a bicycle pedal, for instance, play an *identifiable* role in your experience as you just read the previous sentence? If I change my image of a bike pedal from metal to plastic, if I alter *any* concept at all, do *all* of my experiences necessarily change in identifiable ways? If this is so, then each and every one of my experiences would change with every new notion learned. But this is clearly absurd, for what would it then mean to learn something? I can only learn within a coherent set of experiences which are part of a single consistent background for any experience.

Yet Katz does not specify just which concepts enter into just which experiences. He implies that *religious* concepts play the principal role. Articles by Moore, Gimello, and others may be viewed as elucidating some of the relevant concepts that construct these experiences.[38] But here the problem is again an embarrassment of riches. If we take these articles seriously, not only do notions like "God" play a role, but so too do the following effect mystical experiences:

religious architecture; religious music and dance forms; epistemological and rhetorical teachings; dogmatic principles and traditional
beliefs; religious institutions; religious practices; one's concepts,
expectations, and intentions; and even the mystic's wider cultural
background.[39] We are back to an "every concept effects every experience" claim. Clearly we are in need of a plausible delimitation of
the relevant concepts.[40]

But this the constructivist will probably be unwilling to do, for
to do so would be to undercut the logical foundation of the (anti-
perennialist) pluralism thesis. If differences in some concepts do
not imply changes in mystical experiences, then the perennialist
might argue that concepts like *shunyata* and *samādhi* are "close
enough" to warrent a claim of parallel experiences. Phillip Almond
argues that despite minor differences, parallels *can* be found in the
doctrines of medieval Jewish, Christian, and Sufi mystics in as
much as they were all deeply indebted to neo-Platonism.[41] A similar set of parallels could probably be argued for mystics of Hinduism, Buddhism, and perhaps Taoism. Hence, if the constructivist
delimits his contextualistic claims, he is in danger of threatening
the very underpinnings of his pluralism.

The incompleteness of the constructivist case may serve as a
protective device. It allows Katz to say that, as quoted earlier, "just
setting this Buddhist understanding of the nature of things over
against the Jewish should, in itself, already be strong evidence for
the thesis that what the Buddhist experiences as *nirvāna* is different from what the Jew experiences as *devekuth*" (38)—without
showing in detail how this is so. Were he to show precisely which
concepts differed and how they created actually different experiences, someone else could point to *parallels* in concepts and thus
argue for experiential parallels. Thus, as used, vagueness serves to
systematically protect the case for pluralism.

Sense and Reference

Katz implicitly assumes a one-to-one relationship between concept
and experience. This leads to absurdities, I argued. Let us grant him
the lesser but more defensible claim of a one-to-one relationship
between the concept of the mystical "object" and the mystical expe-

rience. There must be a difference between the Hindu's experience of the object *(sic)* he encounters as *samādhi* (or its equivalents) and the Buddhist's experience of the object *(sic)* he encounters as *śūnyata* (or its equivalents).

However, even this more defensible claim would be fallacious. It implicitly denies the possibility that there may be two terms with different senses which have the same referent. As Friedreich Frege pointed out, two terms—such as the North Star and the Pole Star—may have different senses but the same referent. So too, it may be that a single *experience* can plausibly be referred to with two different terms.

This is not a mere logical nicety. Certainly there have been people who have participated in one tradition and were later converted to another, and themselves used two different terms to think or speak of one experience. "I used to think of that experience as *samādhi*, but now I think of it as *śūnyata" makes sense*. Yet on Katz's account of the incomparability between experiences in different traditions, this sentence should be utter nonsense, since the experience of *samādhi* must be so different from the experience of *śūnyata* as to render them utterly incomparable.

Extending this, given care in communication, I see no reason that different people could not refer to one experience differently. Were a Hindu Guru and a Buddhist Roshi to hear someone report some experience, it would make sense that one might say, "that's an instance of *samādhi*," while the other might say, "oh, you've experienced *śūnyata*." Whether this is in fact what they would say is not a matter for a philosopher to determine in advance, strictly on the basis of some assumed epistemological theory. It is an empirical matter. The Roshi, not the philosopher, should decide whether someone's experience qualifies as an instance of *śūnyata*.

What would it take to show that some religious experiences from different traditions do not differ? Is it enough to note how mystical *texts* differ? As we noted in the last chapter, an exclusive reliance on texts as our source material is dangerous. Texts are particularly unreliable as evidence for the differences between mystical *experiences*. For it has never been shown—and it is *not* true in any obvious way—that if two mystical texts differ then the mystical experiences to which they refer must necessarily differ. I have shown that it is theoretically possible that two different people or traditions may refer to precisely the same experience type in two different ways. In other words, to determine whether or not experiences from two or more traditions differ, it is not enough to only compare mystical texts.

To determine whether or not different people may be referring to the same experience type, then, again we must go beyond the mere comparison of texts. One easy way of establishing this would be to have a practitioner from one tradition describe his or her experiences in language that was laden with a minimum of jargon, i.e., least highly ramified, in Ninian Smart's terms, to a spiritual master from a different tradition. If that guru accepts the description as an adequate description of something in his, the second, tradition, then we have a *single* experience description that is taken as an instance of something in two different traditions. One experience type (sense) will be taken in two different traditions (reference). This may give us the evidence we need to check the pluralism claim.

Let me offer then the following interview I conducted with the Venerable Piya Tissa. A highly respected teacher from the Vipassyana Theravada tradition, Piya Tissa is the abbot and head of the American Sri Lankan Buddhist Society. The interview happened to be conducted in front of a small gathering of Buddhist practitioners. I detailed to him my own experiences of pure consciousness, much as I described them in the last chapter. Again, these did not occur during the practice of a Buddhist technique, but rather occurred in conjunction with my neo-Advaitan (Hindu) meditation program. Thus here was *prima facie* a cross-traditional discussion of a single experience. Here are excerpts from that interview:

> Q: I've been meditating for about twenty-one years, and I meditate about two times a day. The thing that I don't quite understand in Buddhist terms is this: sometimes in meditation my thoughts get very quiet, everything gets very quiet, and the object of meditation passes out of my awareness. I'm inside, yet the object of meditation is going away, fading out of my awareness, and thoughts too are fading out of my awareness. And I'm left just quiet inside, completely without thoughts inside, not aware of the object of meditation, not aware of my body. Just quiet inside. And I'm not exactly sure what this is about.
>
> P.T. That is actually known as *samādhi*, concentration. . . .

Here is a clear case of an experience description from one tradition being accepted as a common experience type in another. He called this *samādhi* and soon equated it with "one-pointedness." After a brief discussion I asked of *samādhi* in the well-known Theravadin text, the Visuddhimagga.

Q. Does the Vissudhimaggha describe *samādhi?*

PT. Oh yes.

Q. Where does *samādhi* come with reference to the *jhānas?*

PT. *Samādhi* is prior to *jhānas.*

Q. Ah.

PT. First one is *samādhi*, concentration. [This is] when one pointedness comes to mind. And then that must be developed.

At this point he asked me whether a white light appeared just before or after this experience, which I confirmed.

Q. So when we talk about one-pointedness of mind—I've seen where [the Visuddhimagga] talks about one-pointedness of mind—in my meditation when all the thoughts go away and all the awareness of breathing goes away, and all sensations go away, no sensations, and I'm not particularly aware of the white light, and I just go into this state—then is this *samādhi before* the first *jhāna?*

PT. Yeah. This is actually still *samādhi.* Not *jhāna, samādhi.*

I believe Piya Tissa is well within normative Abhidharma thought to call my experience *samādhi.* The Vissuddhimaggha, refers to *samādhi* as the "profitable *cittass ekaggata*, unification of mind," which means the bringing to one-pointedeness the various competing directions of the mind. It is roughly like focusing a search-light (II:2:1,n.2).

It is concentration *(samādhi)* in the sense of concentrating *(samādhana).* What is this concentrating. It is the centering *(adhana)* of consciousness and consciousness-concomitants evenly . . . " "Concentration has non-distraction as its characteristic . . . It is manifested as non-wavering." [42]

And I too would say that, despite the fact that I am not a Buddhist, the key characteristic of my experience *is* its steady, non-distracted, nonwavering character.

Now, is mine *precisely* the same experience as that which is meant by "*samādhi*" in Theravada Buddhism? I can say several things. First, at least for his disciples, Piya Tissa qualifies as an authority on what his tradition means by this term. In order to ascertain if it is an experience of *samādhi* he asked me precisely the same sorts of questions he might have asked a disciple as he tried to determine whether or not that person had indeed had an experience of *samādhi*. Since he confirmed my experience, it can be assumed that he would confirm that a disciple had an experience of *samādhi* in a similar way.

Second, let us turn this around. Let us assume that the constructivist thesis is true, and that background expectations do indeed shape mystical experiences. When Piya Tissa confirmed my experience, we can assume that hearing his confirmation, the Theravadin disciples in the room would have now gained expectations that they would have an experience *just like mine*. If experiences are indeed a product of expectations, then these Buddhists would have an experience *just like* a neo-Advaitan (Hindu) meditator's, and the pluralism claim that different traditions' experiences are never identical would be clearly false.

Through much of early Indian history, Buddhists and Hindus coexisted in many parts of India. Buddhists and Hindus were often at the same courts, and had discussions and debates, some of which were quite renowned. It seems likely that through history, there were probably Hindu meditators like me who went to Buddhist teachers. And we must assume that they talked with Buddhists who were not teachers. Thus, we must assume that if the constructivist thesis is indeed true, and there was cross-communication, then the pluralism thesis must be false, for Buddhist experiences would have been shaped by Hindu thought and vice versa.

I was surprised not only that Piya Tissa accepted my experience as a legitimate instance of *samādhi*, but that when he asked me questions about concomitant experience, i.e., a light, this also matched my experiences. (The experience of light is itself very common in various traditions.) Thus, if my neo-Advaitan experience counted as Buddhist *samadhi* for Piya Tissa, should it not count for us?

Piya Tissa thus provided very strong evidence that participants in two different traditions, despite the differences in their conceptual set and background, *can* accept the same experience in different terms. This is strong evidence countering the pluralist hypothesis.

Post Hoc or *Propter Hoc?*

Even if we grant Katz that the mystical experience of someone always does match his tradition (which I do not), in making his causal claim Katz may still be accused of committing the fallacy of *post hoc ergo propter hoc,* i.e., if B follows A, then B is necessarily caused by A. Wainwright offers the compelling example of a Frenchman's and an Eskimo's gastrointestinal experiences.[43] Their cultures differ; probably their gastrointestinal experiences will differ. Probably too their expectations about those feelings and sensations will be highly correlatable with them. But that does not mean that either their culture or their expectations *caused* those digestional experiences. The relationship between experience and expectation may be contingent, not necessary.

The Horse Cart

The final failing with this article, and with constructivism in general, is the most damning: in the constructivist approach, mysticism becomes virtually an epiphenomenon of language and culture. Constructivism has an underlying emphasis, if not an outright claim, that tends toward *cultural reductionism.*

Its conservative—backward looking—character is seen especially clearly in Katz's second essay.

> What one reads, learns, knows, intends and experiences along the path creates to some degree . . . the *anticipated* experience made manifest. That is to say, there is an intimate, even necessary connection between the mystical and religious texts studied and assimilated, the mystical experience had, and the mystical experience reported.[44]

One reads, learns, and intends things obviously, *in the past.* This is to say, today's mystical experience is the result of yesterday's indoctrination.

Having described the models the adept learns along the way, Katz writes that,

> There can be no doubt of the significance of models in mystical, as in all, religious groups. And this component tends to exert an essentially conservative influence . . . models play an important role in providing our map of reality and of what is real and, thus, contribute heavily to the creation of experience—I repeat to the *creation* of experience.[45]

Robert Gimello writes:

> All mystical experiences, like all experiences generally, have specific structures, and these are neither fortuitous nor *sui generis*. Rather they are given to the experiences, at their very inceptions, by concepts, beliefs, values, and expectations *already operative* in the mystics' minds.[46]

Similarly, when Wayne Proudfoot focuses his attention on the terms that are used to label a mystical experience, it is clear that those labels were learned previously.[47] Each theorist claims that it is the system of religious indoctrination—the mystic's accumulation of knowledge, language, models, etc.—that stands as the primary formative element.

Mysticism here becomes a kind of delusion fostered by the indoctrination system. But it thereby loses its authenticity. Rather than a contact with any element that is extrinsic to culture and indoctrination, constructivism exclusively emphasizes the role of intrinsic features of culture and language. It, says, as it were, that each mystic *first* learns about mysticism and *then* has the experience. The mystic's background of language and belief is like a horse that pulls the cart of experience. The Greek Orthodox horse always pulls one to a Greek Orthodox experience, the Hindu Water Buffalo to a Hindu experience, and never do they pull their carts to the same place.

The crucial element of this model is that the horse *always* goes before the cart: one learns first and experiences later. But, as we saw in the previous chapter, this is simply wrong. Daido Sensei Loori's first experience of *samādhi* happened on a *photography* workshop with Minor White. He had "had no training in meditation or anything," and was just sitting in front of a tree when it happened. He had not begun Zen practice, but just the reverse. The aftereffects of his experience were so powerful that he spent the next years of his life trying to recreate it, and, as a result of the whole experience, *began* the practice of Zazen. It was the experience that *led* to the doctrine, not the other way around! The cart of experience went *before* the horse.

Concluding Questions

I have shown that, based on problems internal to them, the key constructivist articles do not conclusively establish that mystical experiences are in part shaped, constructed, or formed by the subject's beliefs or expectations. However, despite the flaws of its lead articles, the constructivist approach as a whole raises some very interesting questions. Considering the importance of and depth of agreement in the academy about the constructivist model in general, it is important that we not let the flaws in any particular articulations of this position deter us from considering the applicability of this general model to mysticism. For as I have noted, constructivism has dominated the study of mysticism and religious experience, just as it dominates so much of the humanities today; it won't go away by showing that any particular versions of it are fallacious.

The general question then to which I shall address myself in the next two chapters is: can the constructivistic approach to "ordinary" experience adequately and elegantly explain mystical experience.[48]

In the next chapter, I will explore two doctrines on which much of constructivism rests: Kant's doctrine of the mediation of experience, and Brentano and Husserl's doctrine of intentionality. The Kantian epistemology stands as the foundation of most modern epistemological thought. Husserl's doctrine of intentionality is an extremely well-regarded thesis for understanding much of experience. I will argue, however, that when it comes to an analysis of mysticism, both are ill applied and cannot bear the philosophical weight that has been placed on them. Insofar as any account of mysticism is grounded on these doctrines, it is profoundly flawed.

Then, in chapter 5, I will note that the data of Mahāyāna Buddhism tends to militate against the constructivist model. While with reference to ordinary experience several respected teachers in this tradition offer a view quite similar to modern constructivists', those Eastern authors explicitly *deny* its applicability to mystical experiences.

Mystical constructivism having been substantially challenged, in Part II I will begin to develop my own model for mysticism, which will, it is hoped, do it more justice and make more elegant sense.

Chapter Four

Non-Linguistic Mediation

Over the last several years, some of my work has been given the honor of being read, pondered, and criticized.[1] One of the more common criticisms of my writings is that I have responded to what I took to be the "received view" of mysticism, which is that of a sociolinguistic constructivism. As a result, I have been subject to *its* limitations. Bruce Mangan, for example, points out that my work has "constructivism as its foil. Too much has rubbed off, and Forman's concern with language is still, I think, obsessive."[2] There are other, deeper, forms of construction, he suggests, and mysticism may be better analyzed in their terms. Unfortunately, Mangan does not indicate just what they are.

Matthew Bagger suggests that though my critique may have some plausibility at the conscious level, the "linguistic framework continues to operate and shape experience at a subconscious level."[3] Again, this is but a suggestion, and we need to know just what sorts of subconscious levels may be at work.

But the most powerful critique to date has fleshed out this criticism more clearly. In his thoughtful *Journal of the American Academy of Religion* article, Larry Short argues that there are two more fundamental forms of mediation than the sociolinguistic.

> Working "downward," there is what Wittgenstein called the "pre-linguistic," including for instance, the fact that humans are social and linguistic (regardless of the particulars of any given society and language), that we have certain appetites, and that we come with given physical, perceptual and neurological equipment. Deeper yet (i.e. logically prior) are Kant's categories (time, space, and causality) [which are, according to Kant] necessary characteristics of any intelligence in order to have coherent

experience. Certainly . . . [these categorical elements] are present in our languages, but that is because they underlie our languages, not because they are products of them. They are, in short, forms of mediation that are not solely sociolinguistic and so do not disappear if we "forget" language . . .[4]

Bagger, Mangan, and Short have a good point. There certainly *are* elements that construct our experience in ways that are logically prior to specific language. Wittgenstein's point is certainly well taken: the fact that humans are linguistic and social, for example, certainly does shape my *linguistic* utterances and my *social* interactions. The fundamental ability to say anything meaningful certainly does impact on my ability to say any one thing.

But does the mere fact that I *can* do so *ipso facto* influence my experience when I am *not* speaking or thinking? An analogy: Humans have the "prelinguistic" inner ear ability to balance well enough to ride a bicycle. Does this inner ear ability shape my experience as I am reading these words? Falling asleep? If we say that it "must" shape these experiences, then our claim has clearly become nonfalsifiable. As Short himself puts it, "the prelinguistic . . . underlies our *languages*" (emphasis mine), not "all experiences." Since it is not self-evidently true, the onus of proof rests on Short and the others to show how someone's prelinguistic ability mediates in a significant way their particular non-*linguistic* experiences.

Short turns to Kant. Kant may offer a more plausible way to understand non-linguistic mediating. After all, Katz and his colleagues are fond of the Kantian term "mediation," and seem to regard his doctrines as the logical foundation of their own. To see whether Short's and the mystical constructivists' arguments are valid, then, let us ask, do Kant's presentations of space, time, and the categories militate for the claim that a mystical event like the PCE must be mediated in terms of his "logically prior" *a priori* elements? Let us look at Kant's *Critique of Pure Reason*, where he articulated these claims. Do its arguments have anything to teach us about the mediation or construction of mystical experiences?

Following that, we will look at another kind of possibly universal sort of non-linguistic construction, the fundamental epistemological structure called "intentionality," which is another of the claims on which constructivism is grounded. Here again we will ask if it can serve as a reliable philosophical basis for our understanding of mysticism.

I should warn the reader that in this chapter I will be exploring and responding to the specific arguments of Kant, Brentano, and Husserl. Though I believe that this chapter is philosophically very important, it may seem relatively technical or "dry." The less philosophically minded reader may prefer to jump immediately to chapter 5.

Kant and the PCE

Do Kant's arguments lead us to believe that all experiences, including the PCE and perhaps other mystical experiences, are mediated by his categories? On the very first page Kant tells us that the knowledge to which he will address himself starts with "experience," by which he means the experience of "objects affecting our senses."

> There can be no doubt that all our knowledge begins with experience. For how should our faculty of knowledge be awakened into action did not *objects affecting our senses* partly of themselves produce representations, partly arouse the activity of our understanding to compare these representations, and, by combining or separating them, work up the raw material of the sensible impressions into that knowledge of objects which is entitled experience? (B1)

Thus, from the very start, Kant is clear that what he is analyzing is our experience *of objects*, indeed *sensory* objects. The processes he will portray thus "begin with" objects. Conversely, the *Critique* is *not* about an objectless awareness, or at least not overtly. Kant never, to my knowledge, directly discussed such mystical experiences.[5] An experience that was not an encounter with some object would then, in all likelihood, not be subject to the mediating epistemological structures he will suggest. Let us turn to his epistemological structures to see whether they do indeed account for the kind of experiences we are exploring.

The Transcendental Aesthetic

The first mediating elements of the *Critique of Pure Reason* are, as Short suggests, "space" and "time."

Space. Kant's first two arguments about space center on the following assertion.[6]

> In order that certain sensations be referred to something outside me (that is, to something in another region of space from that in which I find myself), and similarly in order that I may be able to represent them as outside and alongside one another, and accordingly as not only different but as in different places, the representation of space must be presupposed. (A 23 = B 38)

Kant is here analyzing how it is that I can place and refer to sensations *of objects:* in order for me to represent to myself an object as separate from myself, as different or alongside or separate in place from another object, I must posit the notion of 'space'. This is a clear and fascinating argument, and one I am not interested in critiquing for ordinary spatial experience, except to note the following: Kant is quite clear that we must posit the notion of 'space' *in order to plausibly encounter external objects.* He claims nothing about an experience that does *not* involve an external (sensory) object.

Space does not mediate *all* experiences. This can be seen readily from Kant's discussion of what he calls "inner appearances," i.e., thoughts and emotions. For space, he clearly recognizes, does not mediate such experiences. Space, he tells us, serves as a mediating form if and only if one stands in a relationship with an external object.

> Space, as the pure form of all outer intuitions, is so far limited; it serves as the *a priori* condition only of outer appearances. (A 34 = B 50)

If some extended objects were not perceived, we could not represent space (A 292 = B 349). This is what distinguishes spatially mediated experiences from inner states, which Kant explicitly tells us are *not* so mediated. While solving an arithmetic problem, for example, one is not involved with "outer appearances."[7] The entire endeavor is "inner." Since "space [cannot] be intuited as something in us" (A 23 = B 37), and an arithmetic problem is "in us," then space is uninvolved with that activity. We might say that we are simply "forgetting" or "laying aside" for the nonce the mediating category of space. We do not lose the ability to perceive in space; we just are not doing so for the time being. Only when we encounter a spatial object do we perceive something "in space"; the mediating category of 'space' arises hand in glove with our encounter with something spatial. Even with reference to an ordinary "inner" experience, space does not necessarily mediate *all* experiences.

Now, Kant never directly addressed the status of space in the absence of *all* impressions, i.e. a PCE. Yet the implication here is clear. Since space mediates outer experiences only, when we are not engaging and representing outer impressions, the "mediating form" of space simply does not arise. Because in a PCE, as during the solving of an arithmetic problem, one encounters no external impressions, space does not mediate it.

Time. Kant's first two arguments about the *a priori* status of time center on the following:

Neither coexistence [of appearances] nor succession [of appearances] would ever come within our perception if the representation of time were not presupposed as underlying them *a priori*. Only on the presupposition of time can we represent to ourselves a number of things as existing . . . simultaneously or at different times. (A 30 = B 46)

The argument here may be drawn out as follows:

1. I am conscious.
2. I perceive several different "appearances" as objects for consciousness.
3. I represent those appearances as either
   a) Coexistent or
   b) Successive.
4. To represent appearances as coexistent or successive presupposes the representation of time.

What is striking here for our purposes is # 2, that of perceiving several appearances. For this claim assumes that we are talking of an experience of several objects, thoughts, etc. Yet this is precisely what is lacking in the PCE.

Now, according to Kant, time is never, unlike space, laid aside or forgotten. For even inner intuitions are perceived as successive or coexistent.

But since all representations whether they have for their objects outer things or not, belong, in themselves, as determinations of the mind, to our inner state, and since this inner state stands under the formal condition of inner intuition, and so belongs to time, time is an *a priori* condition of all appearance whatsoever ... all appearances whatsoever, that is all objects of the senses, are in time. (A 34 = B 51)

Thus, time is not laid aside temporarily when our attention is directed towards an inner or exterior object.

Nonetheless, I think we might make a parallel argument with that of space. I noted above that space is not called "into action" when we are devoid of the appropriate content. With no objects to mediate, space remains solely an unused "disposition of consciousness," for it is only actualized in the encounter with the appropriate objects. And Kant's argument about time is that all objects for consciousness, external and internal, are known by our "inner sense" and thus in time. If we had an event in which we remained conscious but did not encounter *any* objects, either "inner" or "outer," in it time, just as space was above, would not be called upon to mediate any manifold. For if the parallel with space goes this far, and I believe it does, then time too is actualized in the very process of representing *things* as successive or coexistent. After all, time is a way of handling representations of the inner sensuous manifold. If there is neither an "inner" nor an "outer" manifold, then there is nothing to represent as successive or coexistent. With no manifold to mediate, time, according to Kant's analysis, would remain solely an unused though readily available "disposition of consciousness."

Considering Kant's analysis, then, Short has overstepped the logical boundaries of the argument: not *all* experiences are represented by space and time; only experiences that are representations of *objects* that are (spatially) separable, and/or successive or coexistent are.

The Transcendental Analytic

How about our thoughts and ways of making judgments? Might they be relevant mediators of mysticism? I think not. After all, Kant presents the understanding as the second tier of the epistemological structure, and we have observed that the first tier is clearly concerned with (intentional) objects. Indeed, the understanding is introduced as a way of relating representations of *objects for consciousness:*

> No concept is ever related to an object immediately but to some other representation of it, be that other representation an intuition or itself a concept. [The understanding] is therefore the mediate knowledge *of an object,* that is, the representation of a representation *of it.* (A 68 = B 93)

What this second tier does, we are told, is to "relate representations to one another" (A 56 = B 80). Since a representation is of some object for consciousness, such interrelating of representations is necessarily an objective act.

Interrelating representations is, according to Kant, a process of making judgments (A 69 = B 94). Judgments relate a logical subject and a predicate (A 6 = B 10). That is, I need to see an object (a coat) and relate a predicate to it (brown): "that coat is brown." Thus, the faculty of understanding, a faculty of judgments, is a faculty that relates something to objects for consciousness. This is the only way we can "understand": we relate something to some *object* or *set of objects.* The faculty of understanding, as Kant is presenting it, does not necessarily apply to any experience whatsoever. Rather, Kant clearly and self-consciously is discussing the *objective* mode of experience. In it, one understands something *of some object* for consciousness. His analysis does not hold for a nonobjective (nonintentional) experience. This is only reasonable since, as I suggested above, Kant's *Critique* is, from the first page, exploring the *a priori* structures of *objective* experiences.

The critical role of objects is especially clear when Kant tells us of "The Outcome of this Deduction." Notice the critical role of objects in Paragraph 27:

> We cannot think *an object* save through categories; we cannot know *an object* so thought save through intuitions corresponding to these concepts. Now all our intuitions are sensible; and this knowledge, *in so far as its object is given* [to awareness], is empirical. But empirical knowledge is experience.[8] Consequently, there can be no *a priori* knowledge, except of *objects* of possible experience.

But although this knowledge is *limited to objects* of experience, it is not therefore all derived from experience. The pure
intuitions (of receptivity) and the pure concepts of understanding are elements in knowledge, and both are found in us *a
priori*. (emphasis mine)

Kant's point is that though the knowledge of which he speaks is *of
objects*, it is not *derived* entirely from them. Rather all our knowledge stems partly from the objects of experience, and partly from
the *a priori* elements that we bring to experience. We encounter an
object with only a limited number of possibilities for that encounter, and those we do not derive from the objects of experience, but
rather bring *to* experience.

The upshot is, Short has misunderstood the structure and function of Kant's "Transcendental Aesthetic" and "Transcendental
Analytic." They do not apply to any experience whatsoever, but, as
Kant himself clearly recognizes, concern our experience of objects.
They establish that important elements of our knowledge *of objects*
is derived from *a priori* sources. They establish absolutely nothing
of conscious events that do not involve objects.

The Deductions. I believe my point is made. But just to drive it
home, let us look at the first of the three key deductive arguments.
Here, Kant is suggesting that all objective perceptions must be
integrated into a unitary consciousness. The first two arguments
assert that, without such an integration, one of two absurd consequences would follow. The first is that perceptions would not be
perceived by consciousness. This would be absurd, for I must be
able to say that I am conscious of each of my perceptions in order
to say that I perceive it. In the first edition he puts this:

There might exist a multitude of perceptions, and indeed an
entire sensibility, in which much empirical consciousness would
arise in my mind, but in a state of separation and without
belonging to a consciousness of myself. This however is impossible. For it is only because I ascribe *all* perceptions to one
consciousness (original apperception) that I can say of all
perceptions that I am conscious of them. (A 121–2)

If perceptions were not brought to consciousness, he says in one of
his more famous passages, they

would not then belong to any experience, consequently would be without an object, merely a blind play of representations, less even than a dream. (A 112)

In other words, in order for me to recognize or make a judgment *about an object,* I must bring it to a single consciousness. Otherwise it would be "as good for us as nothing" (A 111). Drawing out this argument: let us assume that I have a perception of some object without being conscious of it. Then my perception would be not encountered by my consciousness. But to say that "I am conscious of a perception" entails that I can ascribe that perception to consciousness. Otherwise, the perception would not be mine, but a "blind play of representations."

The critical assumption here is that I can say "I am conscious *of a perception.*" Yet a perception is just what is not part of a pure consciousness event. It is defined as an event in which no representation *is* thought or perceived by consciousness. Therefore, Kant's argument would not be made, and would be irrelevant, of one in a pure consciousness event. However interesting and valid this argument may be for most experiences, its assumptions are not instantiated in our mystical event.

We could continue in this vein endlessly. Each of Kant's arguments concerns an experience of intentional objects, not *any* conscious event. The point is clear: Kant is irrelevant as a tool to analyze the PCE. Short's employment of Kant fails.

Does Intentionality Explain Mysticism?

Now I would like to look at another "prelinguistic" form of mediation that some constructivists have used to ground their claims about mysticism. It concerns the doctrine of intentionality as introduced by Brentano and Husserl: the characteristic of an act of consciousness that points beyond itself.[9] This assumption is mentioned in virtually every constructivist book and article on mysticism. The argument, simply put, goes like this: "all experiences are 'intentional' in the sense meant by Brentano and Husserl. Mystical experiences are experiences. Hence mystical experiences are intentional. Therefore however we understand intentional experiences, mystical experiences can be understood similarly." Though rarely defended, the claim that mysticism may be understood as we understand intentionality is often crucial to their analysis.

For example, Professor Jerry Gill grounds much of his constructivist account of mysticism on the supposed intentionality of all experience. Gill assumes that all experiences are intentional, and based on this maintains that all experiences are mediated or constructed. I quote Gill at length:

> [H]uman experience is vectorial in nature; that is to say, our awareness of the world is not that of passive observation, but is rather a function of the fact that we come into and at the world seeking meaning. *Our consciousness is always consciousness* of some concrete aspect of the world, of some particular aspect whose reality for us is *constituted by our intentional activity in relation to it.* This intentionality is clearly a mediational factor which undercuts the possibility of unmediated experience. The vectorial character of consciousness gives it a thrust or flow that provides the ever-present and necessary interpretive framework within which all experience is possible and understood.[10] (Emphasis mine)

Gill clarified what he meant by "vectorial" character of experience in his "Religious Experience as Mediated." There he notes that the basic character of mediated experience is what he calls its basic "from-to" structure.

> Mediational awareness is always *of* something, *through* something else, or the prehender can be said to attend *from* certain factors *to* other factors.[11] (Emphasis mine)

Because all experiences are intentional, Gill says, all experiences are constructed. For in attending toward one factor or from one to another, the system of belief enters constructively into the discrimination process. That is, any object of experience must be actively constituted and constructed as *that* object over against others as well as over against myself. In so doing, we introduce relational terms, distinctions, and thereby our whole background "set." (Here Gill is following, and glosses Husserl, whom I shall discuss shortly.)[12] Since all experiences are intentional and constructed, Gill maintains, mystical experiences are too, and hence may be analyzed appropriately in these terms.

Schematically Gill is saying:

G_1: All experiences are intentional;

G_2: All intentional experiences are constructed;

G_3: Mystical phenomena are experiences and hence are intentional;

Therefore:

G_4: Mystical experiences are constructed.

Arguments like Gill's have led many an author to link intentionality and constructivism. As early as 1923, James Leuba used just this assumption to rule out the possibility of contentless consciousness.[13] More recently, John Hick has argued that mystical experience is cognitive just like a sensory perception. "What is going on [in mysticism] is not fundamentally different from what is going on in other forms of awareness which we take to be awareness *of* our environment."[14]

> [R]eligious experience exhibits a common structure, which it shares with all our other cognitive experience, and [that] this is the experiencing of situations in terms of certain concepts. And awareness of a situation as having a certain character includes an appropriate dispositional stance.[15]

This barely conceals a claim like G_3 above, that mystical experiences, like "all our other cognitive experiences," are intentional, and therefore involve linguistic and conceptual constructive activities. Hick goes on to argue in a Kantian vein that because the epistemological structure is thus, the mystic never encounters a religious "noumenon" but only a "phenomenon." On the basis of this claim he makes a pluralistic argument: the variety of mystical experiences are "filtered" through a diverse set of human religious concepts and hence will always differ.[16]

Even when he counters Hick, Terence Penelhum argues that it is impossible to identify a common or shared object between the experiences found in various traditions. But he never questions Hick's underlying thesis that mystical experiences are like sensory experiences, i.e., of some *object*. Instead, he merely denies that the Kantian distinction is relevant: "mystical experience is the one sort of religious experience where the duality of subject and *noumenon* seems *not* to be applicable."[17]

William Wainwright, like Hick, does not use the term *intentionality per se*. Yet he too bases his foundational arguments on a purported parallel between sense experiences, which are obviously intentional, and mystical experiences.[18] He assumes that mystical experiences involve judgments, much like sense perception or memory, and are intentional.[19]

Steven Katz also argues for the intentionality of mystical experience. The passage in which he does so follows his assertion that the mind contributes the generating problem of the mystic and in so doing, shapes the experience that answers to it. The mystic's starting problem sets up the "constructive conditions of consciousness," he says, on the basis of which he or she will have a mystical experience. A good Buddhist nun, for example, would seek Nirvana and, because she has "set up the conditions" of her search in those terms, perceive what she has gained in terms of Nirvana. Katz thus turns to the "intentionality" of all experience:

> This entire area of the "intentionality" of experience and the language of experience as it relates to mysticism is a rich area for further study. . . . if one looks closely at the language of mystics . . . one will find that much of it is "intentional" in the sense suggested by Husserl and Brentano. . . . Their discussion of "intentional language" *per se* is instructive, for it calls to our attention that certain terms such as "expects," "believes," "hopes," "seeks," "searches," "desires," "wants," "finds," "looks for," involve, as Brentano said, "an object in themselves." We must heed the warning that linguistic intentionality does not generate or guarantee the existence of the "intentional object," but we must also recognize the epistemologically formative character of intentional language mirroring as it does intentional acts of consciousness. Using the language modern phenomenologists favor we might say that "intentionality" means to describe a "datum as meant," i.e., to be aware that an action includes a reach for some specific meaning or meaningful content.[20]

In this very obscure passage, Katz is asserting that the "intentions" (in the sense of desires) of the yogi or the Sufi mystic serve to shape his or her experiences. Ask a beginning monk, for example, "Why are you doing such and such?" and he will answer by describing certain "objects" or goals—i.e., *samādhi,* God-Consciousness, *kaivalya*—which he hopes to achieve. When he encounters a mystical goal he will perceive it in terms of just those same terms and expectations: A mystical experience "is [in part] constituted and conditioned by what the object or 'state of affairs' is 'that the mystic believes he will encounter.' "[21] When the monk who believes that he will encounter Nirvana encounters some mystical phenomenon, he will naturally experience it in the very terms (of Nirvana) he used to formulate his goal.[22]

It is clear that part of the foundation of many constructivist accounts of mysticism is a claim that all experiences are intentional. I want to challenge this claim. I do so with fear and trembling, for like the notion of constructivism itself, the doctrine of intentionality is so widely accepted today that it is nearly an act of intellectual heresy to call it into question.[23] My only defense is that, as with constructivism, I am not denying this doctrine insofar as it is applied to ordinary experience. That is not my concern. Though it is not without its failings even here, I think that the notion of intentionality has been undoubtedly useful for describing and thinking about our experiences of tables, other people, our thoughts, our concepts, love, hate, etc. My "heresy," if heresy it is, concerns only mysticism. Perhaps my remarks may be construed as showing that there are limits to the valid range of this model and the philosophical arguments that underlie it, and that some experiences may stand outside those limits.

Brentano and Husserl on Intentionality

When constructivists gloss Brentano and Husserl on intentionality, it is the latter that they generally mean.[24] But to understand Husserl's thought, it is best to start with Franz Brentano's (1838–1917) famous introduction to *Psychology from an Empirical Point of View,* for this is where he introduces "intentionality."[25] Seeking to clarify the differences between mental and physical phenomena by making an empirical investigation of them, Brentano begins by enumerating examples of each—providing "explanation by means of particulars, through examples." These examples serve him as paradigm cases, for with these in hand he examines the key features of each list.

Here is Brentano's paradigmatic list of mental phenomena:

> Every idea or presentation *(vorstellung)* which we acquire either through sense perception or imagination is an example of a mental phenomenon. . . . Thus, hearing a sound, seeing a colored object, feeling warmth or cold, as well as similar states of imagination are examples of what I mean by this term. I also mean by it the thinking of a general concept, provided that such a thing actually does occur. Furthermore, every judgment, every recollection, every expectation, every inference, every conviction or opinion, every doubt, is a mental phenomenon. Also to be included under this term is every emotion: joy, sorrow, fear, hope, courage, despair, anger, love, hate, desire, act of will, intention, astonishment, admiration, contempt, etc.[26]

As examples of physical phenomena, on the other hand, he enumerates: "a color, a figure, a landscape which I see,[27] a chord which I hear, warmth, cold, odor which I sense, as well as similar images which appear in the imagination."[28] Brentano is clear then: not *all* experienced phenomena are necessarily intentional. He is enumerating a *class*.

His famous characterization of the mental, which he bases on these paradigm cases, is as follows:

> Every mental phenomenon is characterized by what the Scholastics of the Middle Ages called the intentional (or mental) inexistence of an object, and what we might call, though not wholly unambiguously, reference to a content, direction toward an object (which is not to be understood here as meaning a thing), or immanent objectivity. Every mental phenomenon includes something as object within itself, although they do not all do so in the same way. In presentation something is presented, in judgment something is affirmed or denied, in love, in hate hated, in desire desired, and so on.[29]

"Intentionality," he maintains, is the common feature of the above-listed class of examples. It may be characterized as a certain kind of directedness toward an object *(Richtung)* or an attitude *(Einstellung)*. As Gill put this, there is a vectorial character to most mental experience; my loves, thoughts, etc. are one and all *about* something. They *refer to* something or someone. Intentionality signifies this pointing feature of the mind.

Brentano's insight is that our *referential* capacity is a philosophical leap forward. If one thinks of the passivity of inorganic matter or merely organic protozoan nature, the leap to beings who can reach out and include something other than themselves as an object is enormous. Dead nature, as it were, rises above itself to include something beyond itself.

However profound this insight, Brentano had difficulty specifying how this directedness relates to a knowing subject. In the above passage he says that the object is as if immanent within the subject: it "intentionally inexists" within the subject.[30] But an object within the subject is not the same as a transcendental object itself, which is not within us. When I kiss my wife, or fear a bear, I am not confronting a watered-down version of either. Rather, I enjoy her lips and fear real claws. Were I only dealing with immanent objects, I would be trapped in solipsism: If I know only immanent objects then how could I get an idea of a bear in the first place? Brentano himself became acutely aware of the problems with the immanence view of intentions: "It is paradoxical in the highest degree," he wrote, "to say that what a man promises to marry is an *ens rationis* and that he keeps his word by marrying a real person."[31]

The other alternative he suggested, principally in the later edition of the *Psychology*, is that the intentional object is a full-fledged physical object, not something immanent within our minds. The problem with this account is, what do we make of cases like unicorns or imagined trysts, where there is no real object at hand? One suggestion was that in such a case the object has the property of nonexistence.[32] But the problems with saying that existence is a predicate are well known. Brentano too was aware of the problems here: "I admit that I am unable to make any sense at all out of this distinction between being and existence."[33]

Enter Edmund Husserl (1859–1938), whose stroke of genius, first presented in the fifth (and most famous) of the *Logical Investigations*, was to separate the concept of intentionality from the notion of the object's immanent inexistence.[34] Such an association, he notes there, can lead to the view that the *object* is included in the experience, as if within a box.[35] So he removed the object from the box. Intentionality became for him a feature of a certain class of *experiences*, i.e., those that relate to objects. [36] This class Husserl called "acts," since they involve certain specifiable activities of the mind. Intentionality thus became a product of the mind's activities. I will show in detail how his notion of intentionality involves just the sort of "construction" out of which Gill, Penelhum, and the others write.

Before doing so let me note that Husserl, like Brentano, did not regard *all* experiences as intentional. "That not all experiences are intentional is proved by sensations and sensational complexes."[37] In addition to these nonintentional experiences, he maintained that within any, e.g., visual experience there could be found certain "part contents," which he sometimes called sense data (*Empfindungen*). These also are not in themselves intentional. "Intentionality" is thus either (1) a feature of a subclass of experiences or (2) an aspect of some experiences. Husserl, like Brentano, never made any logical or legislative claims about all *possible* experiences, nor even about *all* experiences. His was a strictly descriptive or empirical claim about a class of experiences. (Thus, insofar as it is grounded on Husserl, any claim that mystical experiences are intentional should convincingly demonstrate that they belong to the appropriate subclass or include the appropriate aspect.)

Now, what makes an "act" intentional? An experience is intentional if and only if someone encounters sensory input and *takes it as* referring to an object. The key and novel feature of intentionality no longer is some aspect of the object itself or the object's inexistence within the subject, but is part of the structure of the knowing mind.

> "[I]ntentional" names the essence common to the class *of experiences* we wish to mark off, the peculiarity of intending, *of referring* to what is objective, in a presentative or other analogous fashion.[38] (Emphasis mine)

"Intentional" now denotes the property of my mind that is *directed* towards an object. If I take a brown patch *as* a bear, there is a certain peculiarly "intentional" structure of my consciousness in that act. In taking it thus, I actively point to something as an object. I *constitute* or *construct* it as such. Its status as an object is a creation of my mind.

In this one stroke, Husserl solved Brentano's paradox. On the one hand he no longer has the problem of the "intentional inexistence" of the object within the mind. Gone is Brentano's implicit dualism between the transcendent object and the "immanently inexisting" object. The object can remain "out there," transcendent to the subject. Intentionality no longer is a characteristic of the object but is now a feature of the act of perceiving it. The bear I fear becomes the real bear, the lips I kiss are my wife's. It is *my* taking something as "out there" which makes it intentional. Thus, Husserl, unlike Brentano, can talk about "intentional experiences" as opposed merely to "intentional objects."[39]

Husserl's version of intentionality can also account for the problem of nonexistent objects like unicorns. Here, the structure of my consciousness is the same as it is when I see a real object. In the case of a unicorn, our consciousness is structured "as if" there is an object, even though the object does not exist.

With this Husserlian picture of intentionality in hand, I want to draw out the key connections between the notion of "intentionality" and constructivism. For I think that though the connections between these two doctrines are not generally recognized, they are critical. Gill and the other constructivists are right: This notion *is* one of the foundations of the doctrine of constructivism. Here are the principal connections as I understand them:[40]

A. **The mind constructs by objectifying intentions.** As I noted above, we are confronted with a stream of data, which Husserl characterized as sense-data *(Empfindungen)* and later as *hyletic data* . It is the mind that "assigns" such data *to* an object that is itself transcendent to the act itself. This assignation process is a very complex activity, requiring the organization into an object of input from all the senses. This object must be, first of all, distinguished from the subject. Furthermore, thoughts, emotions, etc. are also "assigned" to an object by the mind. Sense data are used as "raw material," and the "object" is constructed "out of" my perception, thought, emotions about it. These Husserl calls the "qualities" as opposed to the mere presentative "matter" of the intention.[41] Such organizing, assigning, referring, etc. may be involved in the "construction" of any perception or thought.

B. **The mind constructs by unifying intentions.** When I look at some object, blink several times, and look again, I must actively "constitute" those distinguishable impressions as belonging to one and the same object. Otherwise I would be left with merely a series of disconnected perceptions.[42] I must synthesize disjunct perceptions, *taking them as* belonging to a single object. I make what-I-take-to-be-a-bear into a pole, as it were, around which I organize and direct my perceptions, thoughts, etc. All this is a form of construction: I *construct* the bear our of a succession of browns and growls.

C. **The mind constructs by relating intentions.** According to the previous point, my mind is active in holding together two nonsuccessive percepts as elements of "the same" object. I must also actively draw together spatially separate percepts which I take as referring to the same object: the body, claws, front, back, growl, and fuzziness as all "belonging" to a single bear. This too is part of the phenomenon of intentionality.

D. **The mind constructs by differentiating intentions.** When I see something "as" a bear but not as a moose, or as this bear and not that one—I am differentiating an object from others. The process of classifying, of distinguishing one object from another, etc., is a very complex one, but it must be attributed again to the mind. This too is part of the constructive nature of an intentional experience.

E. **The mind constructs by constituting intentions.** When we consider the enormous numbers of neural electrochemical signals that are constantly processed and filtered by the brain, and the myriad possible combinations of those signals which we might theoretically take as this or that object—we can only think, as Husserl did after the first edition of the *Logical Investigations* (1901), that the mind must be credited with "constituting" an object of perception as an object. In the second volume of the *Ideas*, which was entitled "Phenomenological Studies Concerning Constitution," Husserl discussed this constitutive function of the mind through what he calls "intentional analysis." Here the notion of construction becomes the dominant one.

In sum, that the mind takes sensory input "as" belonging to an object may be related to the mind's *constructive activities* because the mind: (1) interprets its input in such a way that an object is presented; (2) unifies nonsuccessive input as belonging to a single object or complex; (3) connects various modes of thought and perceptions into one object; (4) differentiates one object from another; (5) in part constitutes objects. These are just the sorts of activities to which mystical constructivists like Gill, Katz, Wainwright, and Hick refer.

They were right to point to the intentional, vectorial character of the mind as a key foundation of the constructivist model.

Are All Experiences Intentional?

Now that we have seen the sources of the notion of intentionality, and in brief the connection between that term and constructivism, I want to show that the arguments undergirding neither Brentano nor Husserl can serve to ground the claim that all human experiences are intentional. What Gill and the others require is that the notion of intentionality can serve in a logical chain, to wit, that "all possible human experiences are intentional" can predetermine the character of some unusual form of human experience (such as mysticism) or rule out some phenomena as impossible.

Generally, philosophers can rule a phenomenon out based on analytical or definitional factors: because of its definition, a married bachelor is "impossible." But no such analytic incoherence allows a philosopher to legislate out mystical experiences.[43] The question then becomes: Can the arguments of Husserl and/or Brentano serve to ground such a claim?

I have already noted that neither Brentano nor Husserl themselves claim that *all* ordinary human experiences are intentional. For both, sensations, twitches, etc., are nonintentional. Brentano calls them mere physical phenomena; Husserl includes them as part of the "raw data" (sense or hyletic data) on the basis of which intentional experiences are constructed. Hence, it would be a mistake to attribute such a universal claim to either philosopher.

In addition, I believe that it is false that all possible conscious events, especially mystical events, are necessarily intentional. My first two reasons concern Brentano and Husserl's arguments for intentionality, the last concerns a more general principle.

Descriptive Endeavor

Both Brentano and Husserl were engaged in descriptive endeavors. Brentano, we saw, enumerated a set of paradigm cases and then articulated the defining feature of that set. He did not pretend to claim anything about "all human experiences," but rather was engaged in the plausible but more modest task of distinguishing two principle types of experiences. Such a descriptive, empirical task tells us nothing about a phenomenon that was not included in his paradigmatic set. "All A's are Y and all B's are not Y" tells us absolutely nothing about all C's.

Husserl's concern, too, as stated in the *Logical Investigations*, was to find an "epistemological critique" of, a firm grounding for, logic.[44] He maintained that logical concepts must have their origin in intuition, and that such concepts must be founded on indefinitely reproducible experiences. To ground the self-evident statement, $A = A$, we must be able to ascertain that this pen is this pen, that this finger is this finger, etc.—so reliably as to form the notion of certainty. Thus, logic is founded, as he sees it, on certain reproducible patterns within experience.

> Our great task is now to bring the Ideas of logic, the logical concepts and laws, to epistemological clarity and definiteness.
>
> Here phenomenological analysis must begin. Logical concepts, as valid thought-unities, must have their origin in intuition: they must arise out of an ideational intuition founded on certain experiences, and must admit of indefinite reconfirmation, and of recognition of their self-identity, on the reperformance of such abstraction.[45]

We must be able to ground our knowledge on some fundamental certainty. This we gain, he tells us, from the reliability of certain experiences, i.e., on the regularity of our constructed, intentional experience of things, i.e., intentional objects. Such an activity of looking at experience at its foundation is clearly *empirical*. Husserl recognizes this when he calls phenomenology "descriptive psychology."[46] Understanding the structure of intentional experience is an *empirical* process:

> Pure phenomenology . . . is, on the one hand, an ancillary to psychology conceived as an empirical science. Proceeding in purely intuitive fashion, it analyses and describes in their essential generality . . . the experiences of presentation, judgment and knowledge, experiences which, treated as classes of real events in the natural context of zoological reality, receive a scientific probing at the hands of empirical psychology.

Phenomenology, on the other hand, lays bare the "sources" from which the basic concepts and ideal laws of pure logic flow, and back to which they must once more be traced, so as to give them all the "clearness and distinctness" needed for an understanding, and for an epistemological critique, of pure logic.[47]

Husserl's endeavor begins, then, in *description* of certain experiences. As such it can serve no legislative value. It was not his intention to comment on all *possible* experiences, nor even on unusual types of experience. *Nowhere* does he discuss or propose characteristics for all possible experiences. If some experience is not descriptively intentional, nothing Husserl says here about intentionality is compelling. And I need hardly note that the distinguishing mark of the pure consciousness event is that it is *not* described as an experience of *something*.

Refusal to Make a Priori Claims

Both Brentano and Husserl were dissatisfied with the Kantian position because it was based on *a priori* presuppositions. Brentano attempted to avoid basing a philosophy on a, to him, dubious *a priorism* by beginning with what he called pure description. He simply aimed to "clarify the meaning of the two terms 'physical phenomenon' and 'mental phenomenon,'" through first providing examples and later chief characteristics.[48] His was not a "definition according to the traditional rules of logic."[49] Hence, distinguishing between mental and physical phenomena was not a logical or *a priori* task, but strictly empirical. As the title implies, his was a *Psychology from an Empirical Standpoint*.

Nor was Husserl attempting to make some *a priori* arguments about the nature of all experience. His was an attempt to epistemologically ground logic. He maintained that you could not ground any natural laws on a Humean "psychologism"; you could at best establish its probability.[50] His attempt was to locate the grounding of the aprioristic, and *that* is no synthetic *a priori* task. It rather is based on a descriptive endeavor, and discovered through "bracketing." As such, no laws about all possible forms of experience are implied by it. If and only if we are speaking of an intentional experience, then *a priori* laws of logic are established. (This does not make them false for a nonintentional experience, just unestablished.) In short, the constructivist's claim that all experiences are intentional cannot be grounded on Husserl or Brentano.

Prescriptive Status of Empirical Arguments

"All experience is intentional" can either be a logical claim (no form of consciousness anywhere, ever, can be anything but intentional) or an empirical claim (no experiences people have undergone have ever been nonintentional). Katz, Gill, and the others who assume that all experiences are intentional or have content for consciousness require that it be of a *logical or legislative* character—or else with reference to a novel experience it will have no force in a logical chain. I have shown that the arguments undergirding the doctrine of intentionality have no logical force for all possible experiences or for mystical experiences, and hence cannot play such a role.

Indeed, it is difficult to see how anyone could make an *a priori* argument about all possible forms of experiences, or for all conscious events. All *possible* experiences must necessarily allow for novel experiences whose structures are *unpredictable*, i.e., that it may or may not obey any specific, generally accepted patterns. To argue that all experiences will necessarily have some empirical characteristic, one must assume some measure of predictability. But to do so would be to assume away the very unpredictability at issue—and thereby deny the assumed condition.

Can an empirical observation have any legislative force for a novel experience? The claim that all experiences are intentional is similar to a claim someone might have made in 1850, that "humans cannot fly." This may have been stated using the most sound, logically unimpeachable aeronautical principles and engineering techniques then known. But it is a contingent truth; as it turned out, there were certain arrangements of materials of which its utterer could not possibly have been aware that made it empirically false. In empirical matters, the possibility of the new and unexpected may always shatter the "obvious," and make one generation's heresy the next generation's common sense.

In sum, it is not the place of the philosopher to decide on empirical matters. It is, in the case of flying, the place of the pilot or the aeronautical engineer to judge possibilities; in mysticism, it is the mystic's. Nothing the philosopher says in advance can possibly determine the shape or even possibility of a novel experience.

Cognitive Status of Non-Intentional Experiences

Finally, I want to address one issue which the astute reader is probably asking. William Wainwright raises it when he notes (quite correctly, as we have seen) that "westerners have usually assumed that consciousness is necessarily intentional, i.e. that the notion of empty consciousness or a consciousness without contents is self-contradictory."[51] But many texts show that this is a false assumption, Wainwright correctly argues. People from many traditions have reported to have been awake though without intentions, as chapter 2 above shows. But, he asks,

> if the experience has no object, can it have any cognitive value? . . . an objectless experience cannot be noetic, i.e. an experience *of* something which is believed to be real, and yet it is difficult to see how it could possibly be cognitive if it is not noetic.[52]

I believe that Wainwright is correct. I also do not see how something can be nonintentional and also be "cognitive," i.e., an experience in which one has knowledge, knows anything in propositional form in the ways we generally understand. The past tense, sentence, "I was awake without thoughts," may have a truth value, and hence be cognitive. But the mere "act" or "experience" of being so is not obviously cognitive.

However, this does not mean the PCE will necessarily be uninteresting or nonvaluable to those of us who think about it, be we mystics or not. There are many things that are not cognitive states but are interesting. The relationship between atoms in a piece of gold foil, the creation of planets out of gas, digestion, and a painting are all interesting, yet none are cognitive states. Many interesting things have been and will be said about such. I believe that mystical experiences too may be interesting and noncognitive.

Like the behavior of atoms in gold foil, a nonintentional mystical experience can serve as data for a theory or thesis about the way the world is. For example, one obvious direction to which it leads is that if consciousness does not "die out" when all content is dropped, if one does not become unconscious when all content drops away, then one might argue that consciousness is distinguishable from its mere contents. This tells us quite a lot about human consciousness; I will ponder what it says in chapter 7.[53] Given a theological belief set like Meister Eckhart's, persisting without content might reinforce the belief that one may momentarily merge with the distinctionless Godhead. Such a state may also reinforce a Buddhist's understandings of Nirvana.

But that mystical experiences are noncognitive does mean that you cannot ground any knowledge claim on such an event in any simple, direct way. An argument from a PCE to some sort of direct claim of the existence of God, for example, would be inherently dubious, given the non-cognitive status and epistemological structure of this particular form of mysticism. A non-intentional experience cannot by itself serve to ground any truth, or even any proposition, since it is not propositional in nature. It is, in this way, rather like a bit of gold foil. It must be analyzed to be interesting, with all the background of belief that implies.

This is a peculiar bit of data, in as much as the mystic him/her self lives through the data, as it were. But with reference to some perennial philosophy, I do not see how one can *ground* a set of beliefs cross-culturally *solely* on the basis of such an experience. Any cognitive knowledge implies a background of beliefs, definitions, behavioral patterns, etc. within which that knowledge has significance, and a mere experience can only be given meaning within such a context. There can be no simple one-to-one correspondence between experience and knowledge claim.

However, if, as I argued, such an experience is found in a variety of cultures, then it may serve as *evidence* for cross-cultural claims of some sort. One such claim is that some mystical experiences are indistinguishable between cultures. Another, Schuon's, is that many systems may be pointing to the same experiences. And these claims are not, after all, uninteresting.

In sum, Kant's arguments for space, time, and the categories, as well as Husserl's and Brentano's doctrine of intentionality, have been of enormous value in understanding our experiences of objects, things, feelings, thoughts, etc. But these are both doctrines that explain a limited class of experiences, not all possible ones. Constructivists who claim that *all* experiences must be mediated have not argued correctly, given their philosophical underpinnings. When someone has a pure consciousness event, he or she is clearly standing outside of the limits of Kant or intentionality. Insofar as a philosophical system has is foundation in these doctrines, it cannot plausibly account for pure consciousness events.

Chapter Five

Buddhists and Constructivists

Yogacara Constructivism

In the last chapter we have shown that much of the philosophical underpinnings of constructivism, both Kantian and the doctrine of intentionality, is being misapplied when it is used in a philosophy of mysticism. I see these arguments as another nail in the coffin of constructivism: however helpful these approaches may have been in analyzing ordinary experience, constructivism is deeply flawed when it is applied to the mystical phenomenon, the pure consciousness event.

An interesting place to look for confirmation that constructivism is the wrong tool to use in understanding such experiences is to the mystical traditions themselves, particularly to traditional Eastern philosophers. For they, more than most Western philosophers, have tried to make sense of both ordinary and mystical phenomena.

We Western philosophers do not generally turn to non-Western philosophers to help us explore philosophical issues. Despite the huge gaps separating their word views from our own, we tend to be relatively quick to turn to Hume, Plato, Kant, or Aristotle to think through our issues, but very slow to turn the likes of Shankara, Nagarjuna, Dōgen, or Paramārtha. In part this is due to ignorance and habit, of course. But I believe that it is also due to a vague but more insidious bias, stemming perhaps from a generally unconscious cultural imperialism, that holds that "third world" thinkers have nothing to teach us. But stated thus, this impulse is obviously wrong. Some of the world's greatest minds have lived nearer the Ganges or the Yangtze than the Thames, the Rhine, or the Charles, and it is time that we included their thoughts.

81

When it comes to exploring the phenomena of religious experiences, Eastern thinkers are particularly well equipped to help us, for of necessity they have been forced to articulate its peculiarities and explore its nature. Furthermore, it turns out that many, especially Buddhists, have developed a surprisingly sophisticated epistemology of ordinary experience—which is remarkably similar to the constructivist's. Thus, when such men[1] deny that constructivism is an adequate model for understanding experiences such as those we have been discussing, it should have a particularly striking impact, and lend support to my thesis.

Many schools of fourth-century Buddhist thought, like modern constructivists, portrayed the ordinary experienced world as being in large part the result of the constructive and conditioning activities of the mind.[2] In the *Laṅkāvatāra Sūtra*, for example, there is a considerable emphasis on the role and power of language. Words and concepts, it says, are a human creation and born of convention. There are an infinite set of possible languages, it states, by any one of which people could communicate and divide up the world differently.

> If, Mahāmati, you say that because of the reality of words the objects are, this talk lacks in sense. Words are not known in all the Buddha-lands; words, Mahāmati, are an artificial creation. In some Buddha-lands ideas are indicated by looking steadily, in others by gestures, in still others by a frown, by the movement of the eyes, by laughing, by yawning, or by the clearing of the throat, or by recollection, or by trembling.[3]

From early on, Buddhism thrived in a multicultural and multilingual world. As its missionaries spread out, they had to wrestle constantly with issues of translation and cross-cultural understanding. Buddhists perforce had to be sensitive to the fact that different languages could slice up the experiential pie differently, and hence are, to a considerable extent, arbitrary and conventional.

According to the *Laṅkāvatāra Sūtra*, the language that we use sets up the categories of thought by means of which we perceive and experience. Separating things by such different names is technically called *vikalpa*. This term, discussed below, is translated as "discrimination" or sometimes even "construction."

Further, Mahāmati, by "discrimination" is meant that by which names are declared, and there is thus the indicating of (various) appearances. Saying that this is such and no other, for instance, saying that this is an elephant, a horse, wheel, a pedestrian, a woman, or a man, each idea thus discriminated is so determined.[4]

When a person uses a particular language and its concepts, he or she inevitably discriminates in the terms provided by that language. As a result, people tend to fall into the habits of perception that their language engenders, and form attachments to, cling to, such linguistically engendered notions.

Mahāmati, [ordinary men] cling to names, ideas and signs; their minds move along (these channels). As thus they move along, they feed on multiplicity of objects, and fall into the notion of an ego-soul and what belongs to it, and cling to salutary appearances.[5]

In the *Laṅkāvatāra Sūtra*, the key discrimination that leads to *duhkha*, suffering, is said to be the notion of the ego or the self. Modern mystical constructivists, to my knowledge, have not offered a corresponding psychological theory. However, I see no reason for them to deny some such psychological claim. The claim that certain key notions of language are critical in the building up of psychological cathexes and attachments would be perfectly in harmony with the theory.

Aside from its emphasis on such attachments, however, this *sūtra's* analysis of constructivism parallels the constructivist's. That is, according to both, the ordinary mind tends to impose labels provided in large part by one's language and beliefs, and thereby develop tradition-informed habits of perception. According to both, in significant ways the subject creates or shapes his/her own experiences. Finally, according to both, one's ideas and expectations significantly shape and determine one's perception.

One of the most systematic Buddhist accounts of the constructed nature of ordinary perception and behavior may be found in the ninth-century translator and philosopher, Paramārtha, especially in his brief *Chuan shih lun* (CSL), The Evolution of Consciousness, which is a translation of and commentary on the

Triṃśikā of Vasubandhu. I turn to Paramārtha, first, because he was a not insignificant writer and translator for Chinese and Japanese Buddhist thought; second, because his presentation is especially clear; and third, because his cognitive psychology is strikingly parallel at key points to the modern constructivists' philosophy of mind. My discussion of Paramārtha must perforce be summary, and I commend Diana Paul's more exhaustive works on Paramārtha to the interested reader.[6] I want to give an overview of his account of experience and then turn to his account of perception in order to draw out the parallels with modern constructivist thought.

In order to allow his readers to gain control of their mental processes, Paramārtha begins this text by offering an account of such processes as they are found in ordinary, everyday states of consciousness. Employing a term as ancient as Buddhism itself, he maintains that our behavior and perception are based on a process of conditioning (*pratītyasamutpāda*).

Following Vasubandhu, Paramārtha maintains that in this conditioning process there are three structural or functional levels within the mind (or, as he puts it, three kinds of perceiver), each of which conditions and constructs behavior and experience.

[Verse 1b:] Next we shall explain the tree kinds of perceiver [or cognizer].

[Verse 2:] (1) The retributive (*vipaka*) consciousness, namely the *ālayavijñāna*; (2) the appropriating consciousness, namely the *ādānavijñāna*; (3) the consciousness of sense data, namely the six [sense] consciousnesses (*vijñaptirvisayāsya*).[7]

Let us look at these in turn. The most fundamental level is called the *ālayavijñāna*, a term for which Yogacara is renowned. It is fundamentally volitional, representing the capacity of the mind to "construct" future acts based upon past habits and behavior.[8] Insofar as we choose what we attend to and which aspects of a perception we focus on, it plays a role in perception as well.

It [the *ālayavijñāna*] is called the fundamental consciousness because all seeds of conditioned phenomena are dependent upon it and [called] the "abode" consciousness because it is the place where all seeds rest. . . . It is also called the "storehouse" consciousness because it is the place (*sthana*) where all seeds are concealed.[9]

The influences of past habits and behavior are said to be "stored" in the *ālayavijñāna* as impressions (*vāsanā*) or habits; these act like seeds (*bīja*) which "sprout" into, that is, condition and form, future behavior and karma. The *ālayavijñāna* both stores latent habit impressions and acts as a "switching network" that delivers them as needed.

The key terms here in the process of forming and storing perceptual habits are "seeds" and "karma." The CSL goes into the character of these two at some length. Vasubandhu's *Triṃśikā* (verse 19) asserted "two kinds of latent impressions from past karma and (2) attachment to the latent impressions from past karma."[10] Attachment to the latent impressions is a second-order function, after the mere having of latent impressions. Attachment denotes the ego-investment in certain discriminated entities. Hence, the primary elements in the constructive process are the "latent impressions" that are stored in the *ālayavijñāna*. What are those impressions?

> Latent impressions from past karma are identical to the discriminated [object] and are discriminated in nature. . . . [T]he [discriminated] object is the sense object; the discriminator is consciousness. . . .

As for "the two kinds of latent impressions from past karma," each impression has two principles:

> (1) the object [discriminated], which is the latent impressions from past karma; (2) the discriminator, which is the attachment to the latent impressions from past karma. The object is [the result of] the nature of discrimination that can produce a panorama of phenomena generated from seeds [in the ālayavijñāna]. This panorama of phenomena is called the latent impression from past karma.[11]

Paramārtha is taking a strong constructivist position here, that the terms by which we pick out an object play a role in composing it. His utterances, "the object is [the result of] the nature of discrimination that can produce a panorama of phenomena," and "the object [discriminated] . . . is the latent impressions from past karma" together suggest that the object cannot be what it is without our constructive, discriminative activities, and those discriminations are based on past experience (Karma). The terms we use to pick something out make up the object in large part or in whole. Discrimination makes the object what it is.

There is a second facet or level of this process. When I encounter something, say, a tall, tan, rectangular door, I think the word *door* to myself. Insofar as I expect the door to act just like the other doors in my experience, I bring expectations to it. I expect it to open relatively easily, to not spit at me, not to have a red-hot doorknob, to open to a level onto which I can step, and so forth. Thus I in part "construct" a door with my expectations. A more subtle aspect of the process of perceiving a door, however, is that I separate it, the object, from me, the subject. The subject, the "discriminator" is, Paramārtha notes, "the attachment to the latent impressions from past karma." That is, I become attached to (involved with) certain past experiences as my "self," and then regard an object (that is, the door) as a something "over against" that self. Thus, my experience is informed by the particular latent impressions that go into my notions of my self and the structure of "my" experience as (in modern parlance) intentional.

Seeds stored in the *ālayavijñāna* can lead to what we might call psychological attachments to objects or processes as well. Let us use as an example a man's neurotic compulsion to paint. This behavioral pattern may be analyzed to be derived from, say, childhood experiences of parental disdain and not being noticed or seen. The impressions of that disdain and its concomitant influences on behavior are said to be "stored" in the *ālayavijñāna* as "seeds" that lead to the future behavior, and end up being expressed as a compulsion to paint and display.

The second level of conscious functioning is the *ādānavijñāna*, the "appropriating subject." This structure conditions all conceptualizations and perceived objects as inherently intertwined with my self, especially with the identification of one's existence "as what one acquires or appropriates."[12] The tendency we all have toward self-aggrandizement should be associated with this level. Such a focus on the self is in turn based on the "four defilements" (ignorance, views of the self, conceit, and self-love).[13] Our neurotic painter's identification of himself with his own fame or wealth may be an example of this level of functioning.

So far, Paramārtha has drawn a psychologically oriented picture of the constructed character of experience. Based on the tendencies and desires set up by the above two functions of consciousness, we encounter the world in terms of certain habituated categories and concepts. We see things in terms of categories and labels that derive from old habits and impressions, just as Monet saw a Gothic arch. Such an encounter occurs through the constructive activities of the third and final structure, the *vijñaptirviṣayasya*, objective apperception, the six "sense consciousnesses," which is the final stage in our contact with the external world.[14]

Such contact, according to Paramārtha, results from the interaction of three elements: sense faculty or intellect (*manovijñāna*), sense data or ideas, and consciousness.[15] Paramārtha, here, like Husserl, maintains that in ordinary experience we are always conscious of some object, be it external and sensory or something internal, such as a thought.[16] Any perception of an object has some conceptual (*samjña*) and some sensory elements (*vedana*). We perceive no object or thought without bringing in terms and concepts, which in part comprise it, according to Paramārtha. Discrimination of any object is conditioned by the characteristics by means of which we pick it out from the world of objects in general and distinguish it from other objects in a similar class. As part of this process we provide it with a name, Paramārtha notes in his *San wu-hsing lun*.[17] This implies that the act of making such distinctions is part and parcel of and stands in relationship to specific language and hence to an experiential system as a whole and is at least in part the product of discrimination processes made by a subject.

The perception of an object thus results in part from the application of conceptual categories. These categories are derived from past experiences and stand as an element of the conceptual set as a whole. There is an obvious parallel between Paramārtha and the modern constructivist on this point. According to both, ordinary perception, thought, and behavior are in significant part the result of mental conditioning or construction.

The Yogacara term for construction (translated above as "discrimination"), *vikalpa*, is interesting here. It derives from the root, *klp*, to order, adapt, arrange. Sometimes it suggests to ornament and to embellish. The poet's ornamented, ordered, but fictitious creations are called *kavikalpana*. The prefix *vi* adds a distributive sense; *vi* + *klp* can mean to create or contrive, set up antitheses, and so forth. As employed by Buddhist thinkers, it connotes the mind's activities of construction and classification. Like the poet's spinning out of a fictitious world, the mind was thought to create (*vikalpana*) a fictional world for itself. The term may be translated as "imagination," although "mental construction" seems nearest.[18] Thus, the constructive activities of the mind involve something akin to the spinning of a conceptual "web" as a whole, and placing any individual entity or experience some place on such a web.

In sum, there are unmistakable parallels between this Yogācārin's account of the constructive activities of the mind and the modern constructivists such as Gombrich, Gill, and the others. All maintain that the mind, as Coleridge noted, "half sees and half creates," drawing upon categories of perception based on habits and language. All maintain that such categories are not absolute, but are largely conventional and derived from language and the general background of experience. All hold to the pluralistic correlative that one person's or one language's conventional distinctions will differ from another's, and hence, that experiences engendered by different languages will differ.

Now, with reference to ordinary experiences, the differences separating Paramārtha and the modern constructivists do not significantly challenge this fundamental agreement. Probably the most important difference centers on the character of the critical formative milieu. For the Buddhist, what shapes experience is "karma," action or experience as a whole. This notion emphasizes the role of experience as a whole more than language per se, whereas the modern constructivist focuses his/her attentions on language (though not to the exclusion of experience).[19] Additionally, according to the Western world view, only one's biographical background in *this* life plays a role. In Yogācāra, while this life's background plays the dominant formative role, karma derived from past lives is also thought to have an influence.

Finally, Paramārtha writes of an "evolution" of consciousness into objects. "Consciousness evolves in two ways: (1) it evolves into selves (*ātman*); (2) it evolves into things (*dharma*). Everything perceived [or cognized] is included in these two objects [of cognition]."[20] The Western constructivist would probably deny such an evolutionary model and would prefer a more neutral picture of objects and subjects mutually conditioning one another, or perhaps appearing together. This seeming discrepancy, however, may be more apparent than real. Paramārtha does not intend "evolve" here with ontological or Darwinian connotations. Rather, he means "evolve" in the psychologically astute way we have been discussing: the notion of "self" gradually develops and with it the notion of objects and the world over against the self. The general picture of the world as a complex web gradually develops with experience.

Thus, Paramārtha and the modern constructivists may disagree about details such as how we began to construct experience or precisely which past habits and concepts shape some experience. But—and this is the critical point—on the fundamental claim that experiences are constructed by language, concept, and past experiences, they agree profoundly: every ordinary experience of an object is in significant ways shaped, delimited, and controlled by our previously learned, habituated perceptual and cognitive categories. And this, it goes without saying, is the key claim in the modern-day constructivist's account of mysticism.

Perhaps no better confirmation could be found that their pictures are parallel than this: in her summary of Paramārtha's cognitive psychology, Diana Paul's description could be, without changing a word, a description of the constructivist picture given by Gill, Gombrich, and others. Here is her summary of Paramārtha up to this point:

How we perceive and construct our world is influenced by associations from past experiences and by the linguistic terms we use to categorize the world we live in. For example, a child's fear of the dark may be due to perceiving monsters lurking in his room at night. These "monsters" may in turn have been shaped by a previous experience in which the child's parents said a monster would spank the child if he or she misbehaved. Every time the child misbehaves, there is the recurrent fear of the dark associated with fear of punishment. This fear affects the child's perception, that is, monsters in the room; the word "dark" can evoke all of these feelings, perceptions, and ideas in the child.[21]

But that it is devoid of affective content, she could equally well have used our example of Monet painting his cathedral.[22]

Paramārtha on Mystical Experience

The modern-day constructivist's epistemological picture stops here. For Katz, Gimello, Hick, and others, language, expectation, and past experiences come together to create mystical experiences in much the same way that Monet's past experience led to his sensory misperception. Mystical experiences are constructed in ways that are similar or identical to sensory experiences.[23] The epistemological structures that define in advance, form, and give shape to sensory experience and thought enclose mystical experiences as well.

Paramārtha, on the other hand, does *not* stop here. Taking the constructivistic process as his problematic, he *begins* here.

Paramārtha describes the nature of the constructive process so that he or she can gain Arhatship, enlightenment, by seeing through and stopping the constructing process: the construction engendered in the *ālayavijñāna* continues unchanged "until the attainment of Arhatship."[24] The functioning of the *ādānavijñāna* "and its associated [mental] states is *eliminated* in the Arhat stage, and [these] are also *eliminated* upon entering cessation-meditation (*nirodhasamāpatti*)."[25] (Italics mine) Since perceptual and behavioral experiences are constructed and shaped so significantly by the intellect and its associated five senses (the *manovijñāna*); it is most significant that Paramārtha writes:

> On what occasions does this intellect (*manovijñāna*) not arise? [Vs. 34:]A: Except for these six states—[cessation] meditation [*nirodhasamāpatti*], [meditation associated with the third level or *dhyāna* in] heavens without conceptualization (*asamjñisamāpatti*), dreamless sleep, drunken stupor, unconsciousness, or a coma—the others always have it [intellect].[26]

In other words, during the first of these states, *nirodhasamāpatti*, cessation meditation, the constructive role played by past experiences and by previously held concepts, habits, and expectations ceases.

Such a claim stands as the soteriological *raison d'être* of the CSL—as indeed of virtually all Yogācāra thought.[27] The picture of the mind as a constructive agent was put forward, as I noted, in order to make clear how the practitioner might bring about its *stoppage*.[28] By seeing that one brings about perception based on convention-founded discrimination, one may stop those discriminations.

Paramārtha, here following Vasubandhu, observes that if one does not perceive or encounter an object, then the conceptual system as a whole does not arise. Verse 28 of the Trimsika says:

> If the cognizer (*vijñāna*) does not apprehend (*upalabhate*) the objects (*ālamabanam*), the two [attachments to objects and to consciousness that grasps the object, i.e., the attachments that are the product of the *ālaya* and *ādānavijñāna*] are not manifested.[29]

When the adept eliminates all objects of perception, the *ālayavijñāna*—the storehouse of seeds which provides the interpretive categories—temporarily ceases functioning. Fleshing this out: if no objects are encountered or discriminated, none of the mind's constructive activities can occur. Paramārtha comments:

> If the cognizer does not apprehend the object, the two [attachments to objects and to consciousness that grasps the object] are not manifested. The "sense objects" are the objects of Consciousness-Only. Because there are no objects, there is [also] no activity of consciousness. . . . These two [sense objects and consciousness] only refer to two [processes of] consciousnesses presented with a sense object before them, but the sense object [presented] before consciousness is already nonexistent.[30]

The upshot is, if someone does not temporarily encounter objects, as in the PCE or *nirodhasamāpatti,* no objects will be either discriminated or perceived. Hence, no activities of the *ālayavijñāna* or the other two aspect of the perceiver can arise. The *ālaya* can play no "seeding" role, the *ādana* can form no deep attachments, and the *manovijñāna* can perform no discriminations. The everyday attachment processes of the ordinary mind, in other words, are simply abolished in *nirodhasamāpatti.*[31]

In sum, Paramārtha, and with him many Yogācārins, tends to lend support to the thesis that, as articulated by modern thinkers, constructivism is simply inadequate to the task of making sense of mystical events.

One other point will serve as a jumping-off point to the next chapters: Paramārtha suggests that there are at least two distinct sorts of experience, and they deserve two distinct sorts of analyses: in which respectively the cognizer (*vijñāna*) does and does not apprehend (*upalabhate*) objects; in which the intellect (*manovijñāna*) does not and does arise. As such, we should proffer *different* forms of analysis of ordinary and mystical experiences. To do so, let us begin by thinking about how language functions as the mystic moves toward a mystical experience.

Part II

A New Model for Pure Consciousness

Chapter Six

Of Horse Carts and Space Capsules
Constructive Language
and Spiritual Techniques

To summarize the argument so far, we have said that constructivists claim that mystical experience, like any experience, results from prior shaping of expectations.[1] This shaping, they say, is of the intentional object. But, we noted, there is no mental or sensory intentional object in the pure consciousness event and thus nothing to shape. Second, we said, their analogy with sensory or visual experience is ill taken. No one has shown what is supposed to play the role of the visual or sensory object in mysticism. Third, it is not clear how language is involved in mystical experiences. The Upanishadic passage we quoted earlier, for example, states that one is to "continue void of conceptions." If one does so continue, he or she will not think in words, entertain any concepts, or make any identifications during his experience. If so, language or its background is not actually encountered in the PCE.

Third, let us consider an Upanishadic mystic. Let us call him "Svetaketu Aruneya," who was, according to Chandogya Upanishad 6:8, the son of the great guru Uddalaka Aruni.[2] Let us assume that Svetaketu has read Maitri 6.18–19, which we quoted in chapter 2, and from it has indeed learned about Brahman and Atman *before* he has an experience of becoming "void of conceptions." The constructivists commit the fallacy of *post hoc ergo propter hoc* when they suggest that merely because Svetaketu learned about Atman before he experienced it, his experience was therefore *caused* by that prior learning. I heard that Indian food makes people's throats burn long before I had Indian food; yet my hot throat was not caused by my prior knowledge, but by the peppers. The horse of expectations does not always pull the cart of later experience; other causes may be at work.

Fourth, if the horse of language and expectation is pulling the cart of experience, then we should never see the cart going before the horse, or certainly never see a horseless carriage. Yet sometimes we see both in mysticism: sometimes we see experiences preceeding an understanding, and sometimes we see mystical experiences that come virtually devoid of intellectual preparation. For example, in my interview with him, Zen Master Daido Sensei Loori told me that he had his first mystical experience five years *before* he had ever learned about mysticism or Zen Buddhism.[3] His cart came five years *before* his horse.[4] Something *besides* his expectations caused his experience.

Well then, if not language and expectation, what sort of processes might bring about mystical experiences? To answer this, let us think about how language functions in the spiritual process.

Language and the Spiritual Process

Let us try to be as accurate as possible about how mystical language might function. Let us ask, just what *is* the role of Svetaketu's background and language in the "creation" of his experience? Are the expectations and understandings he might have gained from reading the Maitri Upanishad necessarily formative of his experience? Does descriptive language always function to create experiences?

Let us divide the mystical processes involved in the creation of his experience into three different periods: "before," "during," and "after." Assuming that Svetaketu actually does what the Maitri instructs him to do, let us think about how reading about the "unity of the one" before he meditated might affect his experience "during," and how his experience "during" might relate to the language he might use "after."

Before on during: Previous Language and the Experience.

Ever since the philosopher A. J. Ayer, we have known that we do things with words. The most famous is "I do," spoken at an altar.

After a woman utters these two words, she will think about herself and act differently. So too, others will think about, act toward, and interact with her differently than before.

Lots of other words do things: "I solemnly swear to uphold the constitution of the United States . . . " spoken while holding his right hand on a Bible, did something very important to Bill Clinton recently. "Ready, aim, *fire*," are words that do something, often something that at least one person definitely does not want done. These words, "I do," "fire," etc., are called *performatives;* we perform or do things with them.

Similarly, "I never want to see you again" also does something, indeed something usually unpleasant. What "I'm leaving you" does is to *undo* some other words, namely, "I do." In fact, just as "I do" is said to "tie the knot," so "I want a divorce" can be said to begin to "untie the knot."

Tying and untying a knot look like the same sorts of acts. When you knot a rope attached to the bow of a red canoe to a rope attached to a green canoe, you place one string over another in a certain order: a square knot is something like placing rope A under then over rope B, then B under then over A. *Un*tying a square knot is then like pulling A out from under B, then B out from under A. These acts look like mirror images of each other. Yet, though these acts are nearly identical, their *consequences* are radically different. The first one can be said to determine the fate of both red and green canoes long into the future. If ropes A and B are tied together, when I pull A, the canoe attached to B will float right along; when I paddle the green canoe, the red one will necessarily follow. Some acts determine future consequences.

Like that, "I do" ties a knot; henceforth she will call me if she runs out of cash, and the police will call *her* if I total the car. "I do," then, like tying a knot, has a shaping and controlling function. It determines the future in clear and specifiable ways: there is a *necessary* connection between these words and two peoples' destinies.

But words such as the following do something different: "I don't love you anymore and I am leaving" serves to *dis*connect a link. Henceforth the phone won't ring at my place when she runs out of cash. In fact, I won't necessarily know if the phone will ring anyplace if she spends all her cash, or even in what city she will spend it.

*Un*connecting a link does not have the same *logical* functions as connecting one. It does not shape or control the future, except insofar as future relationships will be unlike the past. That is a kind of shaping, of course, but only a vague and minimal one. This shapes rather as "I am not married to her" does.[5] (Something I can say of any of two billion women; though it states something about my history, to state it states very little about my relationships or destiny.)

"I'm leaving you" is a *negative performative*, if you will. It undoes or disconnects something. "You're fired" is another negative performative. Similarly when George Bush heard Bill Clinton say, "I solemnly swear to uphold . . . " he *stopped* being commander-in-chief, stopped being near the red phone, stopped having the power to veto Congress's bills. Here someone else's words served as a negative performative for him. After the initial period of adjustment, such utterances cannot be said to lend "content" to a life, but something more like history or background. In other words, connections between a negative performative and my destiny are largely *contingent*.

Now, some language has a shaping function on *perception*. When I look at the cream colored rectangular box atop my desk, I do not think "cream colored rectangular box" but rather words such as "computer," "Word Perfect," and "keyboard," and (with horror) "disk failure." Part of my experience of that box involves the words with which I identify it: the word *computer* shapes and controls how I see, think about, and interact with that box. For example, despite the fact that it is about the same size, I don't look inside the box to see how many cookies the kids have left, I don't set a teakettle on it to cook, and I don't get out my baseball glove and throw the box to my son. I generally don't even notice what color it is, except when I am writing philosophical essays about perception. I have "automatized" my perception of this box. That is, I have linked up a perceptual object with a phrase or word in an automatic or habitual way. This process is well documented. When we encounter the same thing over and over again, we tend to pigeonhole it without looking at it in detail.[6] These are perceptual "automatisms." They allow us to save psychic time and energy and "see" only what we generally need to see. The categories in whose terms we "see" with, our automatizations, are determined by our set, concepts, context, needs, etc.

On the other hand, some language serves to *undo* such automatized connections between words and perceptions. *"Zut alors,* Monet, forget that the cathedral is supposed to be Gothic and just look over there!" "Stop thinking you know what I said and just listen." "In wine tasting, drop your expectations and pay careful attention to the sensations in and around your tongue." However effective they may or may not be, these phrases are actually trying to do something philosophically quite interesting: they are attempting to get us to *de*-link a connection we had made between expectation and perception. They have, in other words, a *performative* function rather like "I'm leaving you." They help us sunder something, i.e., our perceptual automatization. They undo the knot between expectation and experience.

Sundering perceptual automatizations help us *de*construct perceptual experiences. Were someone to say to Monet, "Claude, just look over there," he might, if he was good at this, cease identifying Rouen's arches as Gothic, and he would probably stop carelessly painting them with pointed tops; he would no doubt see them closer to what they are.

In other words, when a text like our *Maitri Upanishad* passage says "*restrain* the breath," "*withdraw* the senses," "*put to rest* objects of sense," and "let the breathing spirit *restrain* his breathing spirit," it is using negative performative language. Indeed, mystical texts nearly always use such locutions: one should "forget," "lay aside," "cease thinking," "restrain the mind," "put behind a cloud of forgetting," come to a "*vergezzenheit*" (state of forgetting), or what have you.

Taking such expressions seriously, the key process in mysticism seems not like the horse of language pulling the cart of experience, but rather more like *unhitching* the experience-cart from the language-horse. Mystical experiences don't result from a process of building or constructing mystical experience, we've suggested, but rather from an *un*-constructing of language and belief. It seems to result from something like a *releasing* of experience from language. Some forms of mysticism, in other words, should be seen as *decontextualized*.[7]

To continue with my analogy, I propose that mysticism is more like a space capsule than like a horse-drawn cart. Pushed by the rocket of language, the capsule of experience is ultimately de-linked from that which had pushed it, and becomes, as it were, weightless and afloat. Except for its history, the experience on the space capsule is no longer conditioned by its vehicle or the gravity in its history. It now results from other, novel factors.

One interesting correlate to the thought that unhitching perceptual automatisms allows for a new experience: even if we know a lot about his background, we will not be able to predict what he will see when Monet looks at Rouen. The arches he notices might be square, ogee (onion shaped), Romanesque, rhomboid, or perhaps just ugly piles of rubble. The principle here is that the more we are able to deautomatize, the weaker become the logical *links* between our set and our perceptions.[8] That is to say, negative cognitive performative language, language that de-links perception from automatism, cannot be said to lend "content" to a perception. Rather, such utterances serve merely to *stop* us from supplying content. From this point on, there is only a *contingent* connection between expectation and experience: one's experience may or may not fit into one's expectational categories.

Notice, these decontrolling utterances often use the *via negativa*: "*cease* looking," "lay your expectations *down*," "*stop* thinking you know what this will look like," etc. In general, *via negativa* language serves this very particular cognitive function. It is designed to get you to *cease* applying your automatized expectations, and get you to open up to the world more immediately. In our Upanishadic text, "put to rest objects of sense and . . . continue void of conceptions" is also couched in the *via negativa*. And it does seem intended to serve more as a *de*constructive than as a constructive instruction. If Svetaketu follows it, it would not create, predict, or control his experience.[9]

Coming back to our original question about the effect of language learned *before* on the mystical experience *during*, I conclude that language does have a role here, but *not* a constructive one. Its *via negativa* language serves a *negative performative* function. It is intended to project the subject beyond the limits of his or her linguistic system.

Such mystical language functions more like a rocket pushing a capsule beyond Earth's gravity than a horse drawing a cart. Except insofar as the experience aboard the capsule is *not* influenced by the gravity of the earth, the rocket no longer serves to shape the astronaut's experience.

Now let me address a question that the reader may be asking. "Hey, wait on," you may be wanting to say, "really we haven't gained much. It may be true that on being told to 'forget Gothicness and look' Monet might come to cease applying his Gothic formulae; but certainly he would not see without *any* of his perceptual automatizations or formulas. Probably he will simply replace his Gothic formula with some *other*—say Romanesque—or if that doesn't suit, adapt, and modify that one still further until the fit is pretty close."[10] Such a process of replacing one schema with another and altering it is perfectly in accord with the constructivist picture—that we move as if horizontally from one conditioned and constructed form of consciousness to another.

Here, however, is one of the places where my analogy between Monet's dropping his Gothic formula and the mystical instructions in the Upanishads falls down. Svetaketu, our mystic, has not been instructed to replace one concept with another, but to restrain his mind from the external *altogether*, and to put to rest *all* objects of sense and *all* thoughts. In other words, he is not to substitute one automatization for another but to cut off all of his thinking.[11] The Maitri is teaching him not to supply some new concepts and schemata, but rather that he should cease employing concepts altogether. Its closer to going beyond any gravity at all.

In sum, language here does not serve a descriptive function but rather an *evocative* one: it is designed to help bring about a process of *dropping* one's pre-formations. It is intended to help bring him to a new state by *de*constructing the old automatized perceptual patterns.

During on After: The Experience and Its Description

In ordinary experiences, the words I use during the experience itself determines the words I will use to describe that experience. As Wayne Proudfoot puts it, I identify the box on my desk "under a certain description"—i.e., a computer. Because this description shapes my experience, it will also determine my description of that experience: "I picked up the computer to find the paper" uses roughly the same words that I thought with while I was grunting to look for the paper. According to Proudfoot, the language we use to talk about an experience is naturally controlled by the language we employ during that experience. Like that, when a mystical experience is identified "under a certain description," he holds, the terms of that description will invariably control any postexperiential characterization.[12]

Now, is Proudfoot right? Linguistically speaking, what is the relationship between what goes on during a mystical experience and what I say about it afterward?

When I have an experience under a certain description, then my description afterward can and indeed must use those very terms, or synonyms, to truly describe my experience. For example, when I see a robin and think, "Oh, there's a robin," if I report on the experience precisely, I will tell you, "Hey, I just saw what I believed was a robin." Again there's a *necessary* connection between the language I employed consciously or subconsciously *during* the experience and the language with which I describe the experience.

What happens when we have an anomalous experience, one that is some distance from our terms and expectations? Let's say I see a little critter hopping around and I think to myself, "Oh, look, a robin." But then I notice, the robin's breast isn't red, it's *yellow*. Now, were I to describe that bird, I would not be able to use a single automatized label. In fact, I would use words that indicate that my language and expectations were *dis*-confirmed. I'd say, "It looked like a robin but it had a yellow breast," much as I did above. This sentence would communicate something about the relationship between my automatizations and my experience, i.e., that they did apply in some ways and not in some others. At the same time, when I indicate that my automatization was disconfirmed, my language would signify that in order to represent my experience accurately, I needed to replace an aspect of my automatism with more immediate sensory data, i.e., the breast was *yellow*. In other words, the language I would use would be controlled a little more by the sensory information in front of me and a little less by my mutual expectations about robins.

In general, there is an inverse relationship between the use of an automatized label and sensory information. When an object or experience falls into my expectations, or when I simply use an automatization and don't look carefully at something, my description (and presumably my experience) will necessarily rely on that automatization. When I describe it, I will use a minimum of immediately descriptive, sensory language: I will say "Robin," not "six inches long," "rust-colored breast" etc. Conversely, when my expectations are disconfirmed in some way, I will turn to more immediately sensory descriptive language: it had a *yellow* breast. The more my expectations control or match my experience, the less descriptive language I tend to use, and vice versa.

Now let's take this one step further. Instead of its looking like a robin, let's change it a little more. Let's say it had a body and wings of a robin but it had a head like a lion, it barked like a dog, and it was a color I had never before seen, which my instruments said was in the infrared range. Now how would I describe it to myself or to you? I could describe it using schema, as I did just now, or in terms of whatever raw sensory language I could think of. But I wouldn't know clearly *what* to call it. Maybe I would go to my local UFO Research group and they would declare that it was a Martian Roe. Yet this would be the first time I had ever heard of a Martian Roe, and I would be learning the name only *after* the event. That is, unlike my experience of a robin, whatever word that I used for this robin-lion-doggie-thing would not have a *necessary* connection to my actual experience of it. Any relationship between its name and my experience here would be entirely *contingent*.

Words used to describe an experience can have a necessary *or* a contingent relationship with the experience itself. While there generally is a connection between the experience and its description, sometimes there may not be. You *can* name something even if you didn't employ that name while you were undergoing the experience. We do this all the time. "I had no idea what that diagram meant until someone told me it was about phagocytosis." Here, the visual experience of the diagram precedes the acquisition of the language I use to describe it.[13]

The less I use automatizations in my experience, the more my descriptions of it will be controlled by raw sensory input. If, as in the Martian Roe experience, few of my automatic labels clearly apply to my experience, then my immediate perceptual input will play a very large role in shaping my description, and prior expectations or automatizations about the object will play virtually no role.

One way we might describe such a novel experience is, once again, by using the *via negativa*. "It was not a bird, not a lion, and not quite a dog." Here, we are not describing the thing exactly, but using our language as if to cross out expectational categories.

Someone might ask, after the experience, "Did it look like a llama?" We may not have asked that question of ourselves during the experience. Nevertheless, we can answer without hesitation, "No, its size was right but the head and neck were all wrong."

Here, we use the immediate sensory data to answer the question, even though the term we are responding to ("llama") was neither a conscious nor even unconscious element of the experience.

Now, let's perform a kind of calculus on our experience. Let's say the role of language decreases toward nil. That seems to be exactly what our Upanishadic passage is after: nothing "external" is experienced; no "objects of sense" are seen; and one is also absolutely "void of conceptions." Now, what happens to the relationship between experience and later description? That is, if absolutely nothing about an experience is controlled by our language, then how do we come to describe it?

First, anything we say about such an experience would necessarily be expressed in language, conceptions, etc. If so, such conceptions must be conjured up *after the fact*, for *ex hypotheosi*, none are encountered there. If that's the case, they will not have a *necessary* but a *contingent* relationship to the way I encountered the experience itself.

Second, whatever we say about it would be controlled by the nature of the experience as we recall it. Svetaketu might say, for example, "It wasn't noisy," or, "It was pretty quiet." These terms would be a kind of *via negativa* set of descriptions that were, again, not determined by the words he thought during the experience itself, but rather by his recollection of that experience.

Now, here the reader may be asking the following question: Well, how can Svetaketu remember *anything* if there is no content? Here I will simply ask the reader to wait until the next chapter for a thorough discussion of this perplexing question.

What then can we say about the relationship of the "during" period with the "after," postexperiential, descriptions? Any descriptions would be determined by what the subject remembers or does not remember about that event, i.e., that they had had no other content, that they had been awake, that there had been no thinking, that it had been beyond words and therefore a mystery, etc. If Svetaketu was clever, he might say that it was unchanging and nonindividuated. If he came to meet the Buddha, and had taken on his language, he might say it was *shunya*, empty of the kind of form he was used to employing in sensory perceptions. But clearly all these descriptions would have not a *necessary* but a *contingent* relationship with that which he "encountered" during the event. He could say, using *via negativa* language: it was quiet; "I had no particular thoughts"; "I just can't recall any content"; "I came to That which is non-thought"; "I thought the un-thinkable," or any of a host of other such *mahavakyas*, great sayings. Indeed, were he to later become a Buddhist, he could perfectly plausibly say he had encountered *samādhi* or *nirodhasamāpatti* or whatever.

It is in this light that I read the mystical claim of "ineffability," which James called in the *Varieties* one of the four "marks" of mysticism. "Ineffability" means it cannot be spoken, that language is not quite adequate to describe it. To say, "This is ineffable," is in part to say that I cannot tell you, but also that "My own expectational categories were not applicable," that this experience was beyond both your and my words. This is to say, "This was something for which my and your background did not and can not have trained us." Ineffability supports the thought that certain mystical experiences are beyond language and expectations, and indeed are outside the usual necessary relationships between language and experience.

The point is that the connection between experience and description here is not *necessary* but *contingent:* any description would do if it seemed to the subject that it fit. As a result, he would be perfectly capable of changing his description later. Unlike ordinary experience, there is no necessary (philosophical) link between the language of his earlier description and any later description. Furthermore, his description and somebody else's description taken from a different religious language *may fit equally well*: a Buddhist could say, "That was *"nirodhasamāpatti*," and a Christian, "That was the prayer of quiet." Both may be equally and utterly correct, given their language and set.

As for fit, that would be determined by the character of the event as one recalls it and the definition of the terms as one understands them. The fit would not be determined by some purported language used during the event. That is, Svetaketu would be unlikely to say, "It was noisy there," or, "I was thinking how nice it was," because these would not describe what he recalls of his experience, i.e., that it was "void of conceptions."

We might say that the nature of the experience would place certain *limiting parameters* on any descriptions of it, but it would not *control* the description as an automatized term would. In short, the description need not be determined solely by the words I do—or do not—use during the experience.

In conclusion, my research into mystical language tends to support Paramārtha's insight that there are two or more epistemological modalities being tapped by the mystic, and each of those modes warrants a different kind of epistemological analysis. In ordinary experience, one's background and language does effect the experience and the language used to describe it. His or her background also shapes the mystic's path and, in part by encouraging him or her to drop or move away from automatized language, bring on the experience. What Svetaketu learned previously may encourage him to take up meditation, and may shape the transformative meditation processes that lead him to become temporarily "void of conceptions." And when he emerges out of such an event, and his mental chatter starts up again, then he will probably describe this event to himself and to others using the language he learned long before. Then his experience as he recalls it will confirm or disconfirm what his concepts and background led him to expect. He might say, "Oh *that* is what they meant about coming to the formless Self within." But merely using language to describe something does not mean that that language was *necessarily* present in the experience itself.

Sometimes the shaping of language goes the other way: the experience itself may cause one to rethink one's expectations and categories. As the modern American mystic Bernadette Roberts said about her experience: It was so beyond her expectations that it "remained incomprehensible in terms of any frame of reference known to me."[14] Her mystical experience challenged her background and understandings to their roots. In fact, she was compelled to write a book about her experiences *because* she felt so unprepared for it, and she wanted others to be better prepared. The shaping processes may very well go the opposite way than the constructivists hold: *from* experience *to* concept.

On the other hand, I believe that we have shown how it is that a new epistemological structure may be understood to be at work in mysticism. If spiritual language is doing what it claims, I have argued, its shaping function stops *here*. It does not shape these experiences; something else, something nonlinguistic and thus noncultural seems to become decisive. There is, in other words, an epistemologically sound space for nonlinguisticality in mysticism.

The path to mysticism, in short, is at times like a horse and cart, and at times like a rocket and capsule. Mystical techniques such as dervish whirling, meditation, chanting, etc. serve in part to shift us from the one epistemological modality to the other. So too the language of texts like the Upanishads may be designed to help bring about just such an epistemological shift: it shifts us from one *use* of language to another. Mystical language may, in other words, be designed to engender an *epistemological shift*, a shift in the way we use language and in the way that we understand language applies to experience.

We scholars must be more sensitive to the way mystics are emptying their transformative language than we have been hitherto. Mystical teachers may be far more alert to the de-constructive powers of language than we have recognized.

Chapter Seven

Knowledge by Identity

You can't know it, but you can be it . . .[1]

—from the *Tao te Ching*

In the last chapter, I suggested a new model for the kind of apophatic mystical experiences described in the Upanishads, the so called "forgetting model." It takes seriously our Upanishadic passage's instructions to "*restrain* the breath," "*withdraw* the senses," "*put to rest* objects of sense," and "let the breathing spirit *restrain* his breathing spirit." Other mystical texts nearly always use such language: one should "forget," "lay aside," "cease thinking," "restrain the mind," "put behind a cloud of forgetting," or come to "*vergezzenheit*" (the state of having forgotten), etc. Taking such expressions seriously, I have suggested that the key process in mysticism is not like one of construction, but more like one of letting go or *un*constructing. Meditative procedures encourage one to gradually lay aside and temporarily cease thinking in language and concepts.[2] If one truly forgets all concepts, beliefs, etc. for some time, then those concepts, beliefs, etc. cannot form or shape the resultant experience(s). Language cannot shape this experience, but acts more like a booster rocket that *releases* a capsule into weightlessness.[3]

Well, two obvious questions emerge. First, what *does* explain the features of this form of mysticism? That is, if culture does not shape these quiet mystical events, then what factors *are* responsible for their peculiar "shape"?

One might answer, well nothing, for during the pure consciousness event one encounters nothing whatsoever and thus no "shape."

109

The problem with this response is that these experiences are not quite blank: one does not simply black out. Many people I interviewed told me that they remember merely being awake inside: "I know I wasn't asleep," or "I was awake."[4] One "just knows" that one wasn't "gone," dead, blacked out, etc. Paradoxically, one emerges both knowing something (that one was awake, that there was a continuity of awareness throughout the event) and also knowing nothing—that one had been aware of no particular mental or sensory content.

But this leads us to our second question: Usually I can *infer* that I was awake, say, yesterday or half an hour ago, based on the fact that I remember something or other: walking up the steps, typing, thinking about the paper, etc. But in the PCE there was purportedly no content to one's mind, and thus no grounds for inference. Yet one still knows that one had been continuously aware for awhile—a few seconds, a minute, or however long the PCE lasted. The question is, without grounds for inference, how can someone know that he or she was continuously present through a PCE?[5] That is, how can someone remember anything at all, even the merest recollection that they had been conscious during the pure consciousness event?

Consciousness, That Dastardly Term

Let us address the first question first: What does account for the features of the PCE? To do so, let us ask: How do mystics speak about what they encountered during these quiet moments? Our Upanishadic text points us to "That which is non-thought, [yet] which stands in the midst of thought." This suggests that when thinking stops, there is something that remains yet which is in the "midst of thought." Elsewhere in the same Upanishad it is stated that what remains is the "understander of understanding, the seer of seeing." By this, it is generally agreed, the Upanishads are speaking of consciousness or awareness itself.[6]

This insight that much of mysticism touches upon consciousness itself is surprisingly common in a wide range of mystics.[7] According to William Chittick, the Sufi Ibn al-Arabi teaches that what is encountered in his mysticism is consciousness or "sheer

awareness." He says that even though only a "small minority of
human beings" ever attain to the experiences of *fana'* and *baqâ'*,
the mystic experiences "utter undifferentiation, pure unity, sheer
consciousness."[8]

According to the modern Hindu teacher Maharishi Mahesh Yogi,
one key feature of the spiritual path is an experience of "transcendental consciousness," which he defines as an experience of one's
own consciousness devoid of any content:

> Through transcendental meditation [TM], the attention is
> brought from gross experience to subtler fields of experience
> until the subtlest experience is transcended and the state of
> transcendental consciousness is gained. . . . This state of tran-
> scendental pure consciousness [is] also known as Self-conscious-
> ness, Self-awareness [or] samadhi.[9]

According to Maharishi, this "transcendental consciousness" is just
the same consciousness that we employ during ordinary experience, only in mysticism it is experienced in an unmixed form,
uninvolved with perception and thought.

In sum, these mystical authors suggest that one is "encountering" the sheerest awareness itself. Apparently this is the selfsame
consciousness by means of which one has always been conscious, but
here it seems to be unalloyed with the usual intentional content.

Now, what do these mystics mean when they say they are
encountering awareness or consciousness itself?

"Consciousness," as is well known, is one of the most perni-
ciously difficult terms to define, principally because that to which
it points resists clear and precise analysis or definition. In part this
is because consciousness can never itself be an object of analysis for
itself, and so resists definition. As Sir William Hamilton observed:

> Nothing has contributed more to spread obscurity over a very
> transparent matter, than the attempts of philosophers to define
> consciousness. Consciousness cannot be defined; we may be
> ourselves fully aware what consciousness is, but we cannot,
> without confusion, convey to others a definition of what we
> ourselves clearly apprehend.[10]

To make matters worse, our mystics are adding to this mountain of obscurity. For what they mean by consciousness is not quite
what most Western philosophers mean. According to most Western

philosophers, consciousness is always intentional, forever focused
on something. "We can no more eliminate [conscious content] and
be conscious without being conscious of something than we can
separate a dog's bark from the dog."[11] Any claim that consciousness
can be contentlessness is therefore a mistake: "A person cannot be
conscious without its being true that he is either perceiving, or
having thoughts, emotions, etc."[12] After all, it seems that in any
introspection, all one ever comes across is the content or objects of
consciousness, never consciousness itself. In a famous passage Hume
stated:

> For my part, when I enter most intimately into what I call
> myself, I always stumble on some particular perception or
> other, of heat of cold, light or shade, love or hatred, pain or
> pleasure. I *never* can catch myself at any time without a per-
> ception, and *never* can observe anything but the perception.[13]

G. E. Moore stated something similar:

> [T]he moment we try to fix our attention upon consciousness
> and to see what, distinctly, it is, it seems to vanish: it seems
> as if we had before us a mere emptiness. When we try to
> introspect the sensation of blue, all we can see is the blue: the
> other element is as if it were diaphanous.[14]

Because consciousness is always attending *to* some content, such
philosophers hold, a definition of "consciousness" must include this
fact, and therefore might plausibly be "awareness of anything at
all."

Despite Hume's and Moore's use of "consciousness" to describe
only their awareness of intentional objects and thoughts, in the
last chapter we have seen that the doctrine of intentionality is just
not plausibly applied to mystical events. And we have now seen
that many mystics apply "consciousness" to that which they experience when they are without intentional content. So to include the
mystics' claims, we must leave room in our definition of consciousness to allow room for human beings to sometimes be able to persist without content. Thus, a synonym of consciousness should not
be something like "awareness of anything (intentional) at all," but
rather "awareness *per se*" which can (and usually does) become
aware of things.

But, you may ask, is it fair to expand our definition thus? After all, most of us have not experienced our consciousness without an object. Maybe Hume and Moore are right that consciousness never can be encountered without content.

Although we and the philosophers we quoted above may be making general philosophical claims about consciousness, our understanding of consciousness is, at bottom, grounded on empirical observations. Hume makes the cogent and correct observation that whenever he entered into himself, he stumbled on perceptions. When he said he never could catch himself without a perception, he was merely generalizing from the fact that experientially *he* never did. Similarly, when G. E. Moore tried to fix his attention on consciousness and found that it vanished when he did so, he too was describing his experience. Both men based their philosophical statements on *their own* experience of consciousness.

But it should be clear that on empirical matters, the statements of philosophers have absolutely no *legislative* force. No matter how many Humes, Evanses, or Moores observe that they cannot catch themselves devoid of perceptions, this tells us nothing about what a Hindu monk, Dominican friar, or Sufi adept might be able to experience after years of yoga, *orationes secreae*, or Sufi dancing. Indeed many mystics *do* report that they have undergone something quite unique.

Probably Hume and Moore tried to "catch" themselves without a perception on two or three quiet, furtive attempts. Furthermore, those attempts were no doubt part of their philosophical projects. Thus, probably without being aware of the experiential implications of their attitude of "trying to see something about consciousness," they could hardly have allowed their intellectual apparatus to "drop away" completely. Who is to say whether one of them might have achieved a silent consciousness after some years of meditation practices, visualizations, or other practices that were without such an ulterior agenda? Who is to say what Professor Moore might have "seen" in his sensation of blue had he performed twenty years of Tantric visualizations of blue mandalas?[15] These matters are *empirical*, not logical or presuppositional. There are enormous differences between ordinary or philosophical attempts to "introspect the sensation" of consciousness and a deeply transformative meditative path.

What is empirically possible for a human being is not something you, I, or Moore can decide *a priori*, with assertions based on what we *have* experienced so far, any more than we can rule out the possibility of experiencing a past life because no one I personally know has.

In short, philosophical mystics such as Maharishi, Upanishadic thinkers, and Ibn al-Arabi suggest that the data of mysticism point toward an expanded sense of the term *consciousness* to include "awareness per se." And we have seen that it may be reasonable to widen our definition with them. Even though we may not personally have directly experienced our awareness per se, we still should leave logical or definitional room for those who may have.

I should point out that this expanded definition has not insignificant implications for psychology and the philosophy of mind. If we accept this new characterization, this does imply that awareness itself is distinguishable from its content and any processing of content. But *nota bene*, this runs counter to virtually every theory of mind propounded since Immanual Kant's *Critique of Pure Reason*.

Knowledge by Identity

Now, how might a mystic be able to encounter his or her own consciousness—and know that he or she has done so? To answer this, let us ask how, in ordinary experience, we know our own awareness? And how do we know that we have been conscious for, say, the last fifteen seconds?

Here it will be important not to begin on the wrong foot. Many philosophers have theorized about how we know ourselves based on an analogy with how we know other people. Certainly we learn some things about ourselves just as we understand other people. But not all. As John Searle wrote:

> It would be difficult to exaggerate the disastrous effects that the failure to come to terms with the subjectivity of consciousness has had on the philosophical and psychological world of the past half century. In ways that are not at all obvious on the surface, much of the bankruptcy of most work in the philosophy of mind and over a great deal of the sterility of academic psychology over the past fifty years, over the whole of my intellectual lifetime, have come from a persistent failure

to recognize and come to terms with the fact that the ontology of the mental is an irreducibly first person ontology.[16]

There is a fallacy in assuming I know about my own consciousness based on the way I know about others. I know about others through an intentional building toward a sense or picture of them as objects. I construct my knowledge and impressions of others through my sensory impressions of them, my conversations with them, thought about those impressions and conversations, etc. I construct my picture of them as objects over against me, if you will.

But do we learn about ourselves in just the same way? Some things we do learn about ourselves from other people. I no doubt learned my name is Robert by hearing others call me Robert over and over. This is, of course, much as I learn other people's names. I probably learned to recognize when I am angry in part by seeing other people who are angry, hearing e.g. my father shout and seeing him flare his nostrils. Then when I feel a certain way and begin to shout and flare my nostrils, I know that this is what anger feels like. I learned thus to associate my aroused feelings with the term *anger*.

But there is a difference between how I learned about anger and how I learned about being conscious. I did not learn what it is to have a consciousness by seeing what my father's consciousness is like. No, it goes the other way: I *assume* I know what it is like for him (or for anyone) to have an awareness per se only by projecting from my own intimate and first-person subjective sense of what it is for me to have an awareness. As John Beloff said,

> There is only one entity in the universe to which we can with certainty ascribe consciousness and that is oneself. Thus I cannot be certain that you who read these lines are conscious— you may, for all that I can prove to the contrary, be an insentient automaton programmed by nature to behave as if you were conscious.[17]

The importance of this difference—between my first-person acquaintance with my own consciousness and my acquaintance with others and with the world—cannot be overestimated.

Drawing this out, we do not come to an acquaintance with consciousness by virtue of some ostensive definition in anything like its ordinary sense. To ostensively define something new, say a kiwi, I might hand you one and say, "Here, this is what I mean by a kiwi." But I cannot hand you a consciousness. I must point you to it through clues or guides to introspection. That is, we know what it means to be conscious by turning to our first-person acquaintance with *being conscious*.[18]

In short, our knowledge of being conscious is connected first and foremost with a firsthand familiarity with it. This can be seen by thinking about how we might set about teaching what it means to be conscious to something that was not conscious—say a Compaq 386 computer. Even before beginning the attempt it is clear that this will be a hopeless enterprise, since what I mean by "conscious" seems available only to some person or entity that knows what it is to be conscious by virtue of being conscious. Even if my computer were to flash the words, "Aha! I know what it is to have a consciousness," I would not believe that it really did know what I meant. For I can only define "consciousness" by using clues to refer the reader (or computer) introspectively toward that consciousness with which s/he already has an intimate familiarity, the sort of familiarity that can come only from *having* a consciousness.[19]

Nor do I come to a familiarity with consciousness by means of some theory or analysis. I did not learn what it is to be conscious by reading Daniel Dennett, Frances Crick, or G. E. Moore. Indeed, I only can relate to what G. E. Moore said about consciousness because I can relate it to the first-person acquaintance I have always had with being conscious.

Three Kinds of Knowledge

To clarify the kind of acquaintance we have with our own consciousness, let us turn to William James's epistemological distinction between "two kinds of knowledge"[20]: *knowledge-by-acquaintance* [which he sometimes calls knowledge-of-acquaintance] and *knowledge-about*.[21] *Knowledge-by-acquaintance* generally involves direct sensory contact; it is operative when we taste a kiwi or see the color blue. Knowledge-about is conceptual or representational knowledge, operative when we *name* the fruit or *compare* it conceptually with other fruit. It is the more constructed kind of knowledge, clearly involving language, memory, concept, etc.

According to James, even though it is inevitably laced with knowledge-about, knowledge-by-acquaintance provides us with a qualitatively different sort of information:

> In training institutions for the blind they teach the pupils as much about light as in ordinary schools. . . . But the best taught born-blind pupil of such an establishment yet lacks a knowledge which the least instructed baby has. . . . A blind man may know all about the sky's blueness, and I may know all about your toothache conceptually; . . . But so long as he has not felt the blueness, nor I the toothache, our knowledge, wide as it is, of these realities, will be hollow and inadequate.[22]

Generally we gain knowledge-by-acquaintance through direct sensory impressions; knowledge-about we gain through thinking about something, comparing or contrasting it to something else, etc. According to Gerald Myers, in James's conception, "feelings are the vehicles of acquaintance and thoughts the vehicles of knowledge."[23]

James's distinction between knowledge-by-acquaintance and knowledge-about may be more a theoretical distinction between ideal types than a sharp chasm. When I taste a kiwi, for example, the word *kiwi* may be present in my experience. So too I will compare and contrast its taste with other fruits, which suggests knowledge-about. In other words, there is a great deal of knowledge-about infused even in direct sensory contact, in which I gain "knowledge-by-acquaintance." On the other hand, knowledge-about is generally grounded in some immediate contact. In short, the two typically appear together.

We might want to leave the border permeable by saying that some experiences seem nearer to the "knowledge-by-acquaintance" side of a continuum, whereas others seem nearer to the purely knowledge-about pole. Yet we should not forget, James reminds us, that there is a "difference between the immediate feltness of a feeling, and its perception by a subsequent reflective act."[24]

It should be obvious that both knowledge-about and knowledge-by-acquaintance are intentional in structure, involving a subject aware of an object, which is perceived through the senses or thought about. In any intentional knowledge, as we saw in chapter 4, three distinct elements must be involved: the knower, the object of knowing, and the epistemological process(es) involved in that knowing.

In the case of my knowledge-by-acquaintance of the taste of a kiwi, the object is clearly distinct from the subject, and I come to it through the sensory process. Similarly, in knowledge-about I know something also not the subject through the process of thinking. In both, the complex mediating or constructing epistemological processes referred to by the constructivists are clearly involved. This is so even in the case of most self-knowledge, in which some aspect of the personality or ego, a disposition or a self-concept serves as an intentional object. If this is the case, all the constructive activities of the mind again come into play.

But the intentional structure of both of these forms of knowledge makes them particularly ill suited to account for the knowledge I have of my own awareness per se. For in any contact with my own consciousness, the subject is *not* distinct from the object. I just have "contact" with "my" awareness constantly.[25]

For these reasons, I suggest that we add to James's binary epistemological division a third form of knowledge, *knowledge-by-identity*.[26]

In knowledge-by-identity the subject knows something by virtue of being it. I know what it is to be conscious, what it is to "have" "my" consciousness, because and only because I am or "have" that consciousness.[27] I am not acquainted with consciousness through a conceptual knowledge of something but because being something in this case carries within itself a non-inferential sense of what it is to be it. It is a reflexive or self-referential form of knowing. I *know* my consciousness and I know that I am and have been conscious simply because I *am* it.

Knowledge-by-identity is similar to knowledge-by-acquaintance because each is not, in theory, known linguistically.[28] As in the [ideal type of] knowledge-by-acquaintance, my knowledge of my own consciousness is, in a real way, direct and "intuitive": it is not known through analysis or thinking but just by some kind of direct "contact." Again, as in knowledge-by-acquaintance, my knowledge of it may or may not demand that I name it.

But knowledge-by-identity is also different in important ways from knowledge-by-acquaintance. First, as James emphasized, knowledge-by-acquaintance is inevitably involved with knowing-about in some way. An actual experience of tasting a kiwi inevitably is bound up with the knowledge of what other fruits are like, the word *kiwi*, the idea of tasting, etc. Yet I have "knowledge" of my consciousness whether or not I am analyzing it, comparing it to things like it, or even using a term like "consciousness."

Second, knowledge-by-acquaintance can generally be grounded on an ostensive definition. I can hand you a kiwi and say, "Taste this." But this is not true of knowledge-by-identity. To teach you what consciousness is like I cannot hand you your own consciousness and say, "Here, this is what I mean." I must count on the fact that you already know it in the same direct and reflexive way that I do, and then refer you to that preexisting acquaintance with your own awareness, perhaps via clues.

Third, knowledge-by-acquaintance is transient. Within a few hours or days of eating a kiwi, I will lose the immediate tang of a kiwi. Over time I may even forget its taste altogether. But unless I die or go into a coma, my "contact" with my own awareness will not change or disappear. It is, in this sense, permanent.

Forth, and most obviously, knowledge-by-identity is not intentional in structure: I do not know my own awareness as an object.

Fifth, knowledge-by-identity seems to be a truly *direct* or *immediate* form of knowledge. With reference to most knowing—knowledge by acquaintance or knowledge about—knowing comes to us through a complex set of epistemological processes, involving memory, expectation, language, concept use, etc. However the knowledge-by-identity that I am and have been conscious is perhaps the only form of knowledge that is *not* "processed through" these "extremely complex epistemological ways." The knowledge that I am aware and have been aware for the last few seconds or minutes is not a matter of language, nor does it stand on the back of prior experiences. I *just know* that I am and have just been aware directly and without complex reasoning. I know it simply by virtue of being aware.

Nor is awareness per se itself *constructed* or formed by language. An understanding *that* I am conscious is certainly linguistically formed. But clearly *understanding that* I am conscious and *being conscious* are not the same thing. The acquaintance someone has of what it means to be conscious cannot be *articulated* without knowledge of a language system, the term "consciousness" (or a synonym), etc. A non-speaking woman's acquaintance with her own consciousness may remain mute; but in order for her to learn what people mean by "being conscious," she must be able to capitalize on her own primary and direct knowledge-by-identity. She will ground that term on her "encounter" with her own consciousness in exactly the same way as will anyone else, i.e., she will capitalize on her own direct acquaintance with consciousness. She will not gain an acquaintance with consciousness by virtue of learning the word *consciousness*, but rather vice versa.

Other than the "encounter" I have with my own awareness, I know of no other cases of knowledge-by-identity. The knowledge that I am aware is, in other words, not a knowledge like any other. It is *sui generis*.

Long after I came up with this thesis about three forms of knowledge, I was reassured that I had rightly understood the mystical sense of this when I came across the following Sufi three-part division of knowledge. It comes from Ibn el-Arabi of Spain:

> The first [form of knowledge] is intellectual knowledge, which is in fact only information and the collection of facts, and the use of these to arrive at further intellectual concepts. This is intellectualism.

In James's language we would say this is "knowledge-about." Ibn el-Arabi is suggesting that such knowledge *only* involves the collection of facts, thus seeming to ignore the nearly inevitable involvement of "knowledge-by-acquaintance." Nonetheless, the parallel with "knowledge-about" is clear.

> Second comes the knowledge of states, which includes both emotional feeling and strange states of being in which man thinks that he has perceived something supreme but cannot avail himself of it. This is emotionalism.

Here, Ibn el-Arabi has in mind primarily our acquaintance with our emotions. I know my anger or joy by feeling them directly. But I believe we should put our acquaintance with tastes, tactile sensations, etc. in the same category. The Sufi also includes paranormal states in this sort of knowledge, about which I have no comment except to say that if they are known, they are also known through what James would call knowledge-by-acquaintance.

> Third comes real knowledge, which is called Knowledge of Reality. . . . The people who attain to truth are those who know how to connect themselves with the reality which lies beyond both these forms of knowledge. These are the real Sufis, the Dervishes who have Attained.

Ibn el-Arabi's third form of knowledge involves "connecting themselves with the reality." The key here is in this phrase "connect themselves," by which I understand not an experience of looking "at" something intentionally, but rather being or sensing oneself as connected with or through it. If I am connected with something, I know it because I am it. Thus, the form of knowledge he describes clearly corresponds with the knowledge-by-identity I have described.

Now, how do I learn about consciousness through knowledge-by-identity? Here we must remind ourselves not to use our knowledge of other people as the model for self-awareness: we *do* actively construct our sense of other people based on our recollections of what they have said, how they have looked, etc. And indeed we constantly adjust and amend our understanding of them, to form an accurate picture of their attitudes, feelings, habits, etc. We do the same for our understanding of our own attitudes, proclivities, habits, etc.

But do we do the same thing for our sense of our own awareness per se? I think not. We *just have* direct "contact" with what we are; we are familiar with our own awareness based on that "contact." Over time and reflection, I may come to learn much about my personality and character, but this does not change my knowledge (by-identity) of my continuous awareness per se.

Indeed, this firsthand knowledge is the basis of my understanding of consciousness: I am more likely to project to a sense of your awareness *based on* my knowledge-by-identity of my own than the other way around. Had I no acquaintance with awareness from being aware, I could not construct a picture of yours, or *even know to ask whether you had a sense of your own continuous awareness.*

Thus, to the question, how do I know my own consciousness, I think we should say I know it because I *am* it or *live* it. I know my awareness per se as a unity, as tying itself together, as something that ties memories and thoughts together with present stimuli, because, in fact, I do all this. I know it as a unity that can become aware of a thought, perception, or what have you, because I am such a unity.

But I know absolutely nothing about the mechanics of how I do this, how I hold myself together through time, or how I know my own awareness per se. This is because such matters are beyond what I *can* know. I do not know about the mechanics of recalling my own being awake for the last fifteen seconds, since my ability to recall anything at all is directly grounded on this self-recollective ability. Nor do I know about the epistemological processes involved in the fundamental act of tying myself together through time in a single awareness, since any epistemological processes are "for" or "by" it. As the Brihadaranyaka Upanishad says, "Lo, whereby would one understand the understander?"[29]

Malcolm quotes Wittgenstein as saying in a lecture that in philosophy it is important to know when to *stop*.[30] If ever there was an instance of knowing where to stop, it is in speculating how we know that we are conscious and have been conscious for the past few seconds and that the unbroken continuity between these two is a single consciousness.

While we cannot tease out any constituent parts within an awareness per se, we can observe several things about this unknowable process. First, because I do not have access to how I know my own awareness, my knowledge-by-identity is *simple* in the sense of utterly without complexity or plurality. As Śankara says, "The Atman which is the object of knowledge is without parts."[31] I cannot phenomenologically tease out its constituent parts or elements: any parts or elements would be known only by consciousness. I can *hypothesize* about its features and abilities, but I cannot directly experience them as I might experience a sunset or the layers of flavor in a fine wine.

Second, to have an awareness involves tying together what, in intentional experience, we call past and present. That is, it involves a kind of memory, one that does not *think* past and present, but rather simply includes the awareness just past and the awareness of the present within something like a big (present/past) now. It does not involve a sense of a temporal period; that involves the concept of time, a clock, etc. Rather, awareness per se simply ties past and present together as one single continuous awareness. That is, being aware transcends time.

Third, there seems to be a kind of knowledge-about implicit in having an awareness. As Sartre suggested, if we were to tie ourselves together over time and not at some level know that what is being tied together is a single thing, a single me, then we would not be able to hold the present perception as being encountered by the selfsame awareness as was the past one. This begins to sound like conceptual or linguistic knowledge, which it cannot be. But we can say that awareness itself must include some sort of "remembering" that I am single and continuous over time. But this "re-membering" remembers only itself.

Remembering Pure Consciousness Events

Now we are in a better position to understand mysticism. Some mystics, we said, write that during certain experiences they are experiencing their own consciousness, without additional content. How is it possible that they can *know* that they have done so?

The answer is, *I do not know how* I know I have been aware in a pure consciousness event. I just know by means of knowledge-by-identity that I was continuously awake. And that's all.

But ignorance here is the only plausible answer. For in order to answer this question I would have to be able to know the answer to this question with reference to ordinary experience, i.e., to say how, in general, I know that I am and have been conscious a moment ago, that there has been an unbroken continuity of awareness between a few moments ago and now, and that I have an awareness per se at all. But, as we have just seen, *I cannot say how I know any of this* because such matters are beyond the purview of conceptual knowledge in general, and beyond what knowledge-by-identity can reveal.

In general, the mechanics of a consciousness knowing itself or tying itself together continuously through time is something we *cannot* possibly know. We just tie ourselves together continuously through time, that's all. And we simply emerge with the certainty that through the PCE we have tied ourselves together, as usual. But we are precisely as in the dark for how we do this during mystical (nonintentional) experiences as we are about how we do this during ordinary (intentional) experiences. In short, there is no special paradox in not knowing how I recall being awake in PCE. I just know through knowledge-by-identity that I was awake during that (blank) period in just the same *sui generis* way as always!

The most obvious alternative to this view is that mysticism is a moment of knowledge-by-acquaintance. This is most powerfully argued by William Barnard in what we might call the Barnard-James thesis of mysticism. Accepting William James's version of knowledge as bipolar (knowledge-about and knowledge-by-acquaintance),

Barnard observes that when mystical techniques strip away the thoughts, memories, etc. that comprise knowledge-about, the mystic shifts along the scale from "largely knowledge-about" toward "largely knowledge-by-acquaintance."

This Barnard-James approach has several advantages. It allows Barnard to make reasonable sense of mystical experiences that seem to involve some dimly perceived language, and understand subtle differences between several similar-sounding experiences. Barnard also seems to be able to explain what W. T. Stace called "extrovertive experiences," those mystical experiences that involve a new relationship with the world. For Barnard they become a combination of both knowledge-by-acquaintance and knowledge-about. Barnard writes:

> The knowledge-by-acquaintance aspect of [a mystical] experience does not appear alone, but rather, comes into consciousness fused with the mystic's knowledge-about, and structured by the mystic's cultural and psychological categories. Furthermore, this mystical experience is not a static moment frozen in time, but rather, it shifts and reforms, with different "percentages" of these two types of knowledge prevalent at different moments in the process.[32]

But the Barnard-James approach fails when we look closely at common mystical experiences. Let us think about experiences of both the pure consciousness type and of the extrovertive or unitive variety, in which a subject perceives him or her self to be in unity with the perceptual "object."[33] Here is an example of that unitive form of experience, particularly clearly described by the German idealist Malwida von Meysenburg:

> I was alone upon the seashore. . . . I felt that I . . . return[ed] from the solitude of individuation into the consciousness of unity with all that is, [that I knelt] down as one that passes away, and [rose] up as one imperishable. Earth, heaven, and sea *resounded as in one vast world* encircling harmony. . . . I *felt myself one* with them . . . [34] (Emphasis mine)

Malwida senses in some sort of immediate or intuitive manner a connection with the things of the world, as if she was a part of them and they part of her. It is as if the membranes of her self, her own consciousness, had become permeable, and she flowed in, with or perhaps through her environment. In short, objects were encountered as fused with the self itself.

But this means that, unlike knowledge-by-acquaintance, neither this form of experience, nor the PCE of which I wrote earlier, is intentional in structure.[35] In other words, though more sensitive to mysticism's peculiar structures than most, Barnard and James have nevertheless, like so many, based their thoughts about how we know ourselves in mysticism on the model of how we know the sensory world and other people. They have used intentionality as the model for nonintentionality.

Indeed, Barnard seems to recognize the inadequacy of his own account. After suggesting that mysticism should be viewed as an example of a "nearly pure" knowledge-by-acquaintance, Barnard offers the following caveat:

> However, to describe what remains during these non-dual experiences as knowledge-by-acquaintance is perhaps philosophically imprudent, since the category of knowledge depends upon an implicit duality of the knower and the known, and it is this very duality which has purportedly disappeared during unitive mystical experiences.[36]

It seems to me that it makes more sense to classify the kind of encounter the mystic has in a PCE or a unitive experience as an instance of *knowledge-by-identity*. For not only is the mystic instructed to let go of her thoughts and concepts, but to let go of her sensory input as well. Our Upanishadic passage teaches that its mystical experiences will arise if and only if one has

> restrained his mind from the external, and the breathing spirit (prāṇa) has put to rest objects of sense, thereupon let him continue void of conceptions.

Hence, the intentional trinities of subject-perceiving-object and the subject-thinking-thought are abolished. Rather than a knowledge-by-acquaintance, one is instructed to let go of intentional knowledge altogether, and come to rest "in" or "through" one's awareness alone. Removing both conceptual knowledge, knowledge-about, and sensory contact, knowledge-by-acquaintance, in *turīya* one comes to employ knowledge-by-identity alone. "That" which one knows when knowing one is aware is *all* that is recalled after he or she has continued "void of conceptions."

This idea, that mysticism is a *sui generis* example of knowledge-by-identity, in which the subject knows only itself reflexively, is seconded by Suzuki's account of the Zen Buddhist's experience of śūnyatā.

> Śūnyatā is to be experienced and not conceptualized. To experience [śūnyatā] means to become aware of, but not in the way in which we become aware of the world of sense-and-intellect. In the latter case, we always have a subject that is aware of something and an object of which the subject is [intentionally] aware. . . . To be aware of śūnyatā, according to Zen, we have to transcend this dichotomous world in such a way as not to be outside it. Śūnyatā is to be experienced in a unique way. This unique way consists in śūnyatā's remaining in itself and yet making itself an object of experience to itself. This means dividing itself and yet holding itself together. . . . Śūnyatā is experienced only when it is both subject and object. . . . "Knowing and seeing" śūnyatā is śūnyatā's knowing and seeing itself; there is no outside knower or spectator; it is its own knower and seer.[37]

When Suzuki suggests that śūnyatā is known as the subject but serves as both subject and object, thus knowing and seeing itself, he is not suggesting that there are two. Rather, he is drawing an analogy with ordinary seeing and suggesting that despite remaining a single subject, the subject reflexively serves the role of the object. In this sense, he is also holding to a doctrine of the subject "knowing" itself through being itself, or knowledge-by-identity.

I might observe that this thesis, that the mystic encounters the PCE and the unitive or extrovertive mystical experience through knowledge-by-identity, has the same advantages as the Barnard-James hypothesis. It too enables us to make reasonable sense of mystical experiences that seem to involve some dimly perceived language or some sensory contact, and understand subtle differences between several similar-sounding experiences. For in such experience, consciousness is aware of itself through knowledge-by-identity and simultaneously is perceiving thought or language intentionally. Furthermore, "extrovertive experiences" can be understood as a life in the world in which knowledge-by-identity does not disappear even while other epistemological structures are active. In such a phenomenon, one would continue to know the self reflectively simultaneously with seeing, acting, thinking, etc.

Concluding Remarks

Despite the assumptions of neo-Kantian or Wittgensteinian constructivists, apophatic mysticism is not the psychological realization of expectations, concepts, or the background set. Rather, such mystics are encountering consciousness itself.

To assume that we know our own consciousness in the same way that we know another person, an apple, or even facets of our own personality would be to commit the fallacy of the displaced object. Our familiarity with our own consciousness is so intimate, so without seams, that we have no way of teasing out its constituent parts. In knowing it we just have an immediate sense of it and of its continuity through what we know (intellectually) as past and present. This intimate acquaintance—what I have called "knowledge-by-identity"—should be distinguished in epistemological structure from all other knowledge. And this epistemological structure is what makes certain apophatic mystical events so paradoxical yet so interesting.

*P*art III

The Dualistic Mystical State

Chapter Eight

Silence, Thinking, and Cutting Carrots
Characterizing an Advanced Mystical State

In our last chapters, we noted that the evidence provided by mystics leads us to distinguish between two concepts that are generally not distinguished: intentional consciousness and awareness per se. Most people have held that there is no difference, that awareness is always awareness of something, and because this is so they can reasonably define consciousness as "awareness of some intentional object." But in the pure consciousness event, we argued, mystics experience their own awareness to be without content. This leads me to suggest a new account in which awareness is understood as experientially and thus analytically distinguishable from its content.

Furthermore, we said, awareness itself functions and remembers itself differently than it remembers content. It does not know or remember itself through any kind of intentional structure, but rather, we said, just unintentionally knows and holds itself together through time. Thus, we can distinguish two distinct epistemological structures: knowing intentionally, which James divided into knowledge-by-acquaintance and knowledge-about, and the nonintentional form of self-knowing, which I call "knowledge-by-identity." Knowledge-by-identity is an epistemological structure that any and every conscious being must have, a knowing what it is to have a consciousness simply by virtue of being conscious. This sort of self-knowledge, awareness's tying itself together through time, cannot itself be linguistically created, for consciousness tying itself together through time must be prior to language: we must be conscious to learn any language and being conscious means tying myself

131

together. Stating that "I am conscious" is linguistic, of course, but the knowledge-by-identity we have of our consciousness is different than stating it, and is prelinguistic. Furthermore, it is not pluralistic: while there is no doubt that being an American is profoundly different than being Japanese, there is a great deal of doubt that the awareness per se of an American will differ from the awareness per se of a Japanese. Consciousness itself is a, or perhaps the only, nonpluralistic feature of what it is to be human.[1]

We also said that consciousness per se is all that the mystic experiences during a PCE. Having eliminated all conscious content, the mystic is left with the barest being conscious, and thus undergoes an experience that is held together and remembered only through the peculiar, contentless, nonintentional knowledge-by-identity.

With reference to the pluralism question, if we are solely encountering consciousness per se and if all consciousness per se is the same in humans, then it makes sense that the pure consciousness event should be indistinguishable between people from any culture. It should be regarded as a nonpluralistic event.

The Experience Reports

One thing I suggested in the last chapter was that the thesis of knowledge-by-identity allows us to make reasonable sense of the more complex advanced mystical experiences that involve some language or sensory contact. I would now like to show how. Let us look at one form of a more advanced or complex experience.

It is important to do so, for despite the philosophical interest in the quiet pure consciousness event, many people have observed that the PCE seems existentially unimportant. I heartily agree. In general, meditation represents only a few minutes of one's day, and even at its most frequent, the PCE lasts for only a few minutes of a meditation. This is hardly the stuff of mystical tomes or religious enthusiasm! And so, keeping in mind our understanding of the PCE, what can we say about the more advanced, and apparently more personally significant, mystical experiences?

Now, before detailing the experiences, I want to warn the reader that I am going to claim something in this chapter that is nearly unheard of in the scholarly literature on mysticism. Ever since William James declared that one of the four features of mysticism is "transiency," scholars have generally assumed that mystical experiences last only a short time. In this view, mysticism represents a taste of the ultimate only, something that lasts for a few glorious moments, a half a day, or in very unusual cases perhaps a few days. I believe that James, and with him most modern scholars, was wrong. Some mystical experiences *are* semipermanent or permanent, being a transformation that, once accomplished, changes the deep epistemological structure of all experience for months, years, or indeed the rest of one's life.

The different opinions about the permanency of mysticism may be the product of a split between scholars who study Eastern and Western mysticism. Those more familiar with Western mystical accounts may assume, largely because of first person reports and possibly because of certain theological assumptions, that the mystical transformation only leads to short-lived peak experiences such as rapture or a "foretaste" of heaven. This may have shaped James's understanding since most of his subjects, all Western and primarily Christian, had short-lived experiences. On the other hand, those who study Eastern mystics often have a different impression. The Buddhist *Nirvana* is commonly assumed to be a permanent or quasi-permanent state. So too is the *sahaja samādhi* (lit. "all time samādhi") described by Ramana Maharshi, as we noted in chapter 1. Maharishi Mahesh Yogi describes a permanent transformation he calls "Cosmic Consciousness." Sai Baba's experiences began at an early age and have continued ever since.

The reports that follow are all of permanent changes. Thus, as we look at them, let us keep in mind that as scholars we are in very new territory. We should not confuse these permanent apples with some temporary oranges.

One further word: I will look here at only one form of an advanced mystical experience. I am not claiming, and I do not believe, that it is the *only* sort of permanent transformation. Nor is it the most advanced form, according to my preliminary analysis. I am looking at it not because it is stressed by mystics, which it but rarely is, nor because it is personally the most important experience. I am looking at it because it seems to represent a natural next *epistemological* development, and it raises some interesting epistemological questions.

Experience 1: Bernadette Roberts

The living American mystic Bernadette Roberts has written one of the clearest descriptions I have see of the sort of experience I would like to explore. Roberts is an ex-nun, mother, housewife, and a woman who has written *The Experience of No Self*. She had been in the habit of meditating in a local chapel, she tells us.

> On previous occasions, I had come upon a pervasive silence of the faculties so total as to give rise to subtle apprehensions of fear. It was a fear of being engulfed forever, of being lost, annihilated or blacking out and, possibly, never returning. . . . [On one particular afternoon, as I was concluding a meditation,] once again there was a pervasive silence and once again I waited for the onset of fear to break it up. But this time the fear never came. . . . Within, all was still, silent and motionless. In the stillness, I was not aware of the moment when the fear and tension of waiting had left. Still I continued to wait for a movement not of myself and when no movement came, I simply remained in a great stillness. . . . Once outside, I fully expected to return to my ordinary energies and thinking mind, but this day I had a difficult time because I was continually falling back into the great silence.[2]

Roberts had often encountered a silence within, more or less unadulterated moments of the pure consciousness event. But that day the silence she had often experienced simply did not lift. Once she had become silent inside, peculiarly, she did not emerge from it. She "remained in a great stillness" even while waiting for it to lift, thinking, and even talking. She experiences herself as "in a great stillness," even though she continues to have sensory experiences, thoughts, etc. Ultimately, she stood up and walked out of the chapel, "like a feather floats in the wind," while her silence continued unabated.

Her interior silence turned out to be *permanent*. It never again left her. Over the next few weeks, months, and indeed years, she experienced an interior "stillness" while walking, talking, laughing, crying, and even, she reports, cutting carrots.

After several weeks of this peculiar state, she was able to formulate that something deep had shifted inside her. Something familiar was now missing. Trying to figure out just what had happened to her, she went to the library to see what others had said about this sort of thing, but the books she found were of little help.[3]

Coming home that day, she realized that an old "unlocalized" sense of herself, her ego, or her individuality used to motivate all her actions. This, she perceived, was what was missing. In its place was a simple emptiness, a silence. Her deepest self was now unutterably translucent, even in the midst of activity.

This, I should again emphasize, was not the final experience that culminates her progression. Our passage is taken from merely page two of her long autobiography. Many other experiences were to ensue over the next year or two. But as scholars, this is certainly quite enough for us to think about, for she clearly describes something peculiar and long lasting.

What can we say about it? The key here seems to be that while there had once been but one, now there were two different levels or aspects of her experience: a thinking, seeing, feeling aspect and some vast still emptiness within. At some deep level inside nothing was moving, yet she was still able to think. It sounds as though she was able to maintain the sort of silence achieved in a PCE simultaneously with intentional experience.

But how is this possible? In general, when we think, things in us change: when I think, I have the sense that "it is I that thinks"; when I worry, my whole gut gets tied up in knots; no part remains unaffected. One might suppose that if she could think, she could not really be in an interior silence. On the other hand, if she was truly entrenched in an interior silence, how could she think, feel, or see? Ms. Roberts does not explain how she could perform this dualistic trick.[5]

The easiest explanation is, of course, that she is kidding herself. She thinks there are two levels at once, but this is a fiction. Really, one might speculate, she has the same sort of ordinary epistemological structure that most of us do. She thinks, sees, etc. in the same intentional way as most of us, but she is either dissembling or delusional.

This explanation is certainly the easiest, for it challenges none of our easy shibboleths about experience, epistemology, etc. It is always easiest to kill the messenger. But such an explanation is dubious for the following reasons. (1) There are other mystics who report something similar, as we will see. (2) While I often make mistakes about short-lived phenomena (viz. I thought Susan entered the room before Rob, but I was mistaken), it is more difficult to imagine how someone might make a mistake about a permanent change such as hers. I may make a mistake whether a twinge of pain was in my elbow or my forearm, but it is hard to imagine how I could make a mistake about a permanent change such as my arm's amputation. I can check out my beliefs about a permanent changes at any time. (3) We might hold that Bernadette is delusional or psychotic. But this particular woman has written a reasonably coherent book, and appears to be a reasonably sane, reasonably intelligent, mature woman. She shows no signs of delusion or a psychosis serious enough to warrant such an accusation. (4) She tells us that even she recognizes that this is an unusual phenomenon, so unusual that she had never heard of such a thing. Indeed, this is the very reason she went to the library to figure it out, and ultimately why she decided to write a book describing it: so that others would be able to understand it if it happened to them. If we want to claim that she was making a mistake, we must explain both the mistake and her recognition that something was amiss here. (5) When you think about it, there is only one good reason to believe that she was mistaken: it is that we assume, even if subconsciously, that all experiences are more or less like our "ordinary" ones. But if there is a *sine qua non* of all mystical experiences, it is that in the beginning they seem odd, extraordinary, and not "normal." One of the reasons they are so interesting is that they *are* unique. Thus, the very peculiarity of her experience suggests that she may be onto something peculiarly mystical.

For these reasons, without strong counterevidence, let us assume that she is telling her story in a reasonably accurate way, and take it as reasonably accurate.

Experience II: A Zen Buddhist Description

I was unaware that experiences such as hers were ever described in the Zen Buddhist literature until I ran across D. T. Suzuki's (1870–1966) famed essay, "The Zen Doctrine of No Mind"[5] which concerns *Hui Neng's Platform Sutra*. Published in 1949, again in 1954, and once again in 1981, this essay has been crucial in helping students of three generations understand Zen and the mystical transformation.[6] [7] [8]

The *Platform Sutra* itself is perhaps the Zen text that has most nearly attained canonical status. Dating from the sixth century, it purports to be the record of the illiterate but highly revered sixth and last Zen patriarch, Hui Neng, but is itself probably a compilation of his words and those of several generations of his followers.[9] This text says,

> To understand the original mind of yourself is to see into your own original nature. . . . Good friends, in this teaching of mine, from ancient times up to the present, all have set up no-thought (*wu-nien*) as the main doctrine, non-form as the substance, and non-abiding as the basis. . . . No-thought is not to think even when involved in thought. Non-abiding is the original nature of man.[10]

This passage focuses on nonthought (*wu-nien*), which, we read, is maintained even while one thinks: "No thought is not to think *even when involved in thought.*" This statement, and others like it, suggests that Hui Neng is referring to an experience much like Bernadette Roberts's twofold experience that "within, all was still, silent and motionless," even while she was involved in thought. Both Roberts and Hui Neng describe a form of life that has, phenomenologically, two aspects or levels: thinking and, at some level, an interior silence that is uninvolved with or maintained concurrently with ordinary thinking.

Hui Neng's key terms here are *wu-nien*, no-thought, and *wu-hsin*, literally also no-thought but more often translated as no-mind. According to Suzuki, these two terms, which "designate the same experience" or point to the same aspect of consciousness, are absolutely key Zen terms.[11]

Let us look first at *wu-hsin*. The character *hsin* originally symbolized the heart as the organ of affection, but came later to signify the seat of thinking and willing. *Hsin* thus corresponds to the consciousness of thoughts and desires, or what we call intentional consciousness. *Wu* negates. Thus *wu-hsin* means "no intentional consciousness," or "no mind." As for *wu-nien*, the *nien* pictograph shows *chien*, "now," over a pictograph of the heart, and thus originally signified something present for consciousness now, i.e., the thought or percept of which I am presently aware. *Wu* again negates. Thus *wu-nien* means not being aware of something now; thus, "not thinking." Again we have the absence of intentional consciousness. Both *wu-hsin* and *wu-nien*, may thus be translated with some precision as "no-intentional-consciousness."

Suzuki sometimes translates *wu-hsin* with the unfortunate term *unconscious*, by which he connotes "that" which is not itself intentionally conscious but stands as the basis of thought. But this term is highly misleading, due to its long association with the Freudian and Jungian psychological lexicons. That is why I believe it is better to translate *wu-hsin* with a new term that indicates that one is devoid of intentional content; perhaps "nonintentionally-conscious."

One might think *wu-nien* implies a blank or dead mind. This might be the case except for one feature that our Zen masters stress: through *wu-nien*, one recognizes or experiences "the nature of one's *tzu-hsing*, self-nature itself," as Suzuki puts it,[12] one's "original nature." In *wu-nien* "self-nature finds its own being when it sees itself."[13] That is, there is a being conscious of one's own nature, reflexively, in *wu-nien*. Such a recognition implies that one can think even while remaining in the non-thinking: a dualistic experience of silence and thought.

Experience III: An Autobiographical Report

My Reasons for Including Autobiography. I would like to offer the following autobiographical account. Why? As I noted earlier, such accounts, I believe, should offer an interesting counterbalance to an exclusive reliance on third party and textual accounts. Religious texts, I noted, are complex documents, generally written for a host of reasons, descriptive, rhetorical, and many others. It is often hard to distinguish descriptive from evocative, theoretical, theological, or other interpretive matter. This problem is exacerbated by the very common problem of translation. Thus, an autobiographical account, written in English or spoken to a relatively "objective" scholar may eliminate some or many of these obfuscating complexities.

I originally thought I would publish the following material as if I (as a scholar) was interviewing someone. (I suspect William James did something similar in the *Varieties*, occasionally describing his own experiences in the third person.) This white lie would lend the material a more impersonal or objective tone, and keep my own personality more or less out of the picture. I feared that presenting my own experience would be taken as a kind of special pleading, or as an occasion for egotistical self-inflation.

I have decided to run these risks for the following reasons. First, to present this in the third person would be lying, whether white or not, which is always dangerous (in scholarship and in life). Second, I feel reasonably confident that I am not presenting this material as a form of self-inflation, but rather for good scholarly reasons. It serves as another link in a chain of experiences described in this chapter, which should clarify the kind of experience I am exploring here.

Third, one of the things we scholars of mysticism lack are good, healthy autobiographical descriptions of mystical phenomena. We find ourselves often trying to tease out phenomenological description from a source's very complex interpretations, and it makes our work that much trickier. In the interest of lending one more experience report to the heap, I have decided to present as clear a phenomenological portrait as I know how, and in my first language, English. Fourth, when I have occasionally published portions of interviews with unknown people, colleagues have occasionally indicated to me that they do not regard those reports as very reliable, since they are so difficult to verify or explore independently. Indeed, while scholars have responded to several of my articles and books, none have given written heed to those interviews; whereas several have explored or mentioned in the literature a very brief autobiographical description of a PCE. I believe that there is good sense in this. Autobiographical reports are stronger "raw material" for the explorations of philosophers, scholars, mysticists (scholars of mysticism), and psychologists. Last, to the extent that this experience indicates something of my personal agenda, presuppositions, and questions, I include it in the spirit of honesty and openness.

It is important to me that as a methodological tool, i.e., as a subject for scholarly investigation, I am not here *solely* exploring my personal experiences. Several of my students have spilled much ink over their own somewhat idiosyncratic experiences, much to their papers' detriment. For obvious reasons, good scholarship requires that we set any one person's experience in the context of others' clearly parallel experiences.

The Account

I have been practicing a neo-Advaitan form of meditation for twenty-nine years. I began on November 2, 1969, and have continued meditating twice a day ever since, missing one infrequently.

The first permanent change happened in 1971. I was on an extended (nine month) retreat. On extended retreats, we meditate much more than usual every day. At this time I was meditating maybe six or eight hours a day, only breaking for meals, yoga asanas, and evening lectures.

This happened in December, I think, so I had been on this course for approximately three months. I had had quite a few interesting experiences in meditation: pure consciousness, visions, insights, intense moments, etc. These were all transient, generally lasting less than an hour or so. But this first transformation occurred over a period of perhaps a week or two. I realized something was changing on the surface of my body. It was as if all over my body I had had very faint pins and needles sensations, but, starting up around my head, they seemed to have ceased entirely. I stopped feeling anything like pins and needles above a certain plane. My skin became as if dead quiet. Over several days or weeks, I experienced something like a plane running roughly horizontally through my body: below it were these faint pins and needles; above it there weren't any. Above this plane, the surface of my body was as quiet as a still lake, but noisy below. Above, my skin itself had become silent, as if there was no background activity in my nerve endings.[14] It's not as though I couldn't feel anything. It was more as if there was no spontaneous ongoing activity under the surface of my skin.

Before this time it had never occurred to me that I had had anything like faint pins and needles sensations all over my body. It is virtually impossible to be aware of something so constant until it changes. It was only *in comparison* that I became aware of these sensations. But it was obvious to me that this slight level of activity had been a constant feature of my epidermis as long as I can remember. It is not as if I could remember it "turning on" earlier in my life.

This horizontal plane (silent above, noisy below) seemed to get stuck around my upper ankles. It was such a vivid, physical sense: I kept checking to see if my socks were on too tight! I rolled down my socks, even didn't wear any for a while, because I was so conscious of this invisible line there. After a while, the ankle-line just disappeared. I didn't notice it moving. After perhaps two or three days, it just wasn't there any more. Ever since that time, the nerve endings in my skin have remained quiet. I can remember that pins and needles feeling, but I have never again felt it: this quiet surface has remained with me ever since.

Except recently, when I have been working on this account, I do not often think about this transformation. I am certain that there is less activity or background noise on the surface of my skin than pre-1971, but I rarely think about this or compare it to what it was like before that time. It has become just the normal character of my everyday life.

About a month or two later, in January 1972, something else quasi-physical shifted. This was somewhat like the previous change, in that it had a physiological character. But this took place inside the back of my neck. It felt as if a series of tubes running down the back of my neck—inside the back of my head[15]—also became utterly silent. This transformation started on the left side. Over several weeks, one by one, all the activity inside these little tubes inside just ceased. There was a kind of a click or a rapid "zipping" sensation, as the nerve cells or whatever became quiet.[16] As in the bodily shift, it was as if there had been this very faint level of activity, again somewhat like faint pins and needles, within these tubes running down my neck. They had been a quiet but constant background noise inside my head. But when one of these tubes became silent, all that noise just stopped entirely in that portion of my skull, and it became perfectly translucent. As with the change in my bodily surface, I had never before noticed the faint activity in my neck. It was just part of what it felt like to be me. I only noticed the interior noise or activity in these tubes in comparison to the silence that "came into" each of these tubes.

One by one, from left to right, these tubes became silent. Each one shifted without warning. It was as if they went *zip,* and then it was absolutely quiet in that area: absolutely no pins and needles, background noise or sensation was there. It was as if these sections of my brain had become a vacuum or transparent. Absolute emptiness inside.[17]

As each one of these tubes or brain sections became silent inside, that section as if disappeared entirely. That is, after, say, the first three had made this shift, they as if joined together, and became one extended silent piece of the back of my head, not three discrete, quiet tubes.

The transformation from one side of my upper neck to the other took several days. I know that because I remember telling several friends about this strange sense of having one side of the back of my head silent, and the rest noisy. It made me a little dizzy, because it felt as if I was listing over. The left was quiet inside, almost light, the right was noisy.

At the time, I did not know what to make of this shift occurring. I had never heard of anything like this, from my teacher, my reading, nor from anyone else. Nor since this time have I ever met anyone or heard of anyone who has had a shift involving something like these tubes. At first I thought I was getting ill. I wondered if maybe I had cancer or some brain disease which was systematically destroying bundles of nerves. But this did not seem convincing since this was neither unpleasant nor painful, and it had no ill effects.

One by one these tubes continued to become quiet, from left to right. It took a few weeks for the process to complete itself. Finally the last one on the right went *zip,* and that was it. It was over.

After the last tube had shifted to this new state, I discovered that a major though very subtle shift had occurred. From that moment forward, I was silent inside. I don't mean I didn't think, but rather that the feeling inside of being me was like being entirely empty, a perfect vacuum.[18] Since that time all of my thinking, my sensations, my emotions, etc., has been on a silent background. It is as if what was *me* was now this emptiness. The *silence* was now me, and the thoughts that went on inside have not felt quite in contact with what is really "me," this emptiness. "I" became this silence inside, my thinking has been as if on the outside or somehow in the middle of this silence without quite contacting it. So too, when I saw, felt or heard something, that too has been not quite connected to this silence within me. What is "me" is now this silence; everything else feels somewhat different than this silence within, of a different kind or separate.

It may sound as though I went mad on that day. I know that "separate from everything" sounds very unpleasant, a distancing, or even some sort of mental illness. But this does not strike me as a form of madness. I do not feel *emotionally* unconnected to things. In fact I feel more "connected" than I used to. And I certainly do not believe that I am psychotic. In fact, I like to think I am fairly well put together. The feeling is not one of psychosis or emotional distancing, but almost like a deep shift toward new sense of what I am. This shift inside now allows me to feel quiet inside, even while I think, act, whatever.

As for external changes, I had told my friends about this tube business as it was happening, so when it was over they were probably looking for some external signs of change. Whatever the reason, several of them said that for several weeks after this tube thing had ended, I looked unusually happy. That may have been due to the fact that I was happy and excited because this seemed so important. I am not sure how much to attribute to the excitement about this shift, and how much to attribute to the shift itself.

Over the long term however, it is difficult to clearly attribute any particular personality changes to this inner shift. I have the sense that it has made me somewhat freer, allowed me to do things with less effort. But it is hard to know how much to attribute to *just* this change.

The only external change that I can directly attribute to this phenomenon was that, immediately following this transformation, my visual perception changed. The day after the last tube had become quiet, there were huge thunderheads in the distance, rolling in over the sea, high and gray-white. When I looked at them over the hills, the whole scene—hills, brush, and white-gray clouds—seemed to be more three-dimensional than ever before. It was as if my vision had more physical depth to it. Perhaps we could say that before I was not the witness to all my seeing, and thus the seeing could stand out with more depth. But frankly, I am not sure what this new sense of vision "means" or why I experienced it. I have not seen it described in any of the literature.[19] This change was very noticeable. This increased depth in my vision has remained with me ever since that time.

It also caused one other change, to my sleep life. Before this time, when I had slept, it had been very hard for me to wake up. But ever since that time, it is as if I do not quite go to sleep. I sleep with most of me, I feel, but this quiet part, this part that doesn't change, does not sleep. And so when I sleep it's as if I'm not entirely asleep. This significant change this has brought is that first, I need less sleep than I had. I am not certain that I can attribute this to just this shift. But the second I can: it takes virtually no time for me to wake up, either in the morning, or when one of my children comes into the bedroom in the middle of the night. It is as if I hear him or her walk into the room, and I am already awake. That is actually a pretty useful aspect of this experience: I am just ready for things, even at the depths of sleep.

Indeed, all the changes that befell me in 1971 and 1972 have remained since that time. The sensations of quiet inside, seeing in greater depth, etc. have remained a permanent feature of my experience, at this point (1996), for twenty-four years. While my personality, what I do, my social life, my knowledge, etc. have all changed dramatically since that time, this interior silence has not.

I rarely think about it. It has just become an aspect of who I am. It was very noticeable in the beginning, largely because it was so new and different. But the fact that I am silent inside is just the same as it was that first day. I feel certain of that.

I associate this new form of life with the Hindu and possibly Buddhist concepts of the early stages of enlightenment. I understand this as an unchanging silence inside, which is just what the Upanishads and Advaita Vedanta term "Atman." The emptiness of what I am inside, as well as a sense of not quite being touched by thought and language, I associate with the Buddhist concept of *shunyata*, a key aspect of Nirvana.

But one thing that has was at first hard for me to understand is that, even though I now had this unchanging silence within myself which I associate with enlightenment, little except my vision and my sleep patterns changed. That is, I had the same personality; I still became anxious and worried, etc. From what I had heard of enlightenment, I expected that all my troubles would immediately disappear, like magic. But it was not like that at all. Though I have worked at changing, my personality was little changed immediately from the internal shifts.

Over the years, however, this new experience helped make me more open to change, I believe, and more ready to explore things in new ways. I have worked in a variety of ways to change my behavioral responses and my attitudes so that I would be less anxious and unhappy. I believe that I am more flexible now than I was before these shifts happened. But it was not as if my personality became instantly smooth or graceful. In fact, once the initial thrill wore off, I was actually pretty depressed after it first took place. "This is *it?*" I kept wondering. I had thought life would be perfect, but it wasn't. It was just that I was silent inside.

Over the years though, I can report that things have continued to shift. I now believe that this shift was the beginning of a kind of internal thawing that has continued and moved more rapidly as time has gone on. I like to think I am a more open, authentic person than I would have been otherwise. And I believe I am more confident within myself. But this did not come immediately with the new experience of the self.

Other changes have occurred in my internal experience and my perception over the years. But this is quite enough for us to ponder.

As we have seen before, this is a form of life with two distinct levels or modalities of experience. With the outer mode, I have encountered objects, thoughts, and, of course, language and cognition. The more inner mode, however, which began with some sort of transformation in the back of my neck, is entirely silent. Once again, the silence is associated with the self:

the feeling inside of being me was like being entirely empty, a perfect vacuum.[20] Since that time all of my thinking, my sensations, my emotions, etc. have seemed not connected to me inside as they once had, for it is as if what was *me* was now this emptiness. The *silence* was now me, and the thoughts that went on inside have not felt quite in contact with what is really "me," this emptiness. "I" was now silent inside, my thinking has been as if on the outside or somehow in the middle of this silence without quite contacting it.

As we saw in Bernadette Roberts, the experience is that what is really "me" has become this silent level within. Much like hers, my sense of my *self* is now that of an emptiness or a "vacuum" inside. It is as if transparent.

This experience is also reminiscent of the Zen Buddhist thought of *wu-nien,* no-thought. For, as that Zen term describes, I experience the silence inside as distinct from and uninvolved with my thinking and sensing. This experience matches perfectly the Zen description that through *wu-nien*, one recognizes or experiences "the nature of one's *tzu-hsing*, self-nature itself," or one's "original nature." For it makes perfectly good sense to say that I am consciously aware of my own nature (my original nature) which is, I now perceive, an empty silence. To be quite precise, we should say the silence itself, which I now associate with the self itself, is reflexively aware of itself "as" the silence.

Experience IV: Meister Eckhart's Geburt

In my *Meister Eckhart: Mystic as Theologian,* I have shown that Meister Eckhart, famed thirteenth-century Christian mystic, discusses what he calls *gezucken*, a state of being enraptured without sensory or intellectual content.[21] This state, experienced as an utter silence, Eckhart understands as a transient encounter with what he calls the innermost within the soul, or the "summit" of the soul, wherein God exists in purity.

> God is nowhere so truly as in the soul, and . . . in the inmost soul, in the summit of the soul.[22]

> There is something in the soul in which God is bare and the masters say this is nameless, and has no name of its own . . . God is always present and within it. I say that God has always been in it, eternally and uninterruptedly . . .[23]

This ground, he suggests, that is one with the infinite ground that is God, is the true basis, the highest or deepest element of human beings. It is experienced in its purity during the time of *gezucken,* but what is most interesting for our purposes is that the experience of this ground can be brought into activity, he suggests.

What I have written about less is Eckhart's notion of the more advanced relationship between contemplative silence and the active life. In one passage he writes:

> If a person wanted to withdraw into himself with all his powers, internal and external, then he will find himself in a state in which there are no images and no desires in him and he will therefore stand without any activity, internal or external.

Here Eckhart is describing what has become familiar as a silence like the pure consciousness event. It is without internal activity or external activity; i.e., thinking, sensing, or acting. One "withdraws" all of one's powers—i.e., of sensing and of acting—from their objects, thus paying attention to neither sensation, image, thought, etc. But he goes on to suggest that one should not merely forget this form of experience, jumping headlong into activity. Rather, he continues:

> Not that one should escape from the inward man, or flee from him or deny him, but in him, with him, and through him, one should learn to act in such a way that one breaks up the inwardness (*innicheit*) into reality and leads reality into inwardness, and that one should thus become accustomed to work without compulsion.[24]

What does "break up the inwardness (*innicheit*) into reality" mean? "Inwardness" is what is encountered in that moment when one is "without any activity, internal or external." Eckhart instructs his listener to as if drag the inwardness outward, as it were, bringing it into activity. One is to act in such a way that reality—activity, thought, perception, etc.—is perceived and undergone while not losing the interior silence encountered in contemplation. Conversely, one is to lead "reality into the inwardness," i.e., make the silent inwardness dynamic. In other words, one is to learn to think, speak, walk, and work without losing awareness of the inward silence. This new form of experience Eckhart calls the interior Birth (*Geburt*), or the Birth of the Son (or the Word) in the Soul.

The most striking thing about the transformation leading to the Birth, and many of Eckhart's descriptions of this experience, is its *dualism*. A dichotomy between the inner and outer man, the spiritual and material dimensions, was a common Pauline and Augustinian division. But Eckhart adapts it to his focus on mystical experience. He uses this image to express the notion that there is something that occurs *inside* the soul and is more or less clouded by the preoccupation with the external world.

When Eckhart speaks of the Birth one may undergo, he consistently formulates it in dichotomous language. The Birth of "Nothing" takes place "inside." The Son is born "within" the soul, "inside" of the soul.[25] It occurs within the power "in" the soul, "in the inmost part of the soul,"[26] "in the inmost recesses of the spirit."[27] This is "that which is one's own being and one's own life within oneself."[28] The soul must be "outdrawn" from the world and "indwelling."[29] One is born "there" where all is timeless, not "in the world." One is "pregnant with Nothing" within oneself.

Even the very Birth analogy that Eckhart uses connotes dualism: in a birth, mother and infant become irreversibly separate; following a birth there are two distinct entities. But in Eckhart's spiritual "Birth," rather than a baby's being delivered from its mother's body, the Son is born "within" the self. The separation is not between one person and another, but between our interior and exterior aspects. The dichotomy is between what occurs in the still silent "ground" within the soul and the "powers."

> [Grace] flows out of God's essence and flows into the essence of the soul and not into her powers."[30]

As Eckhart employs it, the Augustinian dichotomy between inward and outward comes down to the dichotomy between the experiences of a silent interior aspect and an active exterior:

> [T]he soul has two eyes, one inward and one outward. The soul's inner eye is that which sees *into* being, and derives its being without any mediation from God. The soul's outer eye is that which is turned towards all creatures, observing them as images and through the "powers."[31]

One of Eckhart's clearest descriptions of this state is from the treatise "On Detachment." It analogizes the two aspects of man with a door and its hinge pin. Like the outward boards of a door, the outward man moves, changes, and acts. The inward man, like the hinge pin, does not move. He—or it—remains uninvolved with activity and does not change at all. This, Eckhart concludes, is the way one should really conduct a life: one should act yet remain inwardly uninvolved. Here is the passage:

> And however much our Lady lamented and whatever other things she said, she was always in her inmost heart in immovable detachment. Let us take an analogy of this. A door opens and shuts on a hinge. Now if I compare the outer boards of the

door with the outward man, I can compare the hinge with the inward man. When the door opens or closes the outer boards move to and fro, but the hinge remains immovable in one place and it is not changed at all as a result. So it is also here . . . [32]

To act and yet remain "in her inmost heart in immovable detachment" depicts precisely two sides within a life. "Our lady" acts, yet at a deep level within she experiences something that does not act. Like a door swinging around a hinge pin, she both moves and does not.

Yet the fact that the silent level within is of a piece with the divinity helps us understand more of this silent interior aspect. First of all, Eckhart repeatedly suggests that the silent or unmoving level is not related to the world. Attachment, he emphasizes, leads one to the world, whereas this element is un-attached, emotionally *de*-cathected (we might say), to the world. Inside, one is in touch with the divine, even while one acts.

The steps in the development process sketched by Eckhart may be drawn out as follows: one detaches oneself from all worldly attachments. Having done so a "nothing" becomes encountered inside. When this "nothing" is encountered briefly, one becomes temporarily enraptured: *gezucket*. But when it is permanently established, the changeover becomes more complete. One experiences then the Birth of the Son of God in the soul. Then and only then will one's actions be in accord with God's will effortlessly. Notice that detachment is only complete when it brings about a complete nothing inside:

> When the detached heart has the highest aim, it must be towards the Nothing, because in this there is the greatest receptivity. Take a parable from nature: if I want to write on a wax tablet, then no matter how noble the thing is that is written on the tablet, I am none the less vexed because I cannot write on it. If I really want to write I must delete everything that is written on the tablet, and the tablet is never so suitable for writing as when absolutely nothing is written on it.[33]

The emphasis in this passage is on the achievement of emptiness within. One has "deleted" everything inside; one comes to a "Nothing" inside; the tablet is "blank." When one is truly empty within, "the Nothing," then what goes on outside is of little significance.

Only once this interior "nothing" is established does one truly begin "acting rightly." Eckhart continues,

> In the same way, when God wishes to write on my heart in the most sublime manner, everything must come out of my heart that can be called "this" or "that"; thus it is with the detached heart. *Then* God can work in the sublimest manner and according to His highest will.[34]

Thus, the emptiness within is experienced as separate from action. When and only when this is "owned" does one find a true change in the relationship to one's actions.

Once again, in Eckhart we see a movement toward and an experience of an epistemologically dichotomous form of life. On the one hand, one acts much as one had, yet one also comes to a sense of being established within at the "innermost ground," experiencing an inactive silence within, something unmoving. Eckhart's conceptual system led him to speak of this unmoving quality in terms of the theology he knew. But the key experiential novelty here is that one encounters a silent interior level, even while one is active. To what we have seen, Eckhart adds that it seems to be attachment to the things of the world that keeps one from encountering this interior silence.

The Character of the Dualistic Mystical Experience

Now, through these four experience descriptions and reports, we have seen several patterns. First, we have an experience of "something" silent and unmoving encountered concurrently with changing external experiences, including thinking and feeling. Second, this silence is felt to be within, at a deep level within oneself. Third, in every case but Eckhart's, the silence is explicitly associated with the self itself.[35] Bernadette Roberts described it as "within myself all was still"; and she realizes that what was now empty was "her nonlocalized sense of her self." In the Zen vocabulary, Dōgen describes it as *tzu-hsing*, "self-nature itself." In my own experience, I said, "It is as if what was *me* was now this emptiness."

Fourth, although none of our reports explicitly say this, it seems fair to say that the silence seems to be associated with that which is *aware*. I can say that unhesitatingly about my own experience. What is aware is *precisely* the silence. Meister Eckhart describes the silence as the highest "power" within the soul, that which watches or "controls" the sensory and mental powers. Bernadette Roberts simply says that inside all was silent, by which I understand that her sense of herself as an aware being was the silence.

If this is the case, then that silence which is the aware self itself, also must be perceiving itself "as" a silence. That is, the silence within is reflexively aware of itself.

In sum, we may characterize this as a new pattern of mystical experiences: the *Dualistic Mystical State*, or DMS. It may be defined as an unchanging interior silence that is maintained concurrently with intentional experience in a long-term or permanent way.

The Janus-Faced Soul
An Epistemology of
The Dualistic Mystical State

The ancient Roman god Janus was the son of Sky, the god of the *outer* world, and Hecate, the goddess of Hades, the *inner* realms. To attend to both of his parents' realms, Janus was given two faces, one turned ever without, toward the Sky and the external world, and the other turned ever *within,* toward the more hidden internal world. When the Romans built their homes, they often installed Janus on their doorstep. With his double-sided head, he could watch that which was within and without at the same time and constantly.

H ow can we make sense of the DMS? Several interrelated questions arise. First, how can it be that we are both aware of the self itself or consciousness itself and also aware of thinking and seeing? Most of us would say that our minds tend to be aware of only one thing at a time, yet here we have a claim of being aware of two things simultaneously. Second, can we make sense of Zen Buddhism's claim that "self-nature" is alert to its own nature?

The Dualism of Jean Paul Sartre

To begin to answer these questions, let us take a hint from D. T. Suzuki, who in several places in "The Zen Doctrine of No Mind,"[1] points toward a parallel between the Zen doctrine of no-mind and the existentialist notion of transcendental or nonpositional consciousness.[2] I will turn to Jean Paul Sartre's *Transcendence of the Ego* and the early sections of his *Being and Nothingness*, to see if he can help us open up this matter, for Sartre has explored the peculiarities of consciousness perhaps more than any other Western philosopher. We will then compare Zen Philosopher Hui Neng with Sartre to develop our own account of this peculiarly dualistic state.

A word of warning: Sartre nowhere discusses the data of mysticism, and especially not the data of a dualistic mystical state, a DMS. He focuses solely on ordinary (i.e., intentional) experiences. But I believe that his analyses will give us an interesting angle with which we can make sense of these sorts of phenomena.

Sartre's insight is that along with any consciousness of an object in any intentional perception there is also a "non-positional consciousness of consciousness itself." When I look at a table, clearly I must direct my attention primarily to its colors and hardness. But in addition, he states in *Being and Nothingness*, there must be some sort of reflexive self-awareness, a cognizance of awareness itself, accompanying my perception:

> For if my consciousness were not consciousness of being consciousness of the table, it would then be consciousness of the table without consciousness of being so. In other words, it would be a consciousness ignorant of itself, an unconscious— which is absurd.[3]

In order for me to be aware of the table, I must both perceive it through my eyes, and also connect this perception with other perceptions and thoughts. To do so I must be not only conscious of seeing the table but also hold the perception within the unity of consciousness—behind or alongside my seeing. I must direct my attention to objects, "without losing sight of the unreflected consciousness."[4] My intentional consciousness must be grounded in what Sartre calls a "non-positional self-consciousness"—the consciousness beyond perception that ties any perceptions together. This consciousness, more fundamental than any percept, cannot itself be an object of intentional knowledge. Sartre argues this through a *reductio ad absurdum:* if we claim that to know is to know intentionally that we know, we must introduce into consciousness itself an intentional subject-object structure, the knower aware of itself as a something known. But this leads to an infinite regress:

when I am aware of an object I must be aware also of the consciousness which is aware of the consciousness that is aware of the consciousness that is aware of the consciousness that . . .

> Are we obliged after all to introduce the law of this dyad into consciousness? Consciousness of self is not dual. If we wish to avoid an infinite regress, there must be an immediate non-cognitive relation of the self to itself.[5]

Consciousness's own self-awareness cannot be intentional; we must posit that it simply knows itself and ties percepts together.[6] This reflexive consciousness of self Sartre names consciousness "*pour-soi,*" for itself, in order to stress the reflexive character of self-awareness. He distinguishes it from its object or that which is "*en-soi*" or in-itself.

If we did not have a reflective self-consciousness alongside of every perception, then we would not know our perceptions but merely respond to them. But we do more than respond; we are *conscious* of our perceptions. And that involves being conscious of consciousness itself.

> Every positional consciousness of an object is at the same time a non-positional consciousness of itself. If I count the cigarettes which are in that case, I have the impression of disclosing an objective property of this collection of cigarettes: they are a dozen. This property appears to my consciousness as a property existing in the world. It is very possible that I have no positional consciousness of counting them. Then I do not know myself as counting. . . . Yet at the moment when these cigarettes are revealed to me as a dozen, I have a non-thetic consciousness of my adding activity. If anyone questioned me, indeed, if anyone should ask, "What are you doing there?" I should reply at once, "I am counting." . . . Thus in order to count, it is necessary to be conscious of counting.[7]

Intentional consciousness is thus grounded in the nonpositional awareness of awareness itself. Implicit in any perception is the dualism of intentional knowing plus consciousness (*pour-soi*) nonpositionally conscious of itself.

Sartre continues: consciousness *pour-soi,* nonpositional consciousness, cannot be part of the world. To tie any seeing or thinking together, awareness must remain transcendent to any perception, thought, or even to any perspective. That is, only because nonpositional consciousness stands apart from perceptions, transcends the world and its objects,[8] can it tie perceptions and thoughts together. Awareness itself, though pure subject, remains aware of itself nonpositionally. Consciousness *pour-soi* is thus an original disengagement, a withdrawal in relation to the *en-soi*.[9]

Thus, for Sartre, the consciousness of ordinary experience has the character of freedom or withdrawal from the world. To experience its fundamental freedom, I must recognize that I transcend my perceptions, my situation in the world, my own past and future, and come to recognize that my particular situation is but one of an infinite range of possibilities for a consciousness. There is, in other words, a gap between the roles I inhabit—father, brother, professor, etc.—and my own consciousness *pour-soi*. Consciousness transcends my particular ego-infused situation.

To my knowledge, Sartre was not acquainted with mysticism: whether he was or not, he maintained that consciousness is only aware of its own uninvolved character in a theoretical way alongside of intentional consciousness. It seems that had he known of a PCE and accepted its significance, or had he known of the DMS, he might have recognized that pure consciousness offers a transient yet uncomplex experience of nonpositional and transcendent consciousness. But he did not, and in his eyes one can sense oneself as a disengaged or withdrawn consciousness *pour-soi* only amidst or behind the encounters with the *en-soi*. For him the two persist simultaneously and are eternally opposed to each other, like a radar dish and an airplane.

This, by the way, sets up the situation of anguish for which Sartre is famed. I am in a situation that is fundamentally different than my inherent nature:[10] I am in a world that is fundamentally unlike the nonpositional consciousness that encounters it.[11] This leads us, he says, to a dual flight. On the one hand, we flee from the anguish which is inherent in our situation in order to escape the inherent and disconcerting freedom of our own consciousness. Identifying with my role, I in effect hide my head in the sand and deny my nonpositional separation from all roles. I become preoccupied with my situation, caught up in my classes, paying my mortgage, and raising my children, and I lose cognizance of my own inherently uninvolved nature.

But this identification is never quite complete: at some level, I know with a deep sense of irony that I am not inherently these roles. Realizing that I am not truly these roles, I "flee" from them. Thus, both my role and my transcendence flee from each other, yet still remain tied together like our radar dish and airplane. I run from my freedom at the same time that I run from my identification with my labels.

Sartre was never able to resolve this tension. He said very little of what it might mean to *not* have consciousness and our identity flee from each other, or be truly authentic, leaving it as only a tantalizing possibility.[12]

To summarize, in his analysis of the human situation, Sartre suggests that in every perception there are two epistemological structures: intentional knowledge and nonintentional nonpositional self-awareness. The two are always encountered together, yet are of deeply different natures. Though most of us overlook the inherently transcendental character of consciousness and identify with our roles, this identification is a mistake: we are not truly our roles, and we all intuitively know it.

Hui Neng's Dualism

I suggest that Sartre and our four mystics are speaking from different perspectives about similar human experiences. To draw this out, let me focus on the Zen Philosopher Hui Neng. I believe that Sartre and Hui Neng are describing similar facets of human experience.

Before doing so, I want to point out that these two authors differ in significant ways. They are writing in obviously different contexts and have different agendas. Writing in twentieth-century France, Sartre was modern, Western, educated, and highly philosophical. Though it is not devoid of therapeutic implications, his intent was primarily explanatory. Hui Neng's *Platform Sutra* was written in a spiritually oriented ancient Chinese context. His intent was only coincidentally explanatory; his goal was primarily therapeutic, i.e., to spiritually transform his hearers and readers by helping them free themselves from their attachments. Perhaps most important, for Sartre the subject remains but *sub*consciously aware of itself as separate, yet it is always engaged with its objects. Hui

Neng holds that it is possible to become aware of the distinction between subject and objects in a new form of direct experience. But I do not believe these differences imply an utter dissimilarity. Rather, I believe that these two men were talking about a similarly transcendent aspect of the self, but that the Buddhist writes with an experience of human capacities that is wider than Sartre's.

Indeed, I believe that Sartre's notion of nonpositional consciousness can help illuminate Hui Neng's doctrine of *wu-nien* and vice versa. We noted above that Suzuki's term *unconscious*, which he uses to translate *wu-nien*, would be better understood as "nonintentionally conscious." If so, his notion is clearly parallel to Sartre's term "nonpositional consciousness." Like non-positional consciousness, thoughts and feelings are to be understood as of a different order than it but "witnessed" by it.[13] *Wu-nien,* like nonpositional consciousness, is understood as *sunyata,* empty of content. Yet it is also said to be nondiscriminating *prajña,* aware of itself reflexively. So is nonpositional consciousness, for it ties itself together and reflexively remembers or senses itself. Both are said to sense their own self-nature. Both are not like perceiving or thinking, i.e., neither has, in itself, an intentional structure. Both are presented as transcendental to the "personal I"—self-nature beyond the personal self, if you will—and are, in this sense, impersonal. In short, it makes sense to see *wu-nien* as a finger pointing to the same moon as nonpositional consciousness or awareness aware of itself.

If this hypothesis is reasonable, then we can use Sartre's vocabulary to paraphrase Hui Neng's statement, "No-thought (*wu-nien)* is not to think even when involved in thought." It becomes, "*wu-nien* is nonpositional awareness remaining reflexively cognizant of itself even when involved in thought." If this is correct, then the experience to which Hui Neng is referring is an enlivened or firsthand realization of that which Sartre recognized philosophically as the nature of consciousness behind or within all perception. In *wu-nien* one directly realizes that one is, in one's core, not this or that perception, but transcendental to it. One is both alert to consciousness per se, one's own "self-nature," and also actively thinking. Only, unlike in our ordinary state of consciousness, one no longer conflates the two. Being alert to or aware of one's own nature, consciousness knowing itself, it need hardly be said, is an act of knowledge-by-identity.

Like Sartre, Hui Neng recognizes that we can all too easily become identified with the "10,000 things," i.e., with our desires, the needs of our self, and with our place in the world. Deluded people "cling to the characteristics of things," he says, "adhering to them."[14] They "cling to external environments,"[15] become "stained" by them, and are not "free to come and go."[16] According to Hui Neng, we grow attached to things and our place in the world, and we become stuck thereby in our roles. This is, of course, reminiscent of Sartre's insight that we are in general identified with our role, thereby fleeing from or ignoring our true nature.

But, unlike Sartre, Hui Neng teaches that, through a meditative process, it is possible to *de*tach from the world, and to experientially separate the self from its intentional content. We realize that what we think of as the self is "no self," i.e., is distinct from the ego and its roles. And this, Hui Neng suggests, is the real point of not thinking "even when involved in thought." He expands:

> Oh good friends, not to have the mind tainted while in contact with all conditions of life, this is to be *wu-nien*. It is to be always detached in one's own consciousness from objective conditions, not to let one's mind be roused by coming in contact with objective conditions.[17]

Even while one is engaged in the world, one is not so deluded as to become identified with that engagement. Removed from the roles and perceptions that had bound one to the world, one's mind is not "roused" or caught up. One learns to distinguish the original nature (*tzu-hsing*) of the self, i.e., nonintentional consciousness, from the role one plays and the objective conditions one sees.

Hui Neng goes on:

> What is there for *nien* to become conscious of? *Wu* is to negate the notion of two forms [the dualism of self and other or, what we would call intentionality], and to get rid of a mind which worries over things, while *Nien* means to become conscious of the primary nature of Suchness (*tathata*); for suchness is the body of consciousness, and consciousness is the use of suchness. It is the self-nature of suchness (*tathata*) to become conscious of itself.

In this new way of existing, one experientially recognizes just what Sartre perceived theoretically. One is no longer entrapped in the world, existentially severed from the association with the world that had caused one to become emotionally entangled with the 10,000 things. One experiences suchness, i.e., the nature or "body of consciousness" itself, becoming "conscious of itself." That is, one becomes conscious of one's nonintentional, nonpositional consciousness itself.[18]

My understanding of this form of mystical life is verified by Hui Neng's pivotal reinterpretation of *samādhi* and *prajñā*. Throughout Buddhist history *samādhi* was, of course, generally used to describe quiet meditative emptiness like the pure consciousness event. *Prajñā*, on the other hand, generally signified wisdom as the Buddhists knew it. Hui Neng was no doubt aware of these associations, but he reworked them, for he saw that the traditional emphasis on *samādhi* as the quiet meditative moments led many to become attached to the those moments as something special.

> The deluded man clings to the characteristics of things, adheres to the *samādhi* of oneness, thinks that straightforward mind is sitting without moving and casting aside delusions without letting things arise in the mind. . . . This kind of practice is the same as insentiency, and is the cause of an obstruction to the Dao.[19]

In part to avoid such clinging, Hui Neng redefines meditation and *samādhi* to signify being utterly quiet inside even while engaged in activity:

> And what do we call Chan (Zen) meditation (*chan-ting*)? Outwardly to exclude form is *chan*; inwardly to be unconfused is meditation. Even though there is form on the outside, when internally the mind is composed, then . . . you are of yourself pure and of yourself in meditation. . . . Separation from form on the outside is *chan*; being untouched on the inside is meditation. Being chan externally and meditation internally, it is known as *chan* meditation (*chan-ting*).[20]

Or, speaking of *samādhi* in particular:

> The *samādhi* of oneness is straightforward mind *at all times*, walking, staying, sitting, and lying. . . . Only practicing straightforward mind, and in all things having no attachments whatsoever, is called the *samādhi* of oneness. (Emphasis mine)

Thus to be in *samādhi* as he redefines it is to live in a twofold mode, knowing intentionally that one is in the world but also, at the depths, remaining uninvolved with it. "Facing all environing objects, the mind remains unstained." Hui Neng's *samādhi* meant being without thoughts at the depths inside even while being in the world.[21] (I conceive of this state as something like the Hindu notion of a *hiryanyagarbha*, a golden womb or shell inside of which we remain aloof and silent, while the world and our own ego and thoughts swirl around us outside.)

Prajña, we noted, had generally meant wisdom. Often applied to the general Buddhist doctrines, it signified the four noble truths, the eight fold path, *pratītyasamutpāda*, etc. Sometimes it meant the knowledge of how to deal with objects in the world. Hui Neng, however, transforms this term into what he regards as the highest knowledge available to the human. The *prajña* he advocates is not learned from the outside or through words, for it is "not apart from your own nature."[22] *Prajña* is, in Suzuki's rendering, the knowledge of *tzu-hsing*, self-nature. "Prajña is another name given to self-nature when the latter sees itself," he tells us.[23] Translating this into Sartre's idiom, it is the self knowing itself in the sense of nonintentional consciousness that is conscious of itself.

> In original self nature itself there is *prajña* knowledge, and because of this, self knowledge. Nature [i.e. consciousness] reflects itself in itself, which is self illumination not to be expressed in words.[24]

Seeing into the nature of consciousness is apt to be taken as intentional knowledge, but this would be wrong: self-knowledge here is a nonlinguistic reflexive consciousness of itself. Not a seeing of something distant, it is more like the self's reflecting its own self, or, in our framework, awareness per se's reflecting itself in a nonlinguistic way.

> When *prajña* with its light reflects [within], and penetratingly illumines inside and outside, you recognize your own Mind (*wu-nien*, non-intentional-consciousness). When your own mind is recognized, there is emancipation. When you have emancipation, this means that you are in the *samādhi* of *prajña*, which is *mu-nen* (no-thought-ness).[25]

And this is the true expression of *prajña*, according to Hui Neng. Suzuki puts this:

> Self nature finds its own being when it sees itself, and this seeing takes place by *prajña*. But as *prajña* is another name given to self nature when the latter sees itself, there is no *prajña* outside of self nature.[26]

This self reflexively knowing itself through knowledge-by-identity, I argued in chapter 7, is the best way to account for the pure consciousness event. But Hui Neng's claim here—and it matches the statements of Bernadette Roberts, Eckhart, and my own experience—is that this sort of consciousness aware of itself is experienced alongside of and simultaneously with intentional content.

Thus, in this phenomenon, two distinct epistemological modalities are enacted simultaneously: intentional seeing and the self's knowing itself through a knowledge-by-identity. This is precisely what Sartre saw through his reflective but theoretical analysis; but the mystic experiences it vividly and directly. Hui Neng describes this epistemological dualism as living in two planes of life simultaneously: *yu-hsin*, the plane of intentional consciousness, and *wu-hsin*, "non-[intentional-] consciousness."

Hui Neng offers a multitude of terms for this twofold form of existence. Sometimes, according to Suzuki, Hui Neng distinguishes between Mind, capitol M, and mind, small m, the Mind's (non-intentional) self-awareness and the mind's cognition of external objects and thoughts.[27] Sometimes he suggests that the Zen adept enjoys two forms of *prajña* at once, the *prajña* of *nen-nien*, thought, i.e., knowing how to deal with the changing world of objects, and the *prajña* of *wu-nien*, nonintentional consciousness. This is the nonintentional consciousness that stands at the source of thinking, he suggests, and constitutes *prajña* in its deeper sense. Thus, the *prajña* mind enjoys the wisdom of the world simultaneously with the introvertive wisdom of "knowing" the nature of the Mind or awareness in itself.

Drawing the Strands Together

Now we are ready to draw these three strands together, the experiences of Bernadette Roberts and myself, the analysis of Hui Neng, and the speculations of Sartre. Sartre perceived that the mind bears an implicitly double epistemological structure, but he understood it to be solely implicit and known only through reflection on ordinary (intentional) experience. Hui Neng, as represented by Suzuki, suggests that such a "double" nature can become the day-to-day experience of an (advanced) Zen adept. That is, a Zen practitioner may come to live in such a way that even while acting his or her consciousness is appreciated as free and inherently uninvolved. In Zen language, he or she enjoys both forms of *prajña* simultaneously—the knowledge of the world and the reflexive nonintentional *wu-nien*, nonintentional consciousness. Sartre's understanding that there are two simultaneous functions of the experiencing consciousness—the transcendent or free nature of consciousness itself and its bound, object-oriented intentional aspect—becomes the everyday experience of certain Zen bikshus.

Finally, it is just this sort of dualistic form of life that Bernadette Roberts and I have experienced. Just as Hui Neng described living in two spheres simultaneously, both of our experiences were dualistic as well: outside, each of us continued to see, talk, hear, and cut carrots, even while "within, all was still, silent and motionless." In Ms. Roberts's experience, the silence was present to all her experience, replacing the old "unlocalized" sense of her self. The silent emptiness was now her. Similarly, in my own case, the transcendent *silence* has become me, and my thinking no longer has felt quite in "contact" with what is *really* me. "I" have been the silence inside, my thinking has been as if on the backdrop of or in the middle of this silence, without quite contacting it. Both of these experiences are, in Hui Neng's language, examples of the maintenance of *samādhi* even while active and aware of things through the worldly sort of *prajña*.

Finally, the silence described in all our accounts seemed to have a self-reflexive character, i.e., it was aware of itself. This is precisely how Hui Neng describes *prajña:* "Self nature . . . sees itself, and this seeing takes place by *prajña.* . . . *Prajña* is another name given to self nature when the latter sees itself . . . "[28] *Prajña* is the self 's reflexively knowing itself through knowledge-by-identity.

In Bernadette Roberts's experience the silence that she perceived as having replaced "the non-localized center of herself" was aware of itself *as* that silence. The silence within that was her perceiving center "perceived itself." Both Hui Neng and Roberts describe, in short, two epistemological structures of knowledge (of *prajñā*) being employed concurrently. In each of these accounts, a life of both *nen-nien*, thought or mind is maintained along with *wu-nien*, nonintentional consciousness.

This form of mysticism, in short, seems to represent an encounter with consciousness in a way only dreamt of by Sartre. One encounters one's own consciousness, all the time, alongside all of one's action and thinking. One recognizes, in an entirely new way, the nature of the self, and does not lose contact with that even when one is active. Although this encounter is beyond words, in it one has a direct and permanent experience of the self-referential nature of consciousness itself. It is, in this sense, an entirely new *modus operandi* for human life.

The Transformative Pathway

Now, how can one move from a sensed entanglement with the world to such a twofold existence? That is, how can one move from having a consciousness that is self-reflexive only in theory to one that recognizes itself as self-referring? While Suzuki doesn't address this question directly in this essay, Hui Neng offers several suggestive remarks in the *Platform Sutra*. In ¶20, he draws an analogy between the nature of the self itself and the sun:

> [T]he nature of people in this world is from the outset pure in itself. . . . the sun and the moon are always bright, yet if they are covered by clouds, although above they are bright, below they are darkened, and the sun, moon, stars and planets cannot be seen clearly. But if suddenly the wind of wisdom should blow and roll away the clouds and mists, all forms in the universe appear at once. The purity of the nature of man in this world is like the blue sky; wisdom is like the sun, knowledge like the moon. Although knowledge and wisdom are always clear, if you cling to external environments, the floating clouds of false thoughts will create a cover, and your own natures cannot become clear. (¶20)

The key phrase here is that our self-nature "is from the outset pure in itself." If Sartre and Hui Neng are both talking about the nature of human awareness per se, then as Sartre suggests, this awareness remains what it is from the start, and the Zen adept only becomes aware of what *has been the case all along*. Hui Neng's sun and moon image expresses this admirably. Just as both the sun and the moon in themselves remain bright even when dark clouds float in front of them, so too the self remains what it is, even when hidden by the "floating clouds of ignorance." When ignorance is eliminated through the winds of wisdom, then what is revealed is not something new but something that has been the case throughout even the darkest hours of ignorance. That is, we are what we are, even before we recognize it about ourselves. This tends to agree with Sartre's perception that we are nonpositional consciousness, free, even if we do not recognize it.

Meditation and other spiritual pathways, in other words, do not create something new but rather uncover an "original" feature of ourselves. It simply reveals the self-reflexive nature of awareness itself that, if Sartre is correct, has been with us from the beginning.

Just how does it "get covered"? As we observed, Hui Neng suggests that "cling[ing] to external environments" is the key problem. He does not say just how clinging effects us so, but in the passages in which he speaks of becoming unattached, he suggests something of the attachment process. In ¶31 he writes:

> The *dharma* of no-thought means: even though you see all things, you do not attach to them, but always keeping your own nature pure, cause the six thieves [the six fields of the senses, i.e. seeing, hearing, etc., plus discerning] to exit through the six gates [the five sense organs (eyes, ears, etc., plus thinking mind)]. Even though you are in the midst of the six dusts [six qualities produced by the objects, sight, sound, etc. plus ideas], you do not stand apart from them, yet are not stained by them, and are free to come and go. This is the *prajña samādhi*, and being free and having achieved release is known as the practice of no thought.

Reading the opening sentence in reverse, as a description of the unenlightened person, then we have the following: "When the unenlightened sees things, she or he becomes attached to them." That is, things somehow become part of one. We might say one becomes psychologically hooked into or cathected to objects. Perhaps I become drawn to a woman, and lose myself in that attraction. Or perhaps I get lost in my role of professor. Then Hui Neng goes on: in the enlightened, "The six sense fields of the senses do [not] exit through the six sense organs; when the [un]enlightened sees something, he or she becomes stained by it, and is not free to come and go." That is, most people become personally involved with what they see and hear, and thus they lose sight that they are free of it. This is, of course, reminiscent of Sartre's insight that we come to identify ourselves with our roles, denying the nonpositional transcendence of our own consciousness from them. We thereby lose sight of the inherent freedom of awareness per se, and we become entangled in the perceived world. In this sense, our consciousness, by becoming involved with the perceptual world, itself becomes "stained" by its contact with it. Mistakenly thinking that I am truly this person and really am this role, I lose sight of the transcendent nature and freedom of awareness itself.

The process that leads to enlightenment involves coming to perceive the sensory world as "not me," i.e., to "cause the six thieves to exit through the six gates." This allows us to discover the distance between consciousness itself, self-nature, and the experienced world. Though perceived, the world and my roles in it are seen as not fundamentally connected to the silence that is the nature of my "own" awareness itself, which is, as it were, glowing brightly within.[29] By unlinking myself and hence my awareness from the perceptual world, I remove the "clouds" that had hidden the "sun" of consciousness. I no longer remain stained by my contact with the world. And yet, paradoxically, by virtue of the "twofold existence," I still participate actively in the world.[30]

The human problematic is that, for some complicated set of reasons, we come to think of ourselves as identified with our self, our roles and our world. We objectify ourselves and our world, and we come to see ourselves as "truly" our role, and "truly" connected with the world. The meditative or transformative process is one of coming to distinguish the consciousness that is our true nature from everything it has objectified. And in so doing, we can allow the self to "glow" in itself. Then we become "unstained by [passions], and are free to come and go."

The transformative process ends simple, one-sided attachment. Yet it does not result in mere nonattachment. Rather it results in the paradox of simultaneously being nonattached and also participating in the world of attachments. Bernadette Roberts remained attached to her husband, children, house, and cutting carrots to make a good dinner, no doubt. Yet in the context of her deeper nonattachment, as I understand it, these "attachments" lost their deep connection to her. She was not in an ultimate way attached to them. She both was and was not caught up in the world, "in but not of" the world.

We can return to a radar analogy: If the pure consciousness event is like a radar system that is turned on and functioning but without any airplanes flying by, this more advanced experience may be imagined as like a radar system that, even while it reflects airplanes, also reflects the radar dish itself back to itself. It, as it were, provides its own constant self-referential thrum, even while it picks up the reflections from airplanes. One of these processes is fluid and constantly changing, the other is unchanging: the active stands over against, but concurrently with, the silent interior.

Conclusions: The Janus Faced Soul

In conclusion, at this stage of the mystic's spiritual development, we see a consistent pattern of a twofold form of life: a silence within is encountered concurrently with perception and activity without, and they are experienced as distinct from each other.[31] Hui Neng, through Suzuki, also suggests that this is like coming to a twofold form of life, becoming cognizant of both the intentional world and the nonintentional consciousness simultaneously. The twofold quality of both Bernadette's and my own experience is matched nicely by both Sartre's theoretical picture and Hui Neng's experiential portrait of this degree of enlightenment as epistemologically dualistic—a knowledge-by-identity of an empty (nonintentional) consciousness along with an intentional knowledge of the world. Sartre suggests that even though most never perceive it, in conscious experience there are always two conceptually distinct epistemological modalities existing side by side.

In conclusion, it is reasonable to think that the life of the mystic, at this stage, is epistemologically twofold; thus it deserves a double form of epistemological analysis. Both sides exist simultaneously, Janus-like, with their faces pointing in opposite directions, one within and one without. And yet each illuminates the nature of the other.

Chapter Ten

Concluding Remarks

As I reflect on the directions and patterns that have emerged in this book, I am reminded of the insight of John Searle:

> [M]uch of the bankruptcy of most work in the philosophy of mind and over a great deal of the sterility of academic psychology over the past fifty years, over the whole of my intellectual lifetime, have come from a persistent failure to recognize and come to terms with the fact that the ontology of the mental is an irreducibly first person ontology.[1]

Searle observes that so much in the philosophy of mind has been sterile because philosophers have looked at the mind in the same way they have looked at our knowledge of the external world or our knowledge of other peoples' minds. But this, he suggests is a near-catastrophic error.

Really, we know our minds, and indeed we know what it is to be a thinking, feeling conscious being, by virtue of the fact that we *have* a mind, or *are* conscious. It is a peculiarly diaphanous element, consciousness: hard to define, hard to contact, hard to know. But it is only by virtue of our firsthand, first-person acquaintance with this ineffable and *sui generis* phenomenon that we know anything at all, and certainly know anything at all about our own minds. We do not know it as we know the color of the desk or as we know another's fears. We know it in a peculiarly direct way: by virtue of being it.

In general this sort of self-awareness is vague and difficult to articulate. In most situations we do not know our own consciousness except in some unclear, intuitive way. When we try to sense it by looking "at" or "for" it, we end up like a dog chasing its own tail: it is always just out of reach.

But the mystical traditions seem to have developed ways to slow down the mind. They are akin to a mental cooling process sufficient to allow consciousness and the mind to settle down toward the mind's version of absolute zero: being utterly still. At first such stillness is typically experienced in short flashes; these we have called pure consciousness events. Here, the mind has slowed down to "full stop" for a few instants, long enough for us to recognize that "I wasn't thinking just then, yet I was awake inside." This is akin to briefly slowing down the activity of atoms in heat: as you cool the system, the atoms career about less and less until finally they may come to stillness. So too, the mind or consciousness itself comes, in PCE, to persist silently, and be simply what it is with no extra activity.

Now, the constructivists have it that the mystic has the experience of the PCE because of his/her expectations and language; these both lead him or her to have that particular experience, and also give it the shape that it has. But that claim just doesn't hold. Just as it is not the scientists' expectations that slow down the atoms, it is the technique of withdrawing the heat. So too, it is not the *mystic's expectations* that slow down the mind, it is the spiritual or mental techniques of ceasing thought that slow it down. And just as it is not expectations that determine what the atoms do under those circumstances, it is the physics involved, so too it is not language that determines what the experience is like there, it is the nature of our consciousness itself. Thus, the PCE does not represent "the psychosomatic enhancement" of some word or thought, it is just the temporary but pure encounter with what we have been all along.

Some of my critics have suggested that my account is too highly influenced by the linguistic philosophy that I have criticized. This is a well taken criticism. I have been responding to a very particular set of arguments. But in this volume I have attempted to broaden the argument by showing that neither Kant's theories nor Husserl's notion of intentionality are adequate to account for such mystical experiences. Kant, Brentano, and Husserl all *start* with sense data, and progress from there. The far more sensible way of thinking about the mystical is that in it we are encountering the self (i.e., awareness itself) through our strange and peculiar first-person "knowledge by identity" epistemology. In pure consciousness, there is only consciousness, encountering itself through itself.

The situation in the more complex dualistic mystical state, DMS, however, is even more paradoxical. Here the subject is directly aware of consciousness itself, knows itself reflexively in a pure and direct way. And, simultaneously, it is intentionally aware of its content, sensory objects, feelings, thoughts, etc. That means that in the DMS one can be aware of the *nature* of the self and think about it at the same time. Thus, it is striking that we find a deep parallel with the speculations of Sartre, who seemed to be so cognizant of the *sui generis* status of consciousness. The mystic in the DMS seems to be able to know and encounter his own consciousness in ways that seem to verify Sartre's suspicions.

Keeping Searle in mind, it would be a mistake to think that the mystic knows his or her own consciousness in anything like the same way he or she knows a desk or a knee twinge. One does not think about consciousness or know consciousness as one intentionally knows the external world. Rather, one knows it only because one *is* it. And thus the mystic in the DMS is in an unusually good position to tell us about the nature of his or her consciousness. Such knowledge is not *linguistic* at heart, for consciousness itself is pre- or translinguistic; rather, this knowledge is direct and experiential. Talking about it becomes linguistic, of course, but the knowledge itself does not come through the usual linguistic and constructive modalities. Thus, linguistic or cultural or situational or behavioral analyses are simply the wrong ways to understand this phenomenon. To apply the (incredibly valuable) doctrines of linguistic constructivism to this experience is simply wrongheaded. Such a peculiar, *sui generis* "entity" demands that we treat it in a peculiar, *sui generis* manner. Consciousness, awareness in itself, and the experience thereof, must be analyzed in its own terms.

What the mystics seem to have discovered is that consciousness is utterly translucent. It does not come stamped with a shape of its own, but rather is a pure watching presence. Yet this watching presence, we said, is something that can tie things—and itself—together through time. It also is something that can point toward things, be vectorial. It is, in the Hindu lexicon, *cit,* i.e., that which has the ability to tie any knowledge together at all, that is, to be intelligent.

It is also *empty*. In itself it has no shape. And yet, this very emptiness, or the "no self" as Bernadette Roberts calls it, is at the same time full and complete in itself: it is able to register and hold any and all perceptions and thoughts together within itself. Perhaps we should call it an "empty plenitude."

The *sui generis* features of consciousness thus make it peculiarly well adapted to both apophatic (the language of non-sayable, emptiness and the void) and kataphatic (speaking of it as if it is a something or full) forms of spiritual language. It is experienced as "full within itself"; this disposes it to kataphatic language. Yet its absence of specifiable content makes it a perfect candidate for apophatic language as well. Philosophical arguments on the nature of the mind begin only when we insist that consciousness must be either one *or* the other; this insistence forces us to claim that consciousness is a mere emptiness *(śūnyata)*, or a mere fullness (as Ātman is described). But the nature of consciousness in itself is clearly paradoxically both full and empty, and thus lends itself perfectly comfortably to either language game.

In short, mysticism seems to offer a procedure for unveiling certain deep truths of human existence. What it offers, in the end, is not a linguistic truth, but rather a way to slough off the onion layers of illusion and self-delusion, and allow the nonlinguistic inner presence to reflexively reveal itself to itself: consciousness showing itself to consciousness.

In so doing, this nonverbal presence has a great deal to teach about the nature of human life and intelligence.

Notes

Chapter 1

1. James Clark, *Meister Eckhart: An Introduction to the Study of His Works with an Anthology of His Sermons* (Edinburgh: Thomas Nelson and Sons, 1957). Carl Franklin Kelley, *Meister Eckhart on Divine Knowledge* (New Haven: Yale University Press, 1977).

2. This is one of the key influences identified by Reiner Schurmann, *Meister Eckhart: Mystic and Philosopher* (Bloomington, Ind.: University of Indiana Press, 1978).

3. Benedict Ashley, O.P., "Three Strands in the Thought of Eckhart, the Scholastic Theologian," *The Thomist* 42 (1978): pp. 226–239.

4. In the Eckhart secondary literature, David Kenneth Clark, "Meister Eckhart as an Orthodox Christian," Ph.D. Dissertation, Northwestern University Department of Religion (1984), bases the connection explicitly on Katz's work. So too does Bernard McGinn, "Meister Eckhart: An Introduction," in *Introduction to the Medieval Mystics of Europe*, ed. Paul Szernach (Binghamton: SUNY Press, 1984), pp. 237–258.

5. William Wainwright, *Mysticism: A Study of its Nature, Cognitive Value, and Moral Implications* (Ann Arbor: University of Wisconsin Press, 1981).

6. Ninian Smart, "Interpretation and Mystical Experience," *Religious Studies* 1 (1965): pp. 75–87.

7. John Hick, "Mystical Experience as Cognition," in *Understanding Mysticism*, ed. Richard P. Woods, O.P. (New York: Image Books, 1980), pp. 422–437.

8. Terence Penehelum, "Unity and Diversity in Interpretation of Mysticism," in *Understanding Mysticism*, ed. Richard P. Woods, O.P. (New York: Image Books, 1980), pp. 438–448.

9. Jerry Gill, "Mysticism and Mediation," unpublished paper delivered to American Academy of Religion, 1978.

10. Wayne Proudfoot, *Religious Experience* (Berkeley: University of California Press, 1985).

11. Peter Moore, "Mystical Experience, Mystical Doctrine, Mystical Technique," in Steven T. Katz, ed., *Mysticism and Philosophical Analysis* (New York: Oxford University Press, 1978), pp. 101–131.

12. Steven Katz, "Language, Epistemology and Mysticism," in *Mysticism and Philosophical Analysis*, pp. 22–74; Steven Katz, "The 'Conservative' Character of Mystical Experience," in *Mysticism and Religious Traditions* (New York: Oxford University Press, 1983), pp. 3–60.

13. In 1982–84 alone it is glossed in some fifteen articles. Some of them are: Richard Jones, "Experience and Conceptualization in Mystical Knowledge," *Zygon* 18 (1983): pp. 139–165; Dierdre Green, "Unity in Diversity [Typology of Mysticism]," *Scottish Journal of Religious Studies* 3 (1982): pp. 46–58; Jure Kristo, "The Interpretation of Religious Experience: What Do Mystics Intend When They Talk about Their Experiences?" *Journal of Religion* 62 (1982): pp. 21–38; Karel Werner, "Mysticism as Doctrine and Experience," *Religious Traditions* 4 (1981): pp. 1–18; James Horne, "Pure Mysticism and Two-Fold Typologies: James to Katz," *Scottish Journal of Religious Studies* 3 (1982): pp. 3–14. In a recent American Academy of Religion conference (1985), no fewer than seven papers were devoted to considerations of this article.

14. I first discovered its significance through Clifford Geertz's *Islam Observed* (Chicago: University of Chicago Press, 1968) and *The Interpretation of Cultures* (New York: Harper Colophon Books, 1973). In the sociology of knowledge see Peter Berger, *The Social Construction of Reality: A Treatise in the Sociology of Knowledge* (Garden City, N.Y.: Doubleday, 1967); Robin Horton, ed., *Modes of Thought: Essays on Thinking in Western and Non Western Societies* (London: Faber and Faber, 1973); Peter Hamilton, *Knowledge and Social Structure: An Introduction to the Classical Argument in the Sociology of Knowledge* (London: Routledge and Kegan Paul, 1974).

15. A good general introduction is Walter Bromberg, *The Mind of Man: A History of Psychotherapy and Psychoanalysis* (New York: Harper Colophon, 1959). Two recent schools of psychology emphasize the formative role of early experiences: on the personal construct theory; see Robert Neimeyer, *The Development of Personal Construct Theory* (Lincoln: University of Nebraska Press, 1985); on object relations theory see H. Guntrip, *Personality Structure and Human Interaction* (New York: International Universities Press, 1961); and J. Greenberg and S. Mitchell, *Object Relations in Psychoanalytic Theory* (Cambridge: Harvard University Press, 1983).

16. Ever since Duchamp, much modern art has been preoccupied with the role of the viewer's concepts in the experience of art. Dadaism, Pop Art, Superrealism, and other twentieth-century movements have focused their artwork, writings, and written defenses here. See Douglas Davis, *Art Culture: Essays on the Post Modern* (New York: Harper and Row, 1977), esp. pp. 1–28; *Theories of Modern Art: A Source Book by Artists*

and Critics, ed. Herschel Chipp (Berkeley: University of California Press, 1968), esp. Vincent van Gogh, "Paint Your Garden As It Is," pp. 44–45; "Dada and Surrealism," pp. 366–396; et passim.

17. E. H. Gombrich, *Art and Illusion* (Princeton: Princeton University Press, 1960).

18. Iris Murdoch in D. F. Pears, *Nature of Metaphysics* (London: Macmillan, 1956), p. 122.

19. See Bagger's response to *The Problem of Pure Consciousness, Religious Studies* 27: pp. 401–412. See also my reply, pp. 413–420.

20. Roland Fischer, "A Cartography of the Ecstatic and Meditative States," in Richard Woods, O. P., *Understanding Mysticism* (Garden City, N.Y.: Image Books, 1980), pp. 270–285.

21. Benson and Wallace hypothesize the existence of two opposite mechanisms to explain ergotrophic and trophotropic phenomena: the "fight or flight" mechanism, which is characterized by an increase of metabolic rate, and the "stay and play" mechanism, which is marked by a decrease. I am adding that we ought not explain the cognitive changes of the one by the other.

22. Mary Jeremy Finnegan, *Scholars and Mystics* (Chicago: University of Chicago Press, 1962), p. 59.

23. *Bhagāvad Gītā,* 2:64–5, trans. Franklin Edgerton (New York: Harper, 1944).

24. Smart, "Interpretation and Mystical Experience," p. 75.

25. Louis Bouyer, "Mysticism: An Essay on the History of the Word," in Woods, *Understanding Mysticism*, pp. 42–55.

26. W. T. Stace, *Mysticism and Philosophy* (London: Macmillan, 1960), pp. 62–133.

27. Seen for example in Arthur Osborne, *Ramana Maharshi and The Path of Self Knowledge* (New York: Samuel Weiser, 1973), p. 204 et passim. Arthur Osborne, ed., *The Collected Works of Ramana Maharshi* (London: Rider, 1959), p. 47. The term *sahaja,* "having a quality as a disposition or constant feature," is an ancient one. According to Monier-Williams, it was seen as early as the Harivamsa [4238].

28. See here Osborne, *Ramana Maharshi and The Path of Self Knowledge*, pp. 17–19, where the first experience of *samādhi* preceded *sahaja samādhi* by several years. This is also congruent with the suggestion made by John Farrow, "Physiological Changes Associated with Transcendental Consciousness, The State of Least Excitation of Consciousness," in David Orme Johnson, ed., *Scientific Research on the Transcendental Meditation Program* (Livingston Manor, N.Y.: Meru Press, 1977), p. 132.

29. See the articles in Part I of *The Problem of Pure Consciousness*, ed. Robert K. C. Forman (New York: Oxford University Press, 1990).

30. See note 28 above.

Chapter 2

1. Robert Hume, *The Thirteen Principal Upanishads* (Oxford: Oxford University Press, 1921), p. 436.

2. Abbreviations: DW = Josef Quint, ed., *Meister Eckhart: Die deutsche Werke Herausgegaben im Auftrage der Deutschen Forschunggemeinschaf* (Stuttgart and Berlin: W. Kohlhammer Verlag, 1936–). LW = Josef Koch, ed. *Meister Eckhart: Die lateinische Werke Herausgegeben im Auftrage der Deutschen Forschungsgemeinschaft* (Stuttgart and Berlin: W. Kohlhammer Verlag, 1936–). PF = Franz Pfeiffer, ed., *Meister Eckhart* (Gottingen: Vandenhoeck and Ruprecht, 1924). W = M. O'C. Walshe, ed. and trans., *Meister Eckhart: German Sermons and Treatises* 3 volumes (London: Watkins, 1979, 1981, 1987). Clark and Skinner = James Clark and John Skinner, ed. and trans., *Meister Eckhart: Selected Treatises and Sermons* (London: Faber and Faber, 1958). Maurer = A. Maurer, ed. and trans., *Parisian Questions* (Toronto: Pontifical Institute of Mediaeval Studies, 1970). Colledge and McGinn = Edmond Colledge and Bernard McGinn, *Meister Eckhart* (New York: Paulist Press, 1978).

3. The Latin works are found in LW. These are translated in Maurer, Clark and Skinner, Colledge and McGinn; and James Clark, *Meister Eckhart: an Introduction to the Study of His Works with an Anthology of His Sermons*.

4. Number 57 in Quint's translation = Number 1 in Walshe's.

5. PF 4:29–36 = W 1:3.

6. PF 5:8–18 = W 1:4.

7. PF 5:18–23 = W 1:4.

8. PF 7:8–25 = W 1:7. This is one of the above-mentioned cases in which rapture is being described without use of the term *gezucken*. Since St. Paul is so often the archetype of *gezucken* and since the experience being described here is clearly rapturous, I believe that *gezucken* is being spoken of here.

9. DW 5:290:5–8 = Clark and Skinner, p. 101.

10. Norman Waddell and Abe Masao, trans., "Dōgen's *Fukanzazengi* and *Shobogenzo Zazengi*," *Eastern Buddhist* 6, no. 2 (Oct. 1973): p. 119.

11. Waddell and Masao, p. 116.

12. Waddell and Masao, pp. 116–117.

13. Except where noted, all translations from Yuko Yokoi and Daizen Victoria, *Zen Master Dōgen* (New York: Weatherhill, 1976). In this passage, however, Francis D. Cook, *How to Raise an Ox: Zen Practice as Taught in Zen Master Dōgen's Shobogenzo* (Los Angeles: Center Publications, 1979), p. 96, seems clearer than, "Setting everything aside, think of neither good nor evil, right nor wrong. . . . [stop] the various functions of your mind," in Yokoi, p 46.

14. Yokoi, p. 45.

15. Yokoi, p. 46.

16. Cook, p. 97. This again is clearer than Yokoi p. 46," . . . Think of nonthinking. How is this done? Be without thoughts—this is the secret of meditation."

17. Wadell and Masao, p. 125.

18. Yokoi, p. 46.

19. At an American Academy of Religion discussion of these issues, Professor Katz remarked that advocates of this position "always focus" on Zen. It is true that Zen is extremely popular in the West, and that perennialists have focused on it frequently. It is false that they have focused on it to the exclusion of other schools. See Daniel Goleman, *The Varieties of the Meditative Experience* (New York: Dutton, 1977), who mentions Zen along with ten other systems. Goleman focuses on the *Visuddhimagga*, a far earlier work. I believe that in its stress on parallels in a multiplicity of traditions, *The Problem of Pure Consciousness*, ed. Robert K. C. Forman, should have put an end to this sort of critique.

20. Edward Conze, *Buddhist Scripture* (New York: Harper Colophon Books, 1956). See his summary of this form of experience in his introduction, especially his diagram on p. 16.

21. Katz, "The 'Conservative' Character of Mystical Experience," p. 5.

22. Comment at a panel on mysticism, American Academy of Religion, November 1985.

23. Peter Moore's "Mystical Experience, Mystical Doctrine, Mystical Technique," in Katz, *Mysticism and Philosophical Analysis*, pp. 100–130, explores some of the reasons for the distance between experience and a highly interpreted text.

24. Mr. Katz so argues in his second volume.

25. David Hay establishes this with some certainty.

26. September 11, 1990. A transcript of the relevant sections of this interview is available on request.

27. This is not to say he did not emerge with a sense that he had been awake. Furthermore, while noting it is hard to "pin down," he also was clear that this is very different from what we might call spacing out, which we do when we go to a movie or drive a car for hours. "That is more absorption than concentration. There is a different quality to concentration. Its pretty hard to pin it down, other than the effect that it has on a person."

28. A transcript of the relevant sections of this interview is available on request.

Chapter 3

1. Aldous Huxley, *The Perennial Philosophy* (New York: Harper and Row, 1944, rpt. 1945, 1970).

2. Rudolf Otto, *The Idea of the Holy*, trans. John W. Harvey (New York: Oxford University Press, 1923, rpt. 1950). Also *Mysticism East and West*, trans. Bertha Bracey and Richenda C. Payne (New York: Macmillan, 1932).

3. Evelyn Underhill, *Mysticism* (New York: E.P. Dutton, 1911, rpt. 1961).

4. Frithjof Schuon, *The Transcendent Unity of Religions*, trans. Peter Townsend (New York: Harper, 1975).

5. Alan Watts has written numerous books about Zen. The clearest summary of his perennialist position may be found in the introduction to *Myth and Ritual in Christianity* (London: Thames and Hudson, 1954).

6. Huston Smith, *Forgotten Truth: The Primordial Tradition* (New York: Harper and Row, 1976).

7. W. T. Stace, *Mysticism and Philosophy*.

8. Philip Almond, "Mysticism and its Contexts," in Forman, ed., *The Problem of Pure Consciousness,* p. 212.

9. W. R. Inge, "Ecstasy," in James Hastings, ed., *Encyclopedia of Religion and Ethics* (Edinburgh: T & T. Clark, 1912).

10. Rufus M. Jones, *Studies in Mystical Religion* (New York: Russell and Russell, 1909, rpt. 1970), p. xxxiv.

11. Bruce Garside, "Language and the Interpretation of Mystical Experiences," *International Journal for Philosophy of Religion* 3 (Summer 1972): 91–94.

12. R. C. Zaehner, *Hindu and Muslim Mysticism* (New York: Schocken Books, 1961).

13. H. P. Owen, "Experience and Dogma in the English Mystics," in Katz, ed., *Mysticism and Philosophical Analysis,* pp. 148–162.

14. John Hick, "Mystical Experience as Cognition."

15. Steven T. Katz, "Language, Epistemology, and Mysticism," in Katz, ed., *Mysticism and Philosophical Analysis,* pp. 22–74. All further references to this work appear in the text.

16. Wayne Proudfoot, *Religious Experience;* William Wainwright, *Mysticism.*

17. Robert Gimello, "Mysticism and Mediation," pp. 170–199; Peter Moore, "Mystical Experience, Mystical Doctrine, Mystical Technique," pp. 101–131; Frederick Streng, "Language and Mystical Awareness," pp. 141–169; and Ninian Smart, "Understanding Religious Experience," pp. 10–21—all in Katz, *Mysticism and Philosophical Analysis.* Jerry Gill, "Mysticism and Mediation," *Faith and Philosophy* 1 (1984): pp. 111–121.

18. See the essays in *The Problem of Pure Consciousness,* ed. Robert K. C. Forman. Jonathan Shear, *The Inner Dimension: Philosophy and the Experience of Consciousness* (New York: Peter Lang, 1990). James Robertson Price, "The Objectivity of Mystical Truth Claims," *The Thomist* 49, no. 1 (January 1985): pp. 81–98.

19. John Hick, "Mystical Experience as Cognition," in Woods, ed., *Understanding Mysticism,* p. 432.

20. Hans H. Penner, "The Mystical Illusion," in *Mysticism and Religious Traditions,* ed. Katz, p. 89. Penner is here quoting Godelier.

21. Anthony Perovich, "Does the Philosophy of Mysticism Rest on a Mistake," in Forman, ed., *The Problem of Pure Consciousness,* pp. 237–253.

22. With this phrase, Katz seems to present mystical experiences from a variety of traditions as having a single ontological object, a single reality, which are then encountered or experienced differently. One wonders what he means by this notion.

23. Jerry Gill, "Mysticism and Mediation"; John Hick, "Mystical Experience as Cognition"; Hans Penner, "The Mystical Illusion," in *Mysticism and Religious Traditions,* ed. Katz, pp. 89–116; In the same volume see also Robert Gimello, "Mysticism in its Contexts," pp. 61–88.

24. The exception is that there can be causal relationships ascertained even in the absence of explanatory models. If I throw the switch the light will go on, though I do not understand electricity. Such a causal association should be distinguished from a causal model however.

25. William Wainwright's *Mysticism* stresses the parallel. But see my notice in the *Journal of the American Academy of Religion*, Spring 1985.

26. It was also Rouen Cathedral, not Notre Dame. This was pointed out to me by Michael McLaughlin and Emily Mason. To both I am grateful. Interestingly, here is another case of an expectation dominating our experience, in this case Katz's and my own. We all miss what there is because of what we expect!

27. E. H. Gombrich, *Art and Illusion: A Study in the Psychology of Pictoral Representation,* p. 73.

28. For an early study of this effect see for example Jerome Bruner and Leo Postman, "On Perception of Incongruities: A Paradigm," *Journal of Personality* 18 (1949), p. 213.

29. Peter Moore, "Mystical Experience, Mystical Doctrine, Mystical Technique," in Katz, ed., *Mysticism and Philosophical Analysis,* p 110.

30. Wainwright, op. cit.

31. Wayne Proudfoot, *Religious Experience.*

32. Robert Gimello, "Mysticism in its Contexts," p. 85.

33. Ninian Smart, "Interpretation and Mystical Experience," p. 87.

34. Katz, "The Conservative Character of Mystical Experience," p. 41.

35. William Wainwright, *Mysticism*, pp. 19–22.

36. Katz, "The Conservative Character of Mystical Experience," p. 51.

37. Anthony Perovich, "Mysticism and the Philosophy of Science," *Journal of Religion* 65 (1985): 63–82.

38. Peter Moore, "Mystical Experience, Mystical Doctrine, Mystical Technique"; Frederick Streng, "Language and Mystical Awareness"; Robert Gimello, "Mysticism and Meditation," in *Mysticism and Philosophical Analysis*, ed. Katz. Robert Gimello, "Mysticism in its Contexts," Ninian Smart, "The Purification of Consciousness and the Negative Path," and, insofar as he speaks of the key role of models, Steven Katz, "The 'Conservative' Character of Mystical Experience."

39. Moore, in Katz, *Mysticism and Philosophical Analysis*, p. 114, 116.

40. Cf. Anthony Perovich, "Mysticism and the Philosophy of Science": p. 73 ff.

41. Philip Almond, "Mysticism and its Contexts", in Forman, *The Problem of Pure Consciousness*, pp. 211–222.

42. The full quote here concerns the fact that it is the centering of consciousness and consciousness-concomitants evenly and rightly on a single object. But within meditation, Piya Tissa explained to me, we sink so deeply "into the object" that the object itself falls utterly away, leaving the mind utterly alone.

43. Wainwright, *Mysticism*, p. 20.

44. Katz, "The 'Conservative' Character of Mysticism," p. 6.

45. Ibid., pp. 50–51.

46. Gimello, "Mysticism in Its Contexts," p. 62.

47. Wayne Proudfoot, *Religious Experience*, pp. 119–154.

48. This question is my way of asking, Are the conditions of the nomological causal model fulfilled?

Chapter 4

1. In addition to the articles mentioned, I am responding to un- published talks by Robert Gimello, Steven Katz, Huston Smith, and Ewert Cousins at an American Academy of Religion Mysticism Panel, 1990. While these papers are not published, a tape recording is available from the American Academy of Religion tape service.

2. Bruce Mangan, "Language and Experience in the Cognitive Study of Mysticism—Commentary on Forman," *Journal of Consciousness Studies* 1, no. 2 (Winter 1994): pp. 250–252.

3. Mathew Bagger, "Critical Notice: Ecumenalism and Peren- nialism Revisited," *Religious Studies* 27 (1991): pp. 401–413.

4. Larry Short, "Mysticism, Mediation, and the Non-Linguistic," *Journal of the American Academy of Religion* 113, no. 4 (Winter 1995), pp. 659–676.

5. But see here Perovich.

6. The second argument states that space is the condition of ob- jects, not they of it, for we can represent an empty space but not objects devoid of spatiality. This argument clearly presupposes the first.

7. Let us grant, for the sake of the argument, that one visualizes no numerals, and is thus utterly uninvolved with spatially mediated appearances.

8. Not *all* experience, I am showing, but only objective or inten- tional experience. It is this sort of confusion that I have attempted to avoid by calling one form of mystical phenomenon a "pure consciousness *event*."

9. This was recently pointed out to me by Michael Sells at the Forge Institute Conference, Binghamton, N.Y., 1994. I am indebted to him for encouraging me to explore this important but thorny issue in depth.

10. Jerry H. Gill, "Mysticism and Mediation": p. 113.

11. Jerry Gill, "Religious Experience as Mediated," paper delivered to Philosophy Section, American Academy of Religion, November 6, 1980, p. 5.

12. Though not here using the term "intentionality," Katz implies this sort of connection between the constructive activities of the mind and the intentional character of experience when he says that "the 'given' is appropriated through acts which shape it into forms which we can make intelligible to ourselves given our conceptual constitution." Katz, "Language, Epistemology and Mysticism," p. 59.

13. James Leuba, *The Psychology of Religious Mysticism* (London: K Paul, Trench, Trubner, and Co., Ltd.; New York: Harcourt Brace & Co., 1925).

14. John Hick, "Mystical Experience as Cognition," p. 425.

15. Hick, p. 429.

16. Hick, p. 432.

17. Terence Penelhum, "Unity and Diversity in the Interpretation of Mysticism," p. 447.

18. William Wainwright, *Mysticism*. See also his "Interpretation, Description, and Mystical Consciousness," *Journal of the American Academy of Religion* 45 (1977) (Supplement); "Natural Explanations and Religious Experience," *Ratio* 15 (1973): pp. 98–101; "Mysticism and Sense Perception," *Religious Studies* 9 (1973): pp. 257–278; and "Stace and Mysticism," *The Journal of Religion* 50 (1970): pp. 139–154.

19. Wainwright, *Mysticism*, p. 117. For a discussion of Wainwright on intentionality, see the last section of this chapter.

20. Steven Katz, "Language, Epistemology and Mysticism," p. 63.

21. Ibid., p. 64.

22. Note that there is slippage here between two meanings of "intention": let us call them the "volitional" and "cognitive" (or "extrapractical") senses. In its volitional sense "intention" signifies that which I propose or desire to achieve or accomplish. Virtually all of the terms Katz offers as examples of "intentional" words—"expects," "seeks," "desires," etc.— bear this volitional meaning. The other, cognitive, sense of the term was (re-)introduced nearly a century ago by Brentano and Husserl. It signifies a characteristic of an act of consciousness, i.e., referring or pointing beyond itself. I will discuss this meaning in detail in the next section.

Keeping in mind this distinction between practical and extra-practical senses, the passage seems to be asserting something like the following.

K1: Mystics always formulate and express their goal in terms of volitional intentions.

K2: Volitional intentions always entail cognitive intentions which, if fulfilled, will be encountered in terms which are identical or synonymous with those volitional intentions.

K3: All conscious experiences are cognitive intentions.

Therefore:

K4: When a mystic experiences his goal he will have a conscious experience which will be a cognitive intention encountered in terms that are identical or synonymous to those volitional intentions.

This argument is not compelling, and for several reasons. I will take those that are most relevant to my purposes. First of all, K2, that we always encounter results in terms of our original goals, rests on a congruence between cognitive and volitional intentions. But these are not congruent sets. Not every successful volitional intention results in a cognitive intention encountered in its terms. "I hope to forget all sorrow," does not result in an experience of sorrow or even of "forgetting" as a cognitive intention. Rather, forgetting here marks an absence of a set of cognitive intentions, i.e., sorrowful ones. Similarly, an obsessive woman-hater may go into psychotherapy intending to cease seeing in the terms of this pattern, i.e., seeing women as evil. If successful, he will, in time, cease seeing women in terms of the dichotomy evil/non-evil, or evil/good, but in other terms (intelligent, interesting, attractive, etc.). The experience that results from the achievement of his (practical) intention need not necessarily involve the terms in which that intention was formulated. Indeed, if he achieves his therapeutic goal he will simply cease using such a dichotomy altogether. Thus, successful realization of volitional intentions does not always entail cognitive ones expressed in those terms.

Secondly, K4 is false, as shown by novel and surprising mystical experiences. Many mystics' experiences are so unexpected that they are stunned, and they must struggle for years to find or formulate a suitable language. That is to say, they may not have language that seems to satisfactorily "fit" the experience: they may not have "appropriate" labels. Furthermore, even if someone does have a statable "goal," when he "achieves" it he may do so not in the terms with which he anticipated it. Buddha, who originated the Buddhist language game, certainly encountered certain aspects of his experience for which his past linguistic categories had incompletely prepared him. The modern Christian mystic, Bernadette Roberts, searched for years to find language that seemed to adequately express her experiences.

23. Cf. Mark B. Woodhouse, "Consciousness and Brahman-Atman," *The Monist* (Jan. 1978): p. 114.

24. The other option is to look at the more recent work on the nature of intentionality in the analytical philosophical tradition, notably the

work of Chisholm and Marras. Roderick Chisholm, "Intentionality," *Encyclopedia of Philosophy*, 1967 ed.; "Sentences about Believing," in *Intentionality, Mind, and Language*, ed. Ausonio Marras (Urbana: University of Illinois Press, 1972), pp. 31–51; Ausonio Marras, "Intentionality and Cognitive Sentences," in *Intentionality, Mind, and Language*, ed. Ausonio Marras (Urbana: University of Illinois Press, 1972), pp. 31–51; *et passim*.

25. Franz Brentano, *Psychology from an Empirical Point of View*, trans. Antos Rancurello, D. B. Terrell, and Linda L. McAlister, English edition edited by Linda McAlister (London: Routledge and Kegan Paul, 1973).

26. Brentano, p. 79.

27. That Brentano included a landscape as a member of the class of physical phenomena was unfortunate and often criticized, since clearly the seeing of a landscape involves considerable interpretive activities of the mind—much like hearing a sound or seeing a colored object. He was attempting to distinguish here that of which I am aware from the experience of it, but chose a misleading example. I shall refrain from using this in further discussions.

28. Brentano, pp. 79–80.

29. Brentano, p. 88.

30. This hearkens back to the Scholastic copy theory of knowledge, with which Brentano became quite familiar when training to be a priest. In it, the *intentio intellecta* is a likeness, a *similitudo,* or an *imago.* Where Brentano differs from this theory is in his notion of "reference to an object," which is the element of this definition that he retains and that is picked up by his student, Husserl. See Herbert Spiegelberg, " 'Intention' and 'Intentionality,' " in The Scholastics, Brentano and Husserl,": *The Context of the Phenomenological Movement* (The Hague: Martinus Nijhoff, 1981), pp. 5–9.

31. Letter to Oskar Kraus, 1909, published in Kraus's Introduction to Volume I of *Psychologie vom empirischen Standpunkt*, p. xlix. Quoted in Dagfinn Follesdal, "Brentano and Husserl on Intentional Objects and Perception," *Husserl, Intentionality, and Cognitive Science*, ed. Hubert Dreyfus (Cambridge: MIT Press, 1982), p. 32.

32. Alexius Meinong took this route. See "The Theory of Objects," in *Realism and the Background of Phenomenology*, ed. Roderick Chisholm (Glencoe: The Free Press, 1960), pp. 76–117. See Follesdal, p. 32.

33. *Psychologie vom empirischen Standpunct*, vol. II, p. 137, of the *Philosophische Bibliotek* (Hamburg: Meiner, 1874). Quote reference from Follesdal, p. 33.

34. Edmund Husserl, *Logical Investigations*, 2 vols., trans. J. Findlay (New York: Humanities Press, 1970). Except where noted, all references will be to Volume 2.

35. Husserl, *Investigations* 5, Para. 11, p. 557.

36. Husserl, *Investigations* 5, para. 13, p. 562.

37. Husserl, *Investigations* 5, para. 10, p. 556.

38. Husserl, *Investigations* 5, para. 13, p. 562.

39. In the later *Ideas* Husserl formalized this structure of our consciousness when we are performing an act as the "noema." See Dagfinn Follesdal, "Husserl's Notion of *Noema*," in *Husserl, Intentionality, and Cognitive Science*, in Dreyfus and Hall, pp. 73–80, and Hubert Dreyfus, "Husserl's Perceptual *Noema*," in Dreyfus and Hall, pp. 97–124.

40. Here I am indebted to Herbert Spiegleburg, *The Phenomenological Movement* (The Hague: Martinus Nijhoff, 1982), p. 98–99.

41. Husserl, *Investigations* V, para. 20, pp. 586–590; para. 22, pp. 597–598; para. 39, pp. 642–645; *et passim.*

42. In this, Husserl saw himself answering Hume's "psychologistic" account of perception, in which the mind merely mistakes similar sense data for an identical object. I believe that I am looking at an identical object, according to Hume, merely because I create a fiction, make a mistake about its identity. On this account, there can be no well-grounded conception of an object at all. Husserl's account begins, as it were, with a formation or conception of an object. See Aron Gurwitsch, "On the Intentionality of Consciousness," *Philosophical Essays in Memory of Edmund Husserl*, ed. Marvin Farber (New York: Greenwood Press, 1968), pp. 65–83.

43. The reader may object that "experience" (defined as a conscious encountering *of* something) itself carries the implication of intentionality. That is, the reader may want to *stipulatively* define experience as intentional: i.e., something is an experience if and only if an intentional object or content for consciousness is encountered. If we accept this stipulation we would want to rewrite the assumptions about intentionality without the term *experience,* using some other terms, say, *event:* any event a human may consciously undergo must necessarily be intentional. While this is awkward, I would have no objection.

44. Husserl, Introduction to the German edition, Vol. 2, para 2, Eng. Vol. 1, p. 252.

45. Idem.

46. Husserl, *Investigations,* Vol. I, p. 261.

47. Husserl, *Investigations*, Introduction to German edition, Vol. 2, para. 1, English Vol. I, p. 249–250.

48. Brentano, *Psychology*, p. 78.

49. Ibid., p. 18.

50. Husserl, *Investigations*, Prolegomena to Pure Logic, para. 21, Vol. 1, p. 99.

51. Wainwright, *Mysticism*, p. 120.

52. Ibid.

53. See my "What Does Mysticism Have to Tell us About Consciousness," *Journal of Consciousness Studies,* forthcoming, 1997.

Chapter 5

1. There are few female Buddhist or Hindu philosophers.

2. The debate here, which I do not wish to enter, is whether the Yogācāra school saw everything as the creation of language and concept or rather a large part of experience. Is there something "out there" or nothing, or merely something of which we know nothing? Whatever the answer to this conundrum, the fact that experience is the result of the constructive activities of the mind is not at issue.

3. Chris Gudmunsen, *Wittgenstein and Buddhism* (New York: Macmillan, 1977), p. 58, quoting *Lankāvatāra Sūtra,* 226. The Buddhist sensitivity to the possibility of other language systems may be in part attributed to the polyglot and pluralistic society amidst which it was born and grew. That makes another interesting parallel between these two philosophical systems.

4. Gudmunsen, p. 58, *Lankāvatāra Sūtra,* 225.

5. Ibid.

6. Diana Paul, *Philosophy of Mind in Sixth Century China: Paramārtha's Evolution of Consciousness* (Stanford: Stanford University Press, 1984); "An Introductory Note to Paramārtha's Theory of Language," *Journal of Indian Philosophy* 7, no. 3 (Sept. 1979): pp. 231–255; "The Structure of Consciousness in Paramārtha's Purported Trilogy," *Philosophy East and West* 31, no. 3 (July 1981): pp. 297–319.

7. Paul, *Philosophy of Mind*, p. 153; CSL 61c 5–6.

8. Cf. Paul, "The Structure of Consciousness," p. 301.

9. Paul, *Philosophy of Mind*, 153–154; CSL 61c3–4.

10. Ibid., p. 161; CSL 62c 20. Cf. Sarvepalli Radhakrishnan and Charles A. Moore, *A Sourcebook in Indian Philosophy* (Princeton: Princeton University Press, 1957), p. 336.

11. Ibid., p. 161; CLS 62c 20–21.

12. Ibid., pp. 161–162; CSL 63c21–64a6.

13. Ibid., p. 155, CSL 62 a 15, vs. IVa.

14. Paul translates *vijñaptirviṣayasya* as the six sense consciousnesses, which is a somewhat free rendering. *Vijñapti* is a technical term which refers to mental or perceptual events with intentional objects in which something is represented. Her term, if taken literally, misses this nuance. See here Paul Griffiths, *On Being Mindless* (La Salle, Ill.: Open Court Press, 1986), p. 80.

15. Paul, *Philosophy of Mind*, p. 154; CSL 62a6.

16. Theodore Stcherbatsky, *The Central Conception of Buddhism* (London, 1923; rpt. Calcutta, 1961), pp. 46–47: "The element of consciousness according to the same laws (*pratītyasamutpāda*) never appears alone, but always supported by an object (*viṣaya*) and a receptive faculty (*indriya*)." This makes clear that "consciousness" as used here means intentional consciousness.

17. Paul, "The Structure of Consciousness," p. 305.

18. Here I am indebted to Paul Griffiths, "Pure Consciousness and Indian Buddhism," in Forman, ed., *The Problem of Pure Consciousness,* pp. 71–97.

19. Katz, p. 59, asserts that, among other things, "accumulation of past experience" conditions present experience.

20. CSL 61c1–2.

21. Paul, *Philosophy of Mind*, pp. 98–99.

22. Of course, Diana Paul, a modern academic, may be thought to be influenced by the same background of beliefs as the other constructivists I have mentioned. She may be reinterpreting Paramārtha here based on such training. Let me say only that, to my knowledge, no one has criticized her on this point.

23. William Wainwright's *Mysticism* is most explicit on this point. He argues for a parallel between sense experience and mystical experience, implying that the epistemological processes involved are identical in both.

24. Paul, *Philosophy of Mind*, p. 155; CSL 62a 11.

25. Translation Cox's, in *Journal of Asian Studies* (Nov. 1985): p. 126. Paul translation of CSL 62a16 has "being ultimately eliminated upon entering cessation meditation." This was criticized by Cox, whose criticism was repeated by de Jong, p. 131. Cox noted, glossing Sthiramati, that the *ādanavijñāna*, "though eliminated upon entering the equipoise of cessation, *nirodhasamāpatti*, arises again upon emergence from that equipoise" (p. 126); de Jong echoes this observation. Cox's "and are also eliminated" communicates this notion. In her rebuttal to de Jong, Paul replies that "the text, according to Paramārtha's rendering of this verse, does state quite clearly that the *ādanavijñāna* is eliminated absolutely in cessation

meditation " (p. 135). I will not attempt to adjudicate this matter, since the debate does not speak to my point here: during *nirodhasamāpatti* the activities of the *ādanavijñāna* are eliminated either temporarily (which seems more to me a more plausible rendering) or permanently.

26. Paul, *Philosophy of Mind*, p. 158; CSL 62b 17–19. I should note that de Jong accuses Paul of borrowing the two *samāpattis* (*nirodhasamāpatti* and *asamjnasamāpatti*, the dhyāna without conceptualization) from Paramārtha's original source, the *Triṃśikā*, and applying it to Paramārtha's text. If de Jong is correct, I would have to amend the last two sentences of this paragraph to say that the *Triṃśikā* notes that . . . Paul does not address this criticism.

27. What seemed important to them [the Yogācārins] was the statement that the Absolute is "'thought' in the sense that it is to be sought not in any object at all, but in the pure subject which is free from all objects." Conze, *Buddhism*, p. 163.

28. As Alan Sponberg presents it in "Dynamic Liberation in Yogācāra Buddhism," *The Journal of the International Association of Buddhist Studies* 2 (1979: pp. 46–64. The enlightened individual abides in a state of "non-discriminating cognition (*nirvikalpaka-jñana*)" in which the discriminating functions are cut off. This is especially clear in *nirodhasamāpatti*, in which there is an absence of both object and cognition.

29. Paul, *Philosophy of Mind*, p. 166; CSL 63c2.

30. Paul, *Philosophy of Mind*, p. 167, CSL 63c13.

31. Paul Griffiths, in "Pure Consciousness and Buddhism," concurs with this thesis. In his *On Being Mindless*, he argues that this state should not be considered a state of consciousness as we generally understand the term. This is a matter that would require a full article to discuss. But for the present, we can agree that, whatever we are to call this empty event, there are no constructive activities at work in it.

Chapter 6

1. This chapter is an edited version of a plenary talk given at Binghamton University Ancient Philosophy and Neo-Platonism Conference, October 1993. I am grateful to the respondents for their helpful comments.

2. These two are the main characters in Chāndogya Upanishad 6:8. We know very little about Svetaketu, who is presented primarily as a foil for his father. I use his name as an example, not as a portrait.

3. In 1991, I conducted an interview with Daido Sensei Loori, head of the Zen Mountain Monastery in Mt. Tremper, New York. He told me that his first experience of what he calls "absolute samadhi" came during a photography workshop with Minor White, years before he had looked into Zen. He had been out on assignment, photographing this and that, when he came on a tree, "which was basically just a tree, just a plain old tree like a hundred thousand other ones. But this one was very special for some reason. And Minor used to say, sit in the presence of your subject until you have been acknowledged. . . . So I set up my camera and I sat with this tree, and it was in the middle of the afternoon, and that's all I remember until it was dusk, the sun had gone down and it was cold. And I was feeling just totally elated, just wonderful."

From the fact that he had started in the early afternoon and came out after dusk, when it was cold, he deduced that he had sat there for roughly four hours. Yet he had no recollection of anything specific from that entire period. He states he hadn't thought anything odd had happened; by which I came to understand that he had not blacked out or experienced a discontinuity in awareness. He was certain he had not slept.

It wasn't until five years later that he learned the term *samādhi*, which he now believes most adequately describes this experience.

4. Indeed, what is to say that our Upanishadic passage is not describing a vehicle in which somebody rode long *before* they were led into it by the horse of their language? From texts alone—that is, without something like an interview or a clear autobiographical report—how are we to know which came first? In fact, our passage says that Svetaketu's experience would be "unthinkable" and a "supreme mystery!" Doesn't that *mean* that he will have no good language to describe his experience, that his experience will go beyond language and thought? See my remarks below about ineffability. This means that even if he had heard about the experience, that hearing would not be enough to truly predict or prepare him for the precise character of this experience.

5. If I am trying to guess a number between one and two billion and somebody tells me it is not 18,573, that is some help, but it is absolutely minimal.

6. Speaking of the parallel process in behavioral automatisms, Heinz Hartmann writes:

"In well established achievements [motor apparatuses] function automatically: the integration of the somatic systems involved in the action is automatized and so is the integration of the individual mental acts involved in it. With increasing exercise of the action, its intermediate steps disappear from consciousness." The term *automatism* was employed extensively by Heinz Hartmann, *Ego Psychology and the Problem of Adaptation* (International University Press, 1958). Freud described such a process as a "lack of attention cathexis."

7. See Michael C. McLaughlin, *Lonergan and the Evaluation of Theories of Mystical Experience*, Ph.D. Thesis, University of Toronto, 1995.

8. See Arthur Deikman, "Deautomatization and the Mystic Experience," in *Altered States of Consciousness*, ed. Charles Tart (New York: John Wiley & Sons, 1969), pp. 23–44.

9. In our Upanishadic passage I left out something that may look like a positive (formative) utterance:

> When a person sees the brilliant
> Maker, Lord, Person, the Brahma-source,
> Then, being a knower, shaking off good and evil,
> He reduces everything to unity in the supreme Imperishable.
> (Maitri 6:18)

Here again we have a "seeing;" indeed, Svetaketu is to "see" the Lord, Person, and Brahma-source. This sounds like he is seeing a person, something akin to seeing that old guy in a white beard sitting on his heavenly throne.

But, except for the Śvetāśvatara Upanishads, none of the classical Upanishads talk of Ātman or Brahman as a person. Nor, tellingly, does the Maitri. They speak of both in impersonal terms. Brahman is, for example, consistently said to be the formless One, beyond thought and form. Brahman is, in other words, not a thing among things, but beyond all things. It is not a thing you can see, think, or smell at all. Rather than seeing something like a person, one is to come to or reduce all intentional objects for perception "to a unity." Thus, once again, insofar as it is an instruction, this passage is not about seeing some personalistic thing. Rather than being formative, it is again *destructive* of any sort of expectation—perceptual, cognitive, or otherwise. *Via positiva* syntax does not necessarily imply perceptual automatization.

It seems to me that this Upanishadic language is doing something parallel to saying to Monet, "Look at that non-gothic arch." Grammatically it employs the *via positiva*. Nonetheless, it gives only a negative performative instruction. It is equivalent to saying, "stop thinking that is a gothic arch and just look over there."

10. The reader may be thinking of someone like E. H. Gombrich here, who describes just this process of schema trial and correction, which one might adopt when trying to copy a nonsense figure, say, an inkblot or an irregular patch: "By and large, it appears, the procedure is always the same. The draftsman tries first to classify the blot and fit it into some sort of familiar schema—he will say, for instance, that it is triangular or that it looks like a fish. Having selected such a schema to fit the form approximately, he will proceed to adjust it, [by supplying further schemas], noticing for instance that the triangle is rounded at the top, or that the fish ends in a pigtail." E. H. Gombrich, *Art and Illusion,* pp. 73–4.

11. Cf. the author of the thirteenth-century English *Cloud of Unknowing,* who said that one must be rid of: "*all* those things the which

may be known with any of thy five bodily wits without-forth; and *all* those things the which may be known by thy goostly wits within-forth; and *all* those things that be now, or yet have been, though they be not now; and *all* those things that be not now, or yet may be in time for to come, though they be not now. . . . through the overpassing of thyself and *all* other things, and thus making thyself clean from all worldly, fleshly, and natural liking in thine affection, and from *all* things that may be known by the proper form in thy knowing." Translated from Phyllis Hodgson, *The Cloud of Unknowing and Related Treatises,* "Deonise Hid Diuinite," p. 120:5–25. See my "Mystical Experience in the Cloud Literature," in *The Medieval Mystical Tradition in England: Exeter Symposium IV,* ed. Marion Glasscoe (Cambridge: D. S. Brewer, 1987), pp. 177–195.

12. Wayne Proudfoot, *Religious Experience,* pp. 119–154.

13. Sometimes we have an experience that, even while it is occurring, we don't know how to describe it: This is especially common in psychotherapy and in intimate conversations: "I don't know quite what to call this strong feeling I'm feeling just now." Words don't always have a necessary connection to our experiences.

14. Bernadette Roberts, *The Experience of No-Self* (Boston: Shambala, 1984), p. 9.

Chapter 7

1. Steven Mitchell, trans., *Tao te Ching* (New York: Harper, 1988), Chap. 14 (no page).

2. Daniel C. Matt, "*Ayin*: The Concept of Nothingness, " and Franklin, both in Forman, 1990. See also Daniel Brown, "The Stages of Meditation in Cross-Cultural Perspective," in Ken Wilber, Jack Engler, and Daniel Brown, *Transformations of Consciousness: Conventional and Contemplative Perspectives on Development* (Boston: Shambhala, 1986).

3. Michael McLaughlin, *Lonergan and the Evaluation of Theories of Mystical Experience.*

4. Robert K. C. Forman, "Pure Consciousness Events and Mysticism," *Sophia* 25, no. 1 (1986): 49–58. Unpublished interview with Danielle Roman, 1990.

5. This question has been asked of me in public by Steven Katz and Robert Gimello, Mysticism Group of the American Academy of Religion, November 1990. See also Gene Pendleton, "Forman and Mystical Consciousness," *Sophia* 27, no. 2 (July 1988): pp. 15–17, and Bagger's review article of *The Problem of Pure Consciousness, Religious Studies* 27 (1991): pp. 400–413.

6. In the *Māṇḍūkya Upanishad*, for example, the waking dream and deep sleep states, along with the "fourth" *(turīya)* state, are identified as the four quarters of Ātman, or pure consciousness. Ātman as consciousness is said to underlie the first three states and remain unaffected as it moves through them. Furthermore, two of the great sayings *(mahāvakya)* state this directly: "Brahman is consciousness" and "Atman is Brahman" *(Prajñanam Brahma, Aitareya Upanishad* 3.5.3, and *Ayam Atma Brahma Bṛhadāraṇyaka Upanishad* 2.5.19).

7. Though I will not explore his claim here, D. T. Suzuki suggests that Hui Neng, famed Zen Buddhist patriarch, may be teaching something similar. See Suzuki's, "The Zen Doctrine of No-Mind," in *Zen Buddhism: Selected Writings of D. T. Suzuki* 3, ed. William Barrett (Garden City, N.Y.: Doubleday Anchor Books, 1956), pp. 157–228. Suzuki suggests that the Zen doctrine of No-Mind points toward what he calls an "Unconscious" "below" intentional consciousness. As I argued in "Zen and Reflexive Consciousness," a lecture at the University of Helsinki, Finland, October 1994, I understand this to mean the awareness per se, to which we are referring herein. See chapter 9, below.

8. Willliam Chittuck, *The Innate Capacity,* ed. Robert K. C. Forman (NY: Oxford University Press: 1998).

9. Maharishi Mahesh Yogi, *Bhagavad Gita,* A New Translation and Commentary with Sanskrit Texts (Baltimore: Penguin Books, 1971), p. 144.

10. Sir William Hamilton, in Evans, p. 45. When John Dewey defined the "phenomenon of Self," he used the concept of consciousness in a similar way: "The self not only exists, but may know that it exists; psychical phenomena are not only facts, but they are facts of con-sciousness. . . . What distinguishes the facts of psychology from the facts of every other science is, accordingly, that they are conscious facts. . . . Consciousness can neither be defined nor described. We can define or describe anything only by the employment of consciousness. It is presupposed, accordingly, in all definitions and all attempts to define it must move in a circle." John Dewey, *Psychology, Third Edition*(New York: Harper, 1886), p. 2.

11. David Ballin Klein, *The Concept of Consciousness: A Survey* (Lincoln: University of Nebraska Press, 1980), p. 36.

12. Evans, p. 49.

13. David Hume, *A Treatise of Human Nature*, ed. L. A. Selby-Bigge (Oxford: Clarendon Press, 1888), p. 252. Emphasis mine.

14. G.E. Moore, *Philosophical Studies* (London: Oxford University Press, 1960), p. 17.

15. I do not claim that a Hume or a Moore would have necessarily achieved a pure consciousness event had they only had the right technique. Not all meditators get every result.

16. John Searle, *The Rediscovery of the Mind* (Cambridge, Mass.: MIT Press, 1992), p. 95.

17. John Beloff, "Minds and Machines: A Radical Dualist Perspective," *Journal of Consciousness Studies* 1, no. 1 (Summer 1994): pp. 32–37.

18. Strictly speaking, "acquaint" is a misleading verb. One is acquainted with another person, a color, a piece of music. These are one and all intentional contacts, the familiarity with things distinct from the self. Here, my "acquaintance" is with something that is the self; there is no intentional structure. It is in part for this reason that I think we will be on firmer ground to reserve a new term for this epistemological structure.

19. Again, I don't *have* a consciousness as I might *have* a car. There is no ownership of consciousness.

20. For the discussion that follows, I am indebted to G. William Barnard's excellent dissertation, *Exploring Unseen Worlds: William James and the Philosophy of Mysticism*, The University of Chicago, March 1994, pp. 123–134.

21. William James, *Principles of Psychology*, p. 216. We might add to his division "knowing how," the knowledge of how to drive a car or follow a rule, and "formal knowing" the kind of knowledge we might have in understanding a mathematical equation. But when it comes to mysticism, neither is particularly relevant; for both are intentional and high level, i.e, grounded in the more basic "knowledge about" and "knowledge by acquaintance." So, to save space, I will omit both in my discussion.

22. James, *Principles of Psychology*, p. 656. Quoted in Barnard, p. 125.

23. Myers, p. 275. Quoted in Barnard pp. 125–126. These divisions are strikingly similar to Meister Eckhart's division between the knowledge gained by the "inner man," which centers on feelings, and that gained by the "outer man," which focuses on knowledge and understanding.

24. James, *Principles of Psychology*, p. 189.

25. Here, language fails us: "contact" implies a dualism, which is absent here. "My" is also misleading, for again, I do not own my awareness as I own a car.

26. I first came across this term in Franklin Merrell-Wolff, *Pathways Through to Space* (New York: Warner Books, 1976), pp. 93–97. There, it is, however, undeveloped and used in inconsistent and confusing ways. But Wolff is speaking exclusively of mystical experience. It is true, certain mystical experiences are known by means of a new epistemological structure, but so is consciousness even in ordinary life.

27. Here, the terms my, I, etc. are again problematic. So is the idea that I "have" or "own" consciousness, as if it is a property or something I can possess. Consciousness is at once the subject of any first-person appellation yet is also unrelated to anything denoting personality, possession, etc. Some would have consciousness as impersonal; some hold it to be personal. I note only that it is problematic to say either; thus the scare quotes.

28. This is speaking of James's knowledge by acquaintance in its ideal sense. There are, however, absolutely no words in my acquaintance with my own awareness.

29. *Bṛihadāraṇyaka Upanishad* 4.5.15. Translation from Robert E. Hume, *The Thirteen Principal Upanishads*, Second ed., (Oxford: Oxford University Press, 1931), p. 147.

30. Norman Malcolm, *Ludwig Wittgenstein: A Memoir* (Oxford: Oxford University Press, 1958), p. 87.

31. Shankara, *Brahma Sūtra Bhāsya*, 4.1.2. Quoted in William Indich, *Consciousness in Advaita Vedanta* (Delhi: Motilal Banarsidass, 1980), p. 15.

32. Barnard, p. 130.

33. Here, Bernadette Roberts, *The Experience of No-Self*, is a good example. I put scare quotes around "object" to indicate that if some perceptual object is encountered as the self, then there is no experienced distinction between that object and the subject. Thus, the intentional experiential structure behind the intentional grammar is dissolved.

34. *Memoiren einer Idealistin*, 5th Auflage, 1900, iii. 166. Quoted in James, *Varieties*, p. 395.

35. We have discussed this for the PCE most fully. While I do not have space to explore this in as much detail as it warrants, in the more extrovertive unitive experience, the object is encountered as the self. If this is the case, then the object is not experienced as separate from the self, and thus there is no distinction between subject and object as there is in an intentional experience. I hope to develop a fully fleshed out typology of mysticism that includes this form of experience.

36. Barnard, p. 131.

37. D. T. Suzuki, "Existentialism, Pragmatism, and Zen," in *Zen Buddhism: Selected Writings of D. T. Suzuki,* pp. 261–262.

Chapter 8

This is a revised version of a talk first delivered to the University of Helsinki in October 1994. I am indebted to the comments of that audience and of the astute members of their Department of Religious Studies, as well as insightful comments by Louis Nordstrom and Steven Rosen.

1. Here, I want to emphasize that by this I do not mean "universal." I do not see evidence that everyone has experienced this, nor that it is seen in every tradition. Rather, I am making the more modest claim that if one is able to eliminate all conscious content, then the resultant experience will have nonpluralistic characteristics.

2. Bernadette Roberts, *The Experience of No-Self,* p. 20.

3. I should note that, after the onset of this event, she discovered the writings of Meister Eckhart, which she felt did very nearly describe her experiences. We will see why shortly.

4. Following her autobiography, Roberts offers some vaguely monistic philosophical explanations. But even she will admit that, while a mystic and imaginative autobiographer, Roberts is not a trained philosopher. Her scheme is not particularly clear or well worked out.

5. D. T. Suzuki, "The Zen Doctrine of No Mind", in *Zen Buddhism: Selected Writings of D. T. Suzuki,* p. 189.

6. Suzuki, pp. 157–226. It purports to be an explanation of Hui Neng's *Platform Sutra,* but I suspect that the thoughts Suzuki expresses are more Suzuki's than Hui Neng's. But the interersting historical question of "whose insights?" is not particularly important for us here, for I am not interested in the history of Zen thought or in where Suzuki may have gotten his ideas, but rather am just trying to discern the nature of certain advanced mystical experiences, and I found this essay to be helpful in that regard. That Suzuki was an experienced Zen practitioner himself, probably enjoyed the experiences he discusses, and had certain insights about the spiritual process is more than enough for me.

7. Occasionally, I quote herein from Philip Yampulsky's translation of Hui Neng from *The Platform Sutra of the Sixth Patriarch* (New York: Columbia University Press, 1967), which is the best critical edition and translation available to me. To my knowledge Suzuki did not offer a complete English translation. Whenever possible, I will use Suzuki's translations, in order to keep the argument as consistent as possible. It is *Suzuki's* Hui Neng that I found most helpful.

8. I should address another hesitation that several scholars have expressed to me. Is it legitimate to turn to Japanese thinkers such as D. T. Suzuki or Hui Neng for philosophical insights about experiences of Westerners such as Bernadette Roberts or myself? I believe so. Suzuki and Hui Neng purport to be saying something about the nature of human life and human processes in general, not only about Chinese lives or Japanese Zen Buddhist processes. They teach about what they call "self-nature," the fundamental nature of the human being; certainly this should have some relevance for an American's nature.

The question indicates a kind of cultural bias. Don't we Western-ers unhesitatingly tap the philosophical or hermeneutical strategies of Western thinkers such as Derrida, Sartre, Geertz, or Wittgenstein to look at Hindu or Javanese experiences and phenomena? Why then should we hesitate to use Japanese thinkers to look at experiences of two Western-ers? There is a Eurocentric bias that is willing to look at "them" with "our" insights but unwilling to look at "us" with "their" insights. These two Japanese thinkers have thought a very great deal about mysticism, they should have very interesting things to teach about Bernadette's mysticism.

9. See Yampulsky, pp. 111–121.

10. Yampulski, p. 138.

11. Suzuki, p. 188. Another ancient Zen master, Shen-Hui, says, "true reality is the substance of no-thought (*wu-nien*) . For this reason I have set up no-thought as the main doctrine," Yampulski, 138n.

12. Suzuki, p. 175.

13. Ibid., p. 178.

14. Sometimes I think this might represent a decrease in spontane-ous galvanic skin responses, but I had no base line to check this hypothesis.

15. I suspect that these are bundles of nerves in this area but I have no way to determine that.

16. Here I am struck by the parallel with the rapid shifting of a physical system as it becomes coherent. As disorganized light becomes coherent and forms into laser light, it almost instantaneously "shifts" or "zips" into coherence. This is much as my experience was.

17. (I know I'll hear many "empty headed" jokes from my col-leagues now!)

18. Writing this, I think of the parallel between my experience and Bernadette Roberts's sense of having lost the usual "unlocalized sense of herself." For those who suspect some influence here, it is striking to me that I did not read her book until some eight or ten years after this occurred.

19. At one point (p. 30) Bernadette Roberts says that "to see the Oneness of everything is like having special 3-D glasses put before your eyes." This sounds similar to my own 3-D experience. But hers seems to be an analogy; mine was more a perceptual shift.

20. Here I am struck by the parallel between my sense and Bernadette Roberts's sense of having lost the usual "unlocalized sense of herself."

21. *Meister Eckhart: Mystic as Theologian* (Rockport, Mass.: Ele-ment Books, 1991); see also my "Eckhart, *Gezucken,* and the Ground of the Soul," in *The Problem of Pure Consciousness*, pp. 98–120.

22. M. O'C. Walshe, *Meister Eckhart: Sermons and Tractates*, Volume I and II (London: Watkins, 1978, 1982), Volume 1, p. 147. Hereafter noted as W 1 or 2, for volume number, and page number following a colon.

23. W. 2:312–3.

24. James Clark and John Skinner, eds, *Meister Eckhart: Selected Treatises and Sermons,* p. 102.

25. W 2:157.

26. W 2:32.

27. W 1:117.

28. W 2:136.

29. Clark and Skinner, p. 85.

30. W 2:157.

31. W 2:141–(Underlines mine).

32. Clark and Skinner, p. 167.

33. Ibid., p. 168.

34. Clark and Skinner, p. 168. Emphasis mine.

35. Eckhart too associates this with the self itself, but he does so through a relatively complex theological argument. The silence within is defined as the Word of God, which is in turn defined as the highest within the soul. This "highest" within may be associated with what is most central within the soul, and thus is the self itself. But it would take a longer argument than this to establish this claim.

Chapter 9

1. D. T. Suzuki, "The Zen Doctrine of No Mind", in *Zen Buddhism: Selected Writings of D. T. Suzuki,* p. 189.

2. D. T. Suzuki, "Existentialism, Pragmatism, and Zen," in *Zen Buddhism: Selected Writings of D.T. Suzuki.* I have learned much from William Bossart, "Sartre's Theory of Consciousness and the Zen Doctrine of No Mind," in *The Life of the Transcendental Ego,* ed. Edward Carey and Donald Morano (Albany: SUNY Press, 1986), pp. 126–150. See also Stephen Laycock, "Hui-Neng and the Transcendental Standpoint," *Journal of Chinese Philosophy* 12 (1985): pp. 179–196.

3. Jean Paul Sartre, *Being and Nothingness,* p. Liv.

4. Jean Paul Sartre, *Transcendence of the Ego*, p. 46.

5. Sartre, *Being and Nothingness*, pp liv-lv.

6. "Within" is not strictly correct. There is no inside or outside of awareness itself.

7. Sartre, *Being and Nothingness*, lv.

8. This is in the sense that it is not in itself ever an object.

9. In *Being and Nothingness*, pp. 3–6, Sartre argues this with reference to the ability to question and interrogate.

10. Here language fails us: speaking of "my" consciousness, or what "I" inherently am, is to personalize it, which runs counter to Sartre's entire conception of consciousness *pour-soi*.

11. Paul Ricoeur's notion of the chasm that defines the nature of sin may have had its forerunner here.

12. For the substance of the previous paragraphs, I am indebted to William Bossart's insightful presentation of Sartre, pp. 131 -137.

13. Suzuki, "No-Mind," p. 189.

14. Yampulsky, *Platform Sūtra*, 136.

15. Ibid., p. 142.

16. Ibid., p. 153.

17. Suzuki, "No Mind," p. 190. I have changed Suzuki's word order for clarity.

18. Again, grammar is difficult here. I said one "becomes conscious of one's . . . consciousness itself," which implies that one has or owns a consciousness. But clearly consciousness is not something that can be owned or possessed.

19. Yampulsky, *Platform Sūtra,* p. 136.

20. Ibid., pp. 140–141.

21. Suzuki's translation, p. 213. I might mention that in a private interview Professor Louis Nordstrom holds that this "functioning samādhi" is at once the most important contribution of Zen to the West and the least often recognized. Zen seeks no extraordinary moments, he said, but a life transformed in the context of constant *samādhi*.

22. Yampulsky, *Platform Sūtra,* p. 148.

23. Suzuki, p. 178.

24. Suzuki, p. 173, is a translation of paragraph 6. Cf. Yampulsky's *Platform Sūtra,* p. 149, which is a translation of paragraph 28.

25. Suzuki, p. 214.

26. Ibid., p. 178.

27. This puts him in remarkable accord with the Hindu distinction between self (jiva) and Self (Ātman).

28. Ibid., p. 178.

29. Here again, it is hard not to personalize consciousness. But this is, speaking precisely, a mistake.

30. I am indebted to Steven Rosen, personal correspondence, for this clarifying thought.

31. That will change as her book and her life progress. But let us not get ahead of ourselves. Too many mistakes have been made by conflating one form of mystical experience of state of life with another, and thus one epistemological structure with another.

Bibliography

Almond, Philip. "Mysticism and its Contexts." In *The Problem of Pure Consciousness,* Ed. Robert Forman. New York: Oxford University Press, 1990.

Ashley, Benedict, O.P. "Three Strands in the Thought of Eckart, the Scholastic Theologian." *The Thomist* 42 (1978), 226–239.

Bagger, Mathew. "Critical Notice: Ecumenalism and Perennialism Revisited." *Religious Studies* 27 (1991), 401–413.

Barnard, G. William. *Exploring Unseen Worlds: William James and the Philosophy of Mysticism.* The University of Chicago, March 1994.

Beloff, John. "Minds and Machines: A Radical Dualist Perspective." *Journal of Consciousness Studies* 1, no. 1 (Summer 1994), 32–37.

Berger, Peter. *The Social Construction of Reality: A Treatise in the Sociology of Knowledge,* Garden City, N.Y.: Doubelday, 1967.

Bhagāvad Gita. Trans. Franklin Edgerton. New York: Harper, 1944.

Bossart, William. "Satre's Theory of Consciousness and the Zen Doctrine of No Mind." *The Life of the Transcendental Ego,* ed. Edward Carey and Donal Morano. Albany: SUNY Press, 1986, 126–150.

Bouyer, Louis. "Mysticism: An Essay on the History of the Word," In *Understanding Mysticism,* ed. Richard Woods, O.P., Garden City, N.Y.: Image Books, 1980, 42–55.

Brentano, Franz. *Psychology from an Empirical Point of View,* trans. Antos Rancurello, D. B. Terrell, and Linda L. McAllister. English edition edited by Linda McAlister. London: Routledge and Kegan Paul, 1973.

Bromberg, Walter. *The Mind of Man: A History of Psychotherapy and Psychoanalysis.* New York: Harper Colophon, 1959.

Brown, Daniel. "The Stages of Meditation in Cross-Cultural Perspective." In *Transformations of Consciousness: Conventional and Contemplative Perspectives on Development.* Ken Wilber, Jack Engler, and Daniel Brown. Boston: Shambhala, 1986.

Bruner, Jerome, and Leo Postman. "On Perception of Incongruities: A Paradigm." *Journal of Personality* 18(1949), 210–221.

Chipp, Herschel, ed. *Theories of Modern Art: A Source Book by Artists and Critics.* Berkeley: University of California Press, 1968.

Chisholm, Roderick. "Sentences about Believing." In *Intentionality, Mind, and Language,* ed. Ausonio Marras. Urbana: University of Illinois Press, 1972, 31–51.

Chittuck, William. "Between the Yes and the No: Ibn al-'Arabi on Wujud and the Innate Capacity." In *The Innate Capacity,* ed. Robert K. C. Forman. Oxford University Press, 1998, 95–110.

Clark, David Kenneth. *Meister Eckhart as an Orthodox Chrisian.* Ph.D. Dissertation, Northwestern University Department of Religion (1984).

Clark, James, and John Skinner, ed. and trans. *Meister Eckhart: Selected Treatises and Sermons.* London: Faber and Faber, 1958.

Clark, James. *Meister Eckhart: An Introduction to the Study of His Works with an Anthology of His Sermons.* Edinburgh: Thomas Nelson and Sons, 1957.

Colledge, Edmond, and Bernard McGinn. *Meister Eckhart.* New York: Paulist Press, 1978.

Conze, Edward. *Buddhist* Scripture. New York: Harper Colophon Books, 1956.

Cook, Francis D. *How to Raise an Ox: Zen Practice as Taught in Zen Master Dōgen's Shobogenzo.* Los Angeles: Center Publications, 1979.

Davis, Douglas. *Art Culture: Essays on the Post Modern.* New York: Harper and Row, 1977.

Deikman, Arthur. "Deautomatization and the Mystic Experience." In *Altered States of Consciousness,* ed. Charles Tart. New York: John Wiley & Sons, 1969, 23–44.

Dewey, John. *Psychology, Third Edition.* New York: Harper, 1886.

Farrow, John. "Physiological Changes Associated with Transcendental Consciousness, The State of Least Excitation of Consciousness." In *Scientific Research on the Transcendental Meditation Program,* ed. David Orme Johnson. Livinston Manor, N.Y.: Meru Press, 1977.

Finnegan, Mary Jeremy. *Scholars and Mystics.* Chicago: University of Chicago Press, 1962.

Fischer, Roland. "A Cartography of the Ecstatic and Meditative States." In *Understanding Mysticism,* ed. Richard Woods, O.P. Garden City, N.Y.: Image Books, 1980, 270–285.

Follesdal, Gadfinn. "Bretano and Husserl on Intentional Objects and Perception." In *Husserl, Intentionality and Cognitive Science,* ed. Hubert Dreyfus. Cambridge: MIT Press, 1982.

———. "Husserl's Notion of Noema." In *Husserl, Intentionality, and Cognitive Science,* ed. Hubert Dreyfus and Hall, 73–80.

Forman, Robert K.C. "A New Methodology for the Study of Religion: A Proposal." *Doorways of Perception, Festschrift for Ewert Cousins,* ed. Steven Chase. Franciscan Press, 1997.

———. "Eckhart, Gezucken, and the Ground of the Soul." *The Problem of Pure Consciousness,* ed. Robert K. C. Forman. New York: Oxford University Press, 1990, 98–120.

———. "Silence, Thinking, and Cutting Carrots: Characterizing an Advanced Mystical State." Unpublished Talk delivered to the University of Helsinki in October 1994.

———, ed. *The Innate Capacity: Mysticism, Psychology and Philosophy.* New York: Oxford University Press, 1998.

———. *Meister Eckhart: Mystic as Theologian.* Rockport, Mass.: Element Books, 1991.

———. Mystical Experience in the Cloud Literature." *The Medieval Mystical Tradition in England: Exeter Symposium IV,* ed. Marion Glasscoe. Cambridge: D. S. Brewer, 1987, 177–195.

———. "Mysticism and Autobiographies." Unpublished talk, Binghamton University Ancient Philosophy and Neo-Platonism Conference, October 1993.

———. "Pure Consciousness Events and Mysticism" *Sophia* 25, No. 1 (1986), 49–58.

———. "What Does Mysticism Have to Tell us about Consciousness?" *Journal of Consciousness Studies* 5, No. 2 (1998), 185–201.

———. "Zen and Reflexive Consciousness." Unpublished lecture at the University of Helsinki, Finland, October 1994.

———, ed. *The Problem of Pure Consciousness.* New York: Oxford University Press, 1990.

Garside, Bruce. "Language and the Interpretation of Mystical Experiences." *International Journal for Philosophy of Religion* 3 (Summer 1972), 91–94.

Geertz, Clifford. *Islam Observed.* Chicago: University of Chicago Press, 1968.

———. *The Interpretation of Cultures.* New York: Harper Colophon Books, 1973.

Gill, Jerry. "Mysticism and Mediation." *Faith and Philosophy* 1 (1984), 111–121.

———. "Religious Experience as Mediated." Unpublished paper delivered to Philosophy Section, American Academy of Religion, November 6, 1980.

Gimello, Robert. "Mysticism and Mediation." In *Mysticism and Philosophical Analysis,* ed. Steven Katz. New York: Oxford University Press, 1978, 170–199.

Goleman, Daniel. *The Varieties of the Meditative Experience.* New York: Dutton, 1977.

Gombrich, E. H. *Art and Illusion: A Study in the Psychology of Pictoral Representation.* Princeton: Princeton University Press, 1960.

Green, Dierdre. "Unity in Diversity [Typology of Mysticism]." *Scottish Journal of Religious Studies* 3 (1982), pp. 46–58.

Greenberg, J., and S. Mitchell. *Object Relations in Psychoanalytic Theory.* Cambridge: Harvard University Press, 1983.

Griffiths, Paul. "Pure Consciousness and Indian Buddhism." In *The Problem of Pure Consciousness,* ed. Robert Forman. New York: Oxford University Press, 71–97.

———. *On Being Mindless.* La Salle, Ill.: Open Court Press, 1986.

Gudmunsen, Chris. *Wittgenstein and Buddhism.* New York: Macmillan, 1977.

Guntrip, H. *Personality Structure and Human Interaction.* New York: International Universities Press, 1961.

Gurwitsch, Aron. "On the Intentionality of Consciousness." In *Philosophical Essays in Memory of Edmund Husserl,* ed. Marvin Farber. New York: Greenwood Press, 1968, 65–83.

Hamilton, Peter. *Knowledge and Social Structure: An Introduction to the Classical Argument in the Sociology of Knowledge.* London: Routledge and Kegan Paul, 1974.

Hartmann, Heinz. *Ego Psychology and the Problem of Adaptation.* International University Press, 1958.

Hick, John. "Mystical Experience as Cognition." In *Understanding Mysticism,* ed. Richard P. Woods, O. P. New York: Image Books, 1980, 422–437.

Hodgson, Phyllis, ed. *The Cloud of Unknowing and Related Treatises.* Salzburg: Institut Für Anglistik und Amerikanistik, 1982.

Horne, James. "Pure Mysticism and Two-Fold Typologies: James to Katz." *Scottish Journal of Religious Studies* 3 (1982), 3–14.

Horton, Robin, ed. *Modes of Thought: Essays on Thinking in Western and Non Western Societies.* London: Faber and Faber, 1973.

Hui Neng. *The Platform Sutra of the Sixth Patriarch.* Philip Yampulsky, trans. New York: Columbia University Press, 1967.

Hume, David. *A Treatise of Human Nature.* L. A. Selby-Bigge, Ed. Oxford: Claredon Press, 1888.

Hume, Robert. *The Thirteen Principal Upanishads.* Oxford: Oxford University Press, 1921.

Husserl, Edmund. *Logical Investigations,* 2 vols. Trans. J. Findlay. New York: Humanities Press, 1970.

Huxley, Aldous. *The Perennial Philosophy.* New York: Harper and Row, 1944. Reprinted 1945, 1970.

Indich, William. *Consciousness in Advaita Vedanta.* Delhi: Motilal Banarsidass, 1980.

Inge, W. R. "Ecstacy." In *Encyclopedia of Religion and Ethics,* ed. James Hastings. Edinburgh: T & T Clark, 1912.

Johnson, David Orme, ed. *Scientific Research on the Transcendental Meditation Program.* Livinston Manor, N.Y.: Meru Press, 1977.

Jones, Richard. "Experience and Conceptualization in Mystical Knowledge." *Zygon* 18 (1983), 139–165.

Jones, Rufus M. *Studies in Mystical Religion.* New York: Russell and Russell, 1909. Reprinted 1970.

Katz, Steven. "Language, Epistemology, and Mysticism." In *Mysticism and Philosophical Analysis,* ed. Steven Katz. New York: Oxford University Press, 1978, 22–74.

———. "The 'Conservative' Character of Mystical Experience." In *Mysticism and Religious Traditions,* ed. Steven Katz. New York: Oxford University Press, 1983, 3–60.

Kelley, Carl Franklin. *Meister Eckhart on Divine Knowledge.* New Haven: Yale University Press, 1977.

Klein, David Ballin. *The Concept of Consciousness: A Survey.* Lincoln: University of Nebraska Press, 1980.

Koch, Joseph, ed. *Meister Eckhart: Die lateinische Werke Herausgegeben im Auftrage der Deutschen Forschungsgemeinschaft.* Stuttgart und Berlin: W. Kohlhammer Verlag, 1936–.

Kristo, Jure. "The Interpretation of Religious Experience: What Do Mystics Intend when They Talk about Their Experiences?" *Journal of Religion* 62 (1982), 21–38.

Laycock, Stephen. "Hui-Neng and the Transcendental Standpoint." *Journal of Chinese Philosophy* 12 (1985), 179–196.

Leuba, James. *The Psychology of Religious Mysticism.* London: K Paul, Trench, Trubner, and Co., Ltd.: New York: Harcourt Brace & Co., 1925.

Maharishi Mahesh Yogi. *Bhagavad Gita. A New Translation and Commentary with Sanskrit Texts.* Baltimore: Penguin Books, 1971.

Malcolm, Norman. *Ludwig Wittgenstein: A Memoir.* Oxford: Oxford University Press, 1958.

Mangan, Bruce. "Language and Experience in the Cognitive Study of Mysticism—Commentary on Forman." *Journal of Consciousness Studies* In no. 2 (Winter 1994), 250–252.

Marras, Ausonio. "Intentionally and Cognitive Sentences." In *Intentionality, Mind, and Language,* ed. Ausonio Marras. Urbana: University of Illinois Press, 1972, 31–51.

Matt, Daniel C. *"Ayin:* The Concept of Nothingness." In *The Problem of Pure Consciousness,* ed. Robert K. C. Forman. New York: Oxford University Press, 1990.

Maurer, A., ed. and trans. *Parisian Questions.* Toronto: Pontifical Institute of Mediaeval Studies, 1970.

McGinn, Bernard. "Meister Eckhart: An Introduction." In *Introduction to the Medieval Mystics of Europe,* ed. Paul Szernach. Binghamton: SUNY Press, 1984, 237–258.

McLaughlin, Michael C. *Lonergan and the Evaluation of Theories of Mystical Experience,* Unpublished Ph.D. Thesis, University Toronto, 1995.

Meinong, Alexius. "The Theory of Objects." In *Realism and the Background of Phenomenology,* ed. Roderick Chisholm. Glencoe: The Free Press, 1960, 76–117.

Merrell-Wolff, Franklin. *Pathways Through to Space.* New York: Warner Books, 1976.

Mitchell, Steven, trans. *Tao te Ching.* New York: Harper, 1988.

Moore, G. E. *Philosophical Studies.* London: Oxford University Press, 1960.

Moore, Peter. "Mystical Experience, Mystical Doctrine, Mystical Technique." In *Mysticism and Philosophical Analysis,* ed. Steven Katz. New York: Oxford University Press, 1978, 100–130.

Neimeyer, Robert. *The Development of Personal Construct Theory.* Lincoln: University of Nebraska Press, 1985.

Osborne, Arthur. ed. *The Collected Works of Ramana Maharshi.* London: 1959.

———. *Ramana Maharshi and the Path of Self Knowledge.* New York: Samuel Weiser, 1973.

Otto, Rudolf. *The Idea of the Holy,* trans. John W. Harvey. New York: Oxford University Press, 1923. Reprinted 1950.

———. *Mysticism East and West,* trans. Bertha Bracey and Richenda C. Payne. New York: Macmillan, 1932.

Owen, H. P. "Experience and Dogma in the English Mystics." In *Mysticism and Philosophical Analysis,* ed. Steven Katz. New York: Oxford University Press, 1978, 148–162.

Paul, Diana. "An Introductory Note to Paramārtha's Theory of Language." *Journal of Indian Philosophy* 7, no. 3 (Sept. 1979), 231–255.

———. "The Structure of Consciousness in Paramārtha's Purported Trilogy." *Philosophy East and West* 31, no. 3 (July 1981), 291–319.

———. *Philosophy of Mind in Sixth Century China: Paramārtha's Evolution of Consciousness.* Stanford: Stanford University Press, 1984.

Pears, D. F., ed. *Nature of Metaphysics.* London: Macmillan, 1956.

Pendleton, Gene. "Forman and Mystical Consciousness." *Sophia* 27, no. 2 (July, 1988), 15–17.

Penehelum, Terence. "Unity and Diversity in Interpretation of Mysticism." In *Understanding Mysticism,* ed. Richard Woods, O. P. New York: Image Books, 1980, 438–448.

Penner, Hans H. "The Mystical Illusion." In *Mysticism and Religious Traditions,* ed. Steven Katz. NY: Oxford University Press, 1983, 89–116.

Perovich, Anthony. "Does the Philosophy of Mysticism Rest on a Mistake?" In *The Problem of Pure Consciousness,* ed. Robert Forman. New York: Oxford University Press, 1990, 237–253.

Perovich, Anthony. "Mysticism and the Philosophy of Science." *Journal of Religion* 65 (1985), 63–82.

Pfeiffer, Franz, ed. *Meister Eckhart.* Gottingen: Vanenhoeck and Ruprecht, 1924.

Price, James Robertson III. "The Objectivity of Mystical Truth Claims." *The Thomist* 49 (January 1985), 81–98.

Proudfoot, Wayne. *Religious Experience.* Berkeley: University of California Press, 1985.

Quint, Josef, ed. *Meister Eckhart: Die deutsche Werke Herausgegaben im Auftrage der Deutschen Forschunggemeinschaf.* Stuttgart and Berlin: W. Kohlhammer Verlag, 1936–.

Radhakrishnan, Sarvepalli, and Charles A. Moore. *A Sourcebook in Indian Philosophy.* Princeton: Princeton University Press, 1957.

Roberts, Bernadette. *The Experience of No-Self.* Boston: Shambala, 1984.

Schuon, Frithjof. *The Transcendent Unity of Religions,* trans. Peter Townsend. New York: Harper, 1975.

Schurmann, Reiner. *Meister Eckhart: Mystic and Philosopher.* Bloomington, Ind.: University of Indiana Press, 1978.

Searle, John. *The Rediscovery of the Mind.* Cambridge: MIT Press, 1992.

Shear, Jonathan. *The Inner Dimension: Philosophy and the Experience of Consciousness.* New York: Peter Lang, 1990.

Short, Larry. "Mysticism, Meditation, and the Non-Linguistic." *Journal of the American Academy of Religion* 113, no. 4 (Winter 1995), 659–676.

Smart, Ninian. "Interpretation and Mystical Experience." *Religious Studies* 1 (1965): 75–87.

———. "Understanding Religious Experience." In *Mysticism and Philosophical Analysis,* ed. Steven Katz. New York: Oxford University Press, 1978, 10–21.

Smith, Huston. Forgotten Truth: *The Primordial Tradition.* New York: Harper and Row, 1976.

Spiegelberg, Herbert. " 'Intention' and 'Intentionally.' " In *The Scholastics, Brentano and Husserl: The Context of the Phenomenological Movement,* ed. Herbert Spiegelberg. The Hague: Martinus Nijhoff, 1981.

———. *The Phenomenological Movement.* The Hague: Martinus Nijhoff, 1982.

Sponberg, Alan. "Dynamic Liberation in Yogācāra Buddhism." *The Journal of the International Association of Buddhist Studies* 2 (1979), 46–64.

Stace, Walter T. *Mysticism and Philosophy.* London: Macmillan, 1960.

Stcherbatsky, Theodore. *The Central Conception of Buddhism.* London, 1923: Reprinted 1961.

Streng, Frederick. "Language and Mystical Awareness." In *Mysticism and Philosophical Analysis,* ed. Steven Katz. New York: Oxford University Press, 1978, 141–169.

Suzuki, D. T. "Existentialism, Pragmatism, and Zen." In *Zen Buddhism: Selected Writings of D. T. Suzuki,* Vol. #3, ed. William Barrett. Garden City, New York: Doubleday, 1956.

————. "The Zen Doctrine of No-Mind." In *Zen Buddhism: Selected Writings of D. T. Suzuki* Vol. 3, ed. William Barrett. Garden City, N.Y.: Doubleday Anchor Books, 1956, 157–228.

Underhill, Evelyn. *Mysticism.* New York: E. P. Dutton, 1911. Reprinted 1961.

Van Gogh, Vincent. "Paint Your Garden As It Is." In *Theories of Modern Art: A Source Book by Artists and Critics,* ed. Herschel Chipp. Berkeley: University of California Press, 1968, 44–45.

Waddell, Normann, and Abe Masao, trans. "Dōgen's *Fukanzazengi and Shobogenzo Zazengi." Eastern Buddhist* 6, no. 2 (Oct. 1973).

Wainwright, William. "Interpretation, Description, and Mystical Consciousness." *Journal of the American Academy of Religion* 45 (1977) (Supplement).

————. *Mysticsm: A Study of its Nature, Cognitive Value, and Moral Implications.* Madison: The University of Wisconsin Press, 1981.

————. "Mysticism and Sense Perception." *Religious Studies* 9 (1973), 257–278.

————. "Natural Explanations and Religious Experience." *Ratio* 15 (1973), 98–101.

————. "Stace and Mysticism." *The Journal of Religion* 50 (1970), 139–154.

Walshe, M. O'C., ed. and trans. *Meister Eckhart: German Sermons and Treatises.* Vol. 1–3. London: Watkins, 1979, 1981, 1987.

Watts, Alan. *Myth and Ritual in Christianity.* London: Thames and Hudson, 1954.

Werner, Karel. "Mysticism as Doctrine and Experience." *Reigious Traditions* 4 (1981), 1–18.

Woodhouse, Mark B. "Consciousness and Brahman-Atman." *The Monist* (Jan. 1978), 114.

Yokoi, Yuko, and Daizen Victoria. *Zen Master Dōgen.* New York: Weatherhill, 1976.

Zaehner, R. C. *Hindu and Muslim Mysticism.* New York: Schocken Books, 1961.

Index